SPARKS
BENEATH
THE SURFACE

SPARKS
BENEATH
THE SURFACE

A Spiritual Commentary on the Torah

Lawrence S. Kushner
Kerry M. Olitzky

JASON ARONSON INC.
Northvale, New Jersey
London

First Jason Aronson Inc. softcover edition-1995

This book was set in Schneidler by Lind Graphics of Upper Saddle River, New Jersey, and printed by Haddon Craftsmen in Scranton, Pennsylvania.

Excerpt from *The River of Light: Spirituality, Judaism, and the Evolution of Consciousness* by Lawrence Kushner used by permission of Jewish Lights Publishing, P.O. Box 237, Woodstock, VT.

Library of Congress Cataloging-in-Publication Data

Kushner, Lawrence, 1943-
    Sparks beneath the surface : a spiritual commentary on the Torah /
by Lawrence S. Kushner and Kerry M. Olitzky.
        p.   cm.
    Includes bibliographical references and index.
    ISBN 1-56821-016-7 (hardcover)
    ISBN 1-56821-743-9 (softcover)
    1. Bible. O.T. Pentateuch-Commentaries.   2. Hasidism.
3. Spiritual life-Judaism.   I. Olitzky, Kerry M.   II. Title.
BS1225.3.K87   1994
222'.1077—dc20   93-26265

Manufactured in the United States of America. Jason Aronson Inc. offers books and cassettes. For information and catalog write to Jason Aronson Inc., 230 Livingston Street, Northvale, New Jersey 07647.

We want to particularly acknowledge with abiding appreciation
the publishers of *Itturei Torah*
by Aaron Jacob Greenberg
(Tel Aviv: Yavneh Publishing House, 1970)
who have graciously allowed us permission
to translate into English selected chasidic commentaries
for use in this volume.

Contents

Contents

Contents

Contents

Acknowledgments

Thanking people is a holy task; there are so many who have contributed to make this volume possible. In particular, we want to thank the participants of the annual Morris Zimmerman Memorial Institutes held each summer and sponsored by the New York School of Hebrew Union College–Jewish Institute of Religion where many of these ideas and translations were first taught.

We also want to thank the members of Congregation Beth El of Sudbury, Massachusetts, who allow such endeavors to take place. We thank, as well, our colleagues and our students at Hebrew Union College–Jewish Institute of Religion, who have patiently allowed us to try out many of these ideas and supported our work. Specifically, our appreciation is expressed to our colleagues Herman Blumberg, Donald Splansky, and Jeffrey Summit for sharing their interpretations of the text, and to our *rosh yeshivah*, Alfred Gottschalk, and Dean Norman Cohen – for direction and guidance and for providing us with a vineyard in which to sow the seeds of Torah.

Our gratitude also goes to Arthur Kurzweil at Jason Aronson Inc. for his patience and support in preparing this manuscript. A unique publisher, he allows authors freedom of expression, so that they may take their ideas in directions that few other publishers are willing to allow.

Acharon, acharon chaviv, the last is the most beloved – we thank our families for being who they are and for allowing us to be who we are: Karen, Noa, Zachary, and Lev Kushner and Sheryl, Avi, and Jesse Olitzky.

We also want to thank Rabbi Israel C. Stein whose careful reading of our text helped pinpoint specific citations and sources. We are grateful to him for his assistance.

Lawrence Kushner
Kerry M. Olitzky

Tradition's Table: An Introduction

"The problem is not that God no longer speaks," said our teacher Arnold Jacob Wolf many years ago, "it is that God doesn't shut up!" It is a penetrating insight into the difference between Orthodox and Liberal Jewish theology.

For Orthodoxy, God spoke once and for all at Mount Sinai. Not only did God write the Torah and whisper the Talmud (the twofold law), but more importantly, God included in them the necessary mechanisms to anticipate a relevant response to any future legal contingency. God, in other words, no longer speaks, because there is nothing left to say. Like all orthodoxies, it is a total and totally closed system.

We liberals require a higher tolerance for surprises. For us the unavoidability of novelty and our occasionally arrogant assumption that what happens to us could not have been anticipated by previous generations (or God!) require a God who can "keep talking." Each generation brings with it unimaginable questions that demand new answers. Not even the greatest of our sages foresaw electricity, the liberation of women, nuclear winter, or even cholesterol. Or, to put it another way, when we hear the same Torah that was given to our ancestors at Sinai, to our ears, it sounds different.

The tradition already anticipates our dilemma by offering two legends that ring true in our ears. Unfortunately, like traditional and liberal theology, they are mutually exclusive. First, we believe that whatever it was that happened at Sinai was an event of supreme and unique significance, never to be repeated. God may continue to speak, but (even for staunch Liberal Jews) the Torah remains God's longest and best speech. That is why we get so excited on *Shabbat* and holiday mornings when we read it and on Simchat Torah when we begin it again and on Shavuot when we remember receiving it.

On the other hand, there is also a tradition which, with an equal measure of accuracy, holds that each and every day the Divine Voice issues from Sinai. Even stalwart traditional Jews maintain that what was heard then by our ancestors can be heard now, today, by us. Right here and now, God is saying the very same words that were said at Sinai. Not only then is Torah eternally unchanging (the Orthodox myth), it is also always present, always able to be heard anew (the Liberal myth).

Eliyahu KiTov, the great Orthodox Israeli philosopher, poses this problem as two classic religious questions in *Sefer Ha-Parshiyot: Parashat Terumah* (Aleph Publishers: Jerusalem, 1965, p. 128). If Torah is being spoken all the time, then why can't we hear it clearly now (the great problem for liberal Jews)? And second, if indeed Torah is being spoken all the time, then what makes the revelation at Sinai so special (the great problem for traditional Jews)? KiTov then offers a daring solution and a profound insight into the nature of religious consciousness.

The reason Sinai is so special, he suggests, *and* the reason we are unable to hear Torah all the time, is that the background noise, static, and tape hiss of this world create such a racket, they drown out the sound of God's ever-speaking voice. What made Sinai so important was that it was the only time throughout all history when God "silenced the roar." In the language of modern sound-recording technology, God, you might say, switched on the noise-reduction system. When the Torah was given, we could hear what had been there, and continues to be here, all along.

God, then, you might say, is the One who enables us to hear what is really continuously being spoken at the most primary levels of reality, throughout all creation, and all time. And for this reason, each act of personal religious focus becomes a miniature Sinai, now accessible everywhere.

For our traditional brothers and sisters, the problem is how to squeeze from the Torah coherent responses to contemporary social and technological crises – how to hear God's voice anew. For liberal Jews, the problem is how to make sure it is really God we hear and not the voice of our own convenience disguised as God; that is to say, how to hold fast to our religious lifeline back to Sinai.

For liberal and traditional Jews alike, part of the answer comes from a chasidic rabbi, Menachem Mendl of Kotzk. Commenting on the curious word order in Exodus that reads, "we will do and we will hear" (instead of what we would logically expect, "we will hear and then we will do"), Menachem Mendl explains that some actions simply cannot be understood (heard) until they are performed (done). We do not know what is commanded of us until we try it. By doing we understand.

Jewish tradition might be thought of then as a magnificent banquet table, piled high with everything Jews have ever tried in response to God. After three thousand years, it is a very big table. Some of the dishes are immediately tantalizing; if we are not careful, we could fill up on them and leave room for nothing else. Others at first don't look so good; and when we were children, we needed to be persuaded to try them. Often, when we did try them, we were surprised and delighted to discover that they were delicious. There are others we simply may never enjoy, understand, or even get to at all.

We are also permitted to respectfully place on the table one or two recipes of our own creation. If others agree that they are delicious, word will get around and our offering may, after many centuries, gradually move toward the center of the table. But no one is exempt from trying every dish, just as no one is prohibited from reverently offering an addition. In this way, while we may not resolve the logical tension between a God who spoke once and for all at Sinai and a God who continues to speak, we may be able to endure the paradox.

We have set the table for you in the pages that follow. Come and enjoy it with us.

How to Use This Book

This book was designed for people seeking ready access to sacred text but who feel limited by their Hebrew language skills. We have therefore sought to make the treasures of Torah available to a wider audience. Following the format of the traditional *Mikraot Gedolot* (*The Rabbis' Bible*, literally, "The Big Scriptures"), we hope to open another spiritual dimension of traditional learning.

Each text has the following rubrics for study:

Targum: English Translation

Historically, the Torah was translated for the public when it was read aloud. We have translated the text, as well as the surrounding verses that help to anchor a particular passage, in order for it to be studied by the teacher. Since we believe that all translation (*targum*) is interpretation, you may find scriptural verses translated differently as they appear throughout this volume in order to reflect a particular context.

The Teaching

The teaching has been generally selected and translated from the Hebrew anthology *Itturei Torah*. This section is material, taken primarily from classical chasidic teachers, that we believe speaks uniquely to the modern Jew in his or her own search for spirituality.

Scriptural Context

This section provides a summary of the preceding biblical material in a particular Torah portion and provides a context for the teaching that follows.

Perush: Explaining the Teaching

Even the most lucid commentaries are often complex and require further elucidation. Here we offer our own *perush* (explanation) of the teaching.

Background

We offer a glimpse into the biographical and geographical background of the classical chasidic world, as well as anecdotes and other teachings. In some cases, alternative comments by another teacher on the verse under discussion are presented. Biographies are referenced in bold type in the index.

From the Tradition

This section includes material from Jewish tradition that we believe will add more depth to a point under discussion.

While we have, of course, worked closely with each other, Larry assumes the primary responsibility for "The Teaching" section of each chapter, and Kerry has prepared all of the additional material. We have deliberately allowed our occasional differences of interpretation to stand. We hope that in this kind of project especially, our "two heads are better than one."

GENESIS

(1) Bereishit: 600,000 Letters

The Teaching
from *Yalkut Reuveini* citing *Megalleh Amukot*

Bereishit . . . is actually an acronym:

Bet ב with sixty
Resh ר myriads (600,000)
Alef א letters
Shin ש (that) Israel
Yod י (they all) received
Tav ת Torah.

And the word *Yisrael* (Israel) is also an acronym:

Yod י there are
Shin ש sixty
Resh ר myriads (600,000)
Alef א letters
Lamed ל for the Torah.

This teaches that each individual soul in Israel has a corresponding letter in the Torah, and that if so much as one soul from the 600,000 souls of Israel were missing, the Torah could not be received. For this reason, a *sefer Torah* that is lacking so much as one letter is ritually unfit for use.

This is also the reason for the verse in Psalm 19:8, "The Torah of *Adonai* is perfect, restoring the soul." □

Targum: English Translation
Genesis 1:1

1) God created the heaven and earth *at the beginning* [of time and space]. □

Scriptural Context

This portion begins the Torah, which is itself a blueprint for creation – the infrastructure of being. □

From the Tradition

Taking the word *song* for Torah in Deuteronomy 31:19, "Therefore, write down the song and teach it to the Israelites; put it in their mouths so that it may be my witness for them", the personal possession of a *sefer Torah* is regarded as a biblical commandment. *Sandhedrin* 21b further suggests that one should own a *sefer Torah*, even if one inherits a Torah scroll from parents. The individual may write one (as a scribe) or have one written. According to *Menachot* 30, the scroll that is written by the individual for personal study, is as if it had been given to that person on Sinai itself. The scribe is called a *sofer STaM*. STaM itself is an acronym for *Sefer Torah, Tefillin,* and *Mezuzot*, which are the only three places where the rules of sacred "Torah" calligraphy apply. Since one who →

Perush: Explaining the Teaching

Our tradition believes that everything contained in the Torah, like everything contained in a love letter or what one says to one's therapist, is important. This includes such apparently trivial things as the sequence of letters that form the sacred text. Since Torah is addressed to us personally, we draw meaning from every aspect of it. Thus, the first word of Torah, *Bereishit*, is not accidental; it was selected for a particular reason. *Yalkut Reuveini* suggests that *Bereishit* might be understood as an acronym. (This common hermeneutic device of drawing interpretive meaning from the text is called in Hebrew, *notarikon*.) Each soul is dependent on each and every other soul, even those whom we consider to be our inferiors. Each soul is indispensable. From this we also learn that only a ritually fit →

Background *Yalkut Reuveini* (1681) was written by Rabbi Hoeshke ben Hoeshke (Joshua) Katz, of Prague. It is a collection of kabbalistic lore, also called *Ha-Gadol* (to differentiate it from another work of Hoeshke by the same name). It is important because he uses and cites kabbalistic texts and manuscripts from the previous 500 years, many of which have been lost.

Megalleh Amukot was written by Rabbi Nathan Nata ben Solomon Spira in 1795. It is a classic work that relies heavily on gematria. This is a hermeneutic principle that finds meanings in words by establishing numerical equivalents for letters, totaling those numbers, and equating them with other words whose letters (numbers) are of equal value, as a means of developing kabbalistic ideas. □

Perush: Explaining the Teaching *(continued)*

(kosher) Torah scroll, that is, one that has no missing or superfluous letters, can be used. Finally, a verse from Psalms is brought to emphasize that the Torah is perfect and that, perhaps, only once we realize this can redemption come. □

From the Tradition *(continued)*

completes a *mitzvah* is also accounted as if he or she had performed all of it, a scribe writing a "commissioned" Torah will often only outline the words in the first and last passages of the *sefer Torah* so that the individual might symbolically fulfill (or complete) the *mitzvah* of writing his or her own scroll by filling in the letters. The ceremony is called *Siyyum Ha-Torah* (the completion of the Torah). □

(2) Bereishit: The Argument for Truth

The Teaching
from Menachem Mendl of Kotzk

The Kotzker began his teaching by citing *Midrash* (*Genesis Rabbah* 8:5; cf. Psalm 85:11): Rabbi Simon taught that at the time when the Holy One came to creating the first human being, Love said, "Let the creation occur for this creature will do loving things." But Truth said, "Let the creation not occur for the creature will be all lies." Justice said, "Let the creation occur for this creature will do justice." What did the Holy One do? God took Truth and hurled it to the earth.

What good would it do to only banish the Truth? Peace, which had also argued against the creation of human beings, still remained. The answer is that in banishing Truth, obviously there would be Peace. For the root of quarreling is that everyone battles for his own truth. But if Truth is pushed off to one side, then there is nothing left to argue about, no one to denounce Peace. □

Scriptural Context

God had been at work on creation for five days already. And now, in our text, God is ready to create human beings. This part of creation acts like an introduction or synopsis for what follows. □

From the Tradition

Alef is the first letter of the Hebrew alphabet. *Mem* is found in the middle. And the *alef-bet* concludes with *tav*. The three letters form the Hebrew word *emet* ("truth"). This word was placed on the forehead of the Golem of Prague and it gave him life. When the *alef* was removed, the remaining letters *mem* and *tav* spelled *met* or "death." In this manner, the Golem was brought back to life through the truth (*emet*) of Torah. □

Targum: English Translation
Genesis 1: 26–27

26) **And God said, "Let us make a human being, in our image, like us. Let them take care of the fish of the seas, the fowl of the air, and the cattle, all the earth, even every creeping thing on earth." 27) And God created the human being like God, in the Divine image, created it, man and woman, God created them.** □

Perush: Explaining the Teaching

Menachem Mendl of Kotzk spent his life obsessed with the search for truth. Here, as in so many other cases, he is fascinated by the ability of human beings to lie. Like other teachers before him, he is intrigued by the plural form of the verb the text uses as God says, "*Naaseh*" ("let *us* make"). We would reasonably have expected the singular "I will make" here instead. Citing a previous rabbinic tradition, the Kotzker finds a possible answer to the problematic plural by explaining that before creating the primordial human being God took counsel with Love, Peace, Truth, and Justice [the latter three are pillars of the earth according to *Pirke Avot* 1:18]. But Menachem Mendl is dissatisfied with the teaching. Why did God only cast out Truth from the creation process? After all, Peace had voted against the creation of human beings, as well. The Kotzker reasons, however, that if no one is seeking personal truth, then of course Peace will be possible. □

Background The Kotzker was interested in truth and truth alone. He was motivated by a fierce argumentativeness in his obsession with the truth. To reach the level of truth, the Kotzker was prepared to sacrifice all else. There is only one truth and everything else is therefore false. The way to truth in the world is a tortuous one. It must do away with all emotional bias and outward appearances. Every day one must try to find the truth just as if it had been unknown before, said the Kotzker. □

(3) Bereishit: A Real Partner

The Teaching
from Mordechai Yosef Leiner of Izbica
from his *Mei Ha-Shilo'ach*

We can explain this odd phrase in the following way. The desire of the Creator was that there should spring up for the Adam-man a supporter and a helper who was opposite him, as in the relationship of a master and disciple. And thus we find recorded in *Bava Metzia* 84a, "Resh Lakish died and Rabbi Yochanan was plunged into deep grief. Said the rabbis, 'Who shall go to comfort him?' Let Rabbi →

Scriptural Context

According to an orderly plan for creation, God created the world. Each day, for six days, God created light, moon and stars, plants and animals, all living things – including human beings. It is the creation of the second human being that is the focus of our text. □

From the Tradition

Rashi suggests that if Adam is worthy, Eve will be a helpmate to him. If he is unworthy, she will be opposed to him, to fight him. □

Targum: English Translation
Genesis 2:18–20

18) God said, "It is not good for **Adam to be alone.** *And I shall make him a helper, over against him.*" 19) **God formed all the wild beasts and all the birds of the sky out of the earth and brought them to Adam to see what he would call them, and whatever Adam called the creature, that would be its name. 20) And Adam gave names to all the cattle and all the birds of the sky and to all the wild beasts; but for Adam no fitting helper was found. □**

Perush: Explaining the Teaching

Our teacher, as in so many other cases, tries to draw meaning from the peculiar construction of the language of our text. What is the meaning of the awkward phrase *"over against"* him? He reasons that it is not a spouse, a fellow "procreator," as we might readily assume. Instead, Adam and Adam's helpmate should reflect the even higher kind of love between master and disciple. They support each other and help each other. Citing a talmudic text, *Mei Ha-Shilo'ach* offers an example of how a student helps and supports his teacher – by pushing him toward full comprehension of God's way.

But that's not enough. Our text goes one step further. Such loving argument, our teacher reasons, leads to a better understanding of God's way, and therefore ultimately brings us closer to ultimate unity. □

Background Mordechai Yosef Leiner of Izbica (d. 1854) is the author of *Mei Ha-Shilo'ach*. *Mei Ha-Shilo'ach* is probably a literary allusion to Isaiah 8:6 and serves as a metaphor for redemption. Founder of the dynasty and rabbi in Radzn, Mordechai Yosef was a disciple of Simchah Bunem of Przysucha and was Menachem Mendl of Kotzk's star student. According to Mordechai Yosef's grandson, Gershon Henikh, the *rebbe* remained hidden in the cave of Adullam for thirteen years studying the Torah in secret until the time when the word of God came. It is a chasidic custom to "tell great tales" of one's *rebbe*. This story is almost a precise replay of that of Shimon bar Yochai, who is the traditionally ascribed author of the *Zohar* and therefore a central figure in kabbalistic lore. Bar Yochai, one of the few surviving disciples of Rabbi Akiba, avoided Roman persecution by remaining hidden in a cave. In 1840, Mordechai Yosef revealed the Torah of the messianic era in a rather bold and imaginative system. □

The Teaching (*continued*)

Eleazar ben Pedat go, whose disquisitions are very subtle.' So he went and sat before him; and on every dictum uttered by Rabbi Yochanan he observed: 'There is a *baraita* that supports you.' Are you as the son of Lakisha? He complained, 'When I stated a law, the son of Lakisha used to raise twenty-four objections to which I gave twenty-four answers, which consequently led to a fuller comprehension of the law; while you say, 'A *baraita* has been taught that supports you,' do I not know myself that my dicta are right?' Thus he went on rending his garments and weeping, 'Where are you, O son of Lakisha, where are you, O son of Lakisha'; and he cried thus until his mind was turned. Thereupon the rabbis prayed for him, and he died.

And this is the decree of all creation: specifically, that controversy creates unity. □

(4) Noach: Paralysis in the Middle

The Teaching
from Mosheh ben Amram Greenwald

How often it is that spiritual awakening comes even to a person who is not on a high enough level of awareness to be purified and to ascend higher. Instead, in the middle of the journey, his lower instincts overcome him, paralyze him, render him unable to move on.

Then there are the pious and the righteous ones who, as we read in Isaiah 40:4, set their hearts on, "making the rugged level, and the crooked places a plain." They →

Perush: Explaining the Teaching

Mosheh ben Amram Greenwald is perplexed by the contradiction between honoring parents and rejecting idolatry: "How does Abraham honor his father if his father was an idolater?" Greenwald solves the problem by examining the mythic legend of *Lech Lecha*. Terach, Abraham's father, set out for Canaan with a clear vision. But, since he was spiritually unfit, he could only go halfway. Greenwald suggests that since Abraham had found the true God, he could go farther than his father. □

Scriptural Context

At the end of this portion, Torah introduces Abraham as the son of Terach. The Torah text delineates Abraham's genealogy and details his family's journey to Haran. God will call Abraham to journey forward in the next portion. This call of *Parashat Lech Lecha* concludes our teacher's lesson. □

Targum: English Translation
Genesis 11:26–12:1

26) **When Terach was 70, he fathered Abram, Nahor, and Haran.** 27) **This is the genealogy of Terach: Terach fathered Abram, Nahor, and Haran. Haran fathered Lot.** 28) **Haran died in his native land while his father Terach was still alive.** 29) **Abram and Nahor married women. Abram's wife was named Sarai; Nahor's wife was named Milcah; she was the daughter of Haran, Milcah, and Iscah's father.** 30) **But Sarai was infertile; she was childless.** 31) **Together, Terach, his son Abram, his grandson Lot, Haran's son and Sarai, his daughter-in-law, his son Abram's wife, all set out from Ur of the Chaldees for the land of Canaan.** *But when they came to Haran they settled there.* 32) **The sum total of Terach was 205 years and Terach died in Haran.**

12:1) *Adonai* **said to Abram, "Go forth from your native land, from your birthplace, and from your father's house to the land that I will show you."** □

From the Tradition

The Master of the Palace may be an allusion to *Genesis Rabbah* 39:1, offering one description of God's revelation to Abraham: "Said Rabbi Isaac, 'This may be compared to a person who was traveling from place to place when he saw a palace in flames. Is it possible that the palace lacks someone to look after it?' he wondered. Whereupon the Master of the Palace looked out and said, 'I am the owner of the place.' Similarly, when Abraham, our father, said, 'Is it conceivable that the world is without a guide?' the Holy One of Blessing looked out and said, 'I am the Guide, the Master of the Universe.'" □

Background The idolatry of Terach is not in the Torah. Instead, it is found in the *Midrash*. The *Midrash* is the rabbinic method of filling in the gaps in the Torah text. In a sense, the *Midrash* tries to tell the rest of the story, as the rabbis see it. Often, as in the case with Terach's idolatry, the *Midrash* becomes so much a part of the Torah reader's psyche that it is difficult to determine the dividing line between Torah and *Midrash*. Fantasy affects reality, changes it, becomes it! □

The Teaching (*continued*)

clear away every obstacle from the way of the Ruler who ascends to the mountain of *Adonai*. They do not remain frozen in the middle of the journey.

Just this is the difference between Terach and Abraham. For while there was awakened in Terach the clear vision to set out for the Land of Canaan, he changed his mind in the middle of the journey. As it is written: "But when they came to Haran [halfway between Ur and Canaan], they settled there" (Genesis 11:31).

But Abraham, our forefather, was not content to rest. He did not get cold feet in the middle of the journey. For this reason, the "Master of the Palace, blessed is the Name" appeared to him and revealed the Self to him, saying, "Go forth from your native land, from your birthplace, and from your father's house to the land that I will show you . . ." (Genesis 12:1). □

(5) Noach: Exiled to Safety

The Teaching
from Aharon Shmuel Tameret

The people of the generation of the flood did great evil, each person injuring and afflicting his brother. They did their evil gratuitously, they loved doing evil for its own sake. Even Noach was only a righteous person in relation to his generation. Unlike Abraham, our father [who when he heard of God's intention to destroy Sodom and Gemorah was pleased on their behalf], when Noach heard the terrible fate, of how all living creatures would be wiped off the face of the earth, he uttered not one peep in protest against the decree. He was only concerned for his own well-being and building an ark to protect himself.

And accordingly, a suitable punishment was meted out for both the wicked and the righteous of that generation. Noach and his sons, everyone got what he deserved. This is what the Holy One did. God brought the flood. And because →

Scriptural Context

This portion focuses on the story of Noach and the flood. Only six chapters and ten generations ago (in the last *parashah*) the world had been created, yet human beings are already corrupt "beyond repair." So God washed the world clean, shutting up in an ark those whom God chose to be progenitors of all the species on a new earth. □

Targum: English Translation
Genesis 7:12-16

12) It rained for forty full nights [without stop]. 13) That same day [when the rain began], Noach and his family: his wife, his son's wives; they all entered the ark. 14) They and all species of beasts, all animals of every kind, all kinds of creepy crawlers, and all varieties of birds, everything that flies. 15) They joined Noach in the ark, two by two, all living flesh. 16) *They came, male and female, from all flesh they came as God commanded them, and* **Adonai, shut** *[Noach] in [the ark].* □

From the Tradition

Following the flood, "God remembered [*Va-yizkor Elohim*] Noach . . ." (Genesis 8:1). This phrase, which is found frequently in the Bible, reflects a Divine belief in the moral potential inherent in human beings. Thus, it is the phrase used in Jewish memorial prayers as well (*Yizkor Elohim*—"May God remember"). What happens in one's life is not forgotten; it is stored up in Divine memory. Even though, like Noach we may have been punished, God will remember us also. □

Perush: Explaining the Teaching

Superficially, Noach appears in a favorable light–the sole righteous person in his generation. Our commentators, however, debate whether his righteousness could be measured on an absolute scale or was only relative to the wickedness of others in his generation. The prevailing rabbinic opinion assumes that he was *tzaddik im pelz* (holy man in a furcoat)–only concerned about his own welfare. For this reason Rabbi Tameret explains that his closure in that ark was actually punishment through isolation. We diminish our righteousness in not being open to the suffering of our neighbors. If we are not sensitive to their needs, we too will be shut out, not only from them but from God as well. □

Background According to *Midrash Ha-Gadol*, God instructed Noach to build his ark publicly and slowly, hoping that when his fellows saw him at his labor, they would be moved to repent. But they paid no attention to his urgings. □

(5) Noach: Exiled to Safety

The Teaching *(continued)*

of the flood, Noach was forced to flee for his life in the ark. And in this way, both wicked and righteous got what was coming to them: those who were completely wicked were wiped off the face of the earth and Noach and his sons were exiled into the ark.

When someone who has accidentally committed murder [according to biblical law] seeks safety in a city of refuge, he is not just seeking protection from a relative of the deceased who wants to avenge the murder, he is also making atonement and restitution for his own sin. In the same way here, the closing of Noach and his sons into the ark was not only to save them from the waters of the flood, but also the punishment of exile, to repair their perversion, for their hearts were cold to the suffering of their companions.

Scripture hints at this idea when it says: "And *Adonai* shut [Noach] in [the ark]," which is to say that Noach indeed entered the ark to save himself but God closed the door behind him, in the same way that a prisoner, locked into his cell by the jailer from the outside, is not allowed to close the door on his own cell from the inside. □

(6) Noach: Two Pockets

The Teaching
from Yechiel of Alexander

Rashi: This verse can be understood in two different ways. There are those of our rabbis who interpret it as a praise of Noach: if he could be a righteous one in such a generation, imagine how good he could be amidst a generation of good people. And there are those who interpret it as Noach's disgrace: Sure, in that generation he could be a righteous one, but in the generation of Abraham, Noach would →

Scriptural Context

The world was corrupt in the time of Noach, so God washed it clean with a flood. Only Noach and his family were saved – as a result of Noach's righteousness. After the flood, the tower of Babel was built. ☐

Targum: English Translation
Genesis 6:9-11

9) **This is the line of Noach.** *Noach was a righteous man, blameless in his age. Noach walked with God.* **10) Noach begot three sons: Shem, Ham, and Japhet. 11) The earth became corrupt before God; the earth was filled with lawlessness.** ☐

From the Tradition

Martin Buber taught that *shiflut*, usually translated as "humility," refers to the sense that one feels the other as oneself and oneself in the other. This person has "drawing power," for when a person rests in oneself as in nothing, that person is not limited by anything. That person is limitless and God is able to pour God's glory into that person. This humility is neither a virtue nor a practiced value. It is not the result of self-humbling, self-restraint or self-resolve. It is like the glance of an innocent child. It is simply just there. The person who is truly humble in this regard realizes that all souls are one. Each is a spark from the original soul and all of the original soul is in each. ☐

Perush: Explaining the Teaching

In the context of the Noach story, Yechiel of Alexander explains the often-debated righteousness of Noach. Would he indeed be considered a good person had he not lived amid the corruption of his time, or was his world so filled with evil that any act of goodness elevated him beyond the moral decay that was commonplace? Rashi is called upon for the traditional explanation. Rashi reasons that if one could raise oneself up to goodness in a world devoid of any goodness, how easy would it be to be righteous when one did not have to try so hard?

Yechiel cites the teaching of Rabbi Simchah Bunem of Przysucha, who brings together the great struggle of human existence: radical humility or glory. Yechiel applies this well-known teaching to the challenge of good and evil acts. When a person feels in control of the world, a veritable master of the universe, he should remind himself that he is merely dust and ashes. Yet, when she is seduced by her evil impulse into feeling worthless and depressed, she should remind herself that the world was created with her in mind.

Noach, contrary to Rashi's reading, was not so bad. While he was surrounded by evil, he conducted himself according to the way of God understood in the text as "a righteous man, blameless in his age." Had he lived in Abraham's age, he would have realized that, amidst such righteousness, he was merely "dust and ashes." ☐

Background Simchah Bunem had four main disciples: Kotzk, Izbica, Ger, and Alexander. They were called the Przysucha school of Chasidism. An influential dynasty of chasidic rabbis in Poland from the second half of the nineteenth century was founded at Aleksandros Lodzki (in Yiddish, "Alexander"). Unlike other *chasidim* they did not take part in party politics in Poland. Yechiel was the son of the Shraga Feivel Danziger and student of Isaac Vorki (the founding *rebbe* of the dynasty). ☐

The Teaching (*continued*)
not even be worthy of mention at all.

Simchah Bunem of Przysucha used to teach that each person in Israel needs to designate two pockets. In one pocket there should be the verse from Genesis 18:27, "I am dust and ashes." And in the other, the passage from *Sanhedrin* 37, "For my sake was the world created." According to need, the person should draw out the message from either pocket.

When the Evil Impulse wants to show a person how great he or she is, or of the greatness of his or her acts or achievements in the learning of Torah and fulfillment of Divine commandments–in order to bring him or her into the power of arrogance and self-centeredness–the person should draw out the scrap that reads, "I am dust and ashes."

When the Evil Impulse wants to snare a person in the net of sadness and depression and show his or her failures, the person would draw strength from the scrap that reads, "For my sake was the world created."

Now Noach was surrounded by the wicked people of the generation of the flood. Nevertheless he conducted himself in the service of God in the way of "For my sake was the world created," as our text reads, "a righteous one blameless in his age." That is to say that he considered himself blameless and righteous. This behavior was necessary for him in a generation of such wickedness so that he would not succumb to their ways. But it he were to live in Abraham's generation, among great righteous ones, Noach, certainly would consider himself "dust and ashes," seeing himself in his own eyes as if he were nothing at all. □

(7) Lech Lecha: Abraham Saves Terach

The Teaching
from the Maharsha

Rashi: "Unto your fathers . . ." [His father was an idolater and yet (the text) announced to him that (Abraham) would go to (his father)! But] this teaches you that Terach repented of his evil ways.

This interpretation raises some problems. How does Rashi get from this verse that Terach made *teshuvah*? Isn't it more likely that Terach remained obdurate in his idolatry? And yet, despite all this, how could he then be rewarded with the Garden of Eden together with Abraham, his son.

An explanation can be found in →

Perush: Explaining the Teaching

The Maharsha is puzzled by God's revelation to Abraham that he would return to his father, Terach (even though he had been an idolater) in peace – that is, in Gan Eden, paradise. But the only way that Terach could be admitted to Gan Eden is if he had repented of his pagan ways; otherwise, how could Abraham go to him! The Maharsha suggests that we must note →

Scriptural Context

Abraham is the central character in this portion. He is called by God and told to leave his native land and begin his [spiritual] journey. Our text is taken from the middle of what is called the covenant of the pieces. This is the second time Abraham hears the Divine promise and responds to it. Our text is taken from this promise. Shortly after, God sends forth a great flame to seal the Divine covenant, as presented in the promise. □

From the Tradition

According to *Genesis Rabbah* (38: 13ff.), young Abraham was an assistant in his father's idol shop. Once when left alone, Abraham smashed all the idols. When his father returned, he demanded to know who had smashed the idols. "The head god," replied a smirking Abraham. Terach said, "You know that idols made of clay can't do such things. I made them all myself." His precocious son replied, "Then why do you worship them, Father?" □

Targum: English Translation
Genesis 15:12–16

12) **At dusk, Abram fell asleep and a mysterious darkness enveloped him.** 13) [*Adonai*] **said to him, "Know for sure that your offspring will be strangers in a land which is not native to them and shall serve them** [the native citizens] **and afflict them** [the Israelites] **for 400 years.** 14) **Then I will adjudicate against that nation in which they will labor. Afterwards, they** [the Israelites] **will leave with great wealth.** 15) *As a result, you will go to your ancestors satisfied;* **you will be buried at a ripe old age.** 16) **And in four generations they** [the Israelites] **will return from there, for the iniquity of the Amorite is not completed."** □

Background The Maharsha (Moreinu Ha-Rav Shemuel Adels, 1555–1631) was a well-known talmudist who married the daughter of Moses Ashkenazi Heilpern. His mother-in-law, by whose name he came to be known, was a wealthy woman who supported his studies and his disciples from 1585 to 1605. He was appointed rabbi of Lublin in 1614 and opened a *yeshivah* in Ostrog in 1625. In his most famous work, *Chiddushei Halachot*, he criticized the technique of *chillukim*, which utilized *pilpul* simply as an exercise to destroy the arguments of a fellow student. While a critic of *Kabbalah*, he quoted it extensively in his work. □

The Teaching (*continued*)

Sanhedrin 104a, where we read that "a son confers privileges on his father but a father confers no privilege on a son. For it is written, 'Neither is there any one that can deliver out of my hand' (Deuteronomy 32:39)" and furthermore, as we learn from *Yoma* 87a, it would be impossible for the son to be in paradise while the father was in Gehinom.

We can also resolve the problem in another way. Scripture says, "And you will go to your fathers in peace . . ." (Genesis 15: 15). "Fathers" is in the plural, implying that not just Abraham's father, Terach, would be in paradise, but also Nahor, Terach's father, as well. But if Nahor were to be in paradise together with Abraham, his grandson, by what merit could Nahor possibly have earned paradise!

From this we can conclude that Terach must have made *teshuvah* and that [as we learned above in Sanhedrin 104a] since "a son confers privileges on his father . . ." he [Terach must have] earned a place also for Nahor, his father, to be with him in Eden. □

Perush: Explaining the Teaching (*continued*)

that "fathers" is in the plural and does not specifically refer to Terach. Instead, it is even stronger. It refers to all of Abraham's ancestors who were also idolaters. The Maharsha teaches that, like Abraham, we are all in the position to actually "heal" our parents. The righteous acts of Abraham actually heal the idolatrous acts of his ancestors. (If they could produce a child like that, they couldn't be all bad.) Taking the burden of the lesson even further, he suggests that our good acts hold the potential for correcting the sins of our ancestors – directing the path of *teshuvah* (a return to God) all the way back to primordial Adam. Jews do not have a notion of "original sin," but here we see that we do have a way of correcting it! □

(8) Lech Lecha: High Test

The Teaching
from the Sefas Emes, Yehudah Aryeh Leib of Ger

Rashi: For your own benefit and reward.

If God assured Abraham that this would be for his own benefit and reward, it's not such a difficult test to endure. And why would this be the first of the ten trials by which Abraham was tried?

Actually this was a great and very difficult test for Abraham. For the text says that ultimately Abraham did not set out on the journey for his own benefit and reward but [simply], "And Abraham went as God had told him" (Genesis 12:4), which is to say that he went

Scriptural Context

This portion begins with the call to Abraham, the first of the ten tests of Abraham. He is told to leave his native land, the land of his ancestors, and journey into a new place where God will direct him. □

Targum: English Translation
Genesis 12:1–4

1) Then *Adonai* said to Abram, *"Go forth from your land*, from your community of birth, from your ancestral home to the land I will show you.* 2) [If you do this] I will turn you into a great nation. I will bless you and establish for you a mighty reputation. You will be a blessing. 3) I will bless [all] those who bless you and curse those who curse you. Because of you, all of earth's families will be blessed. 4) *And Abraham went as God had told him.* Lot went with him. Abram was seventy-five years old when he left Haran. □

From the Tradition

According to *Pirke Avot* 5:3, Abraham underwent ten trials or tests of faith. While different lists of these trials are given, the sages maintain that only the righteous, who are certain to pass the test, are tried (*Genesis Rabbah* 55:1–2). For example, take a look at *Avot de Rabbi Natan* 33:2, *midrash* to Psalms 18:25,98 and *Pirke de Rabbi Eliezer* 26. □

only because of the command of God, without any other specific motive. The test therefore was whether, after all these assurances of reward, he would be able to preserve the purity, doing as God wanted, without contaminating the act with his own motives or confusing it with his own benefit. □

Perush: Explaining the Teaching

This was a simple command by God to Abraham, literally, "Go for yourself," an emphatic construction in Hebrew. And Abraham goes, just as God has commanded him – wouldn't you? The Sefas Emes wants to know what motivated Abraham, for what is at stake is the purity of the motive. Did Abraham know he would personally reap the benefit of his journey? If he did, would that not minimize the power of the test to leave home? Rashi says yes. The Sefas Emes says no. Abraham knew he would be rewarded but dismissed any notion of self-benefit and simply followed God's instructions. And this was his true merit. □

Background One teacher explains that the verse means "Go *to* yourself." Go back to your essence in order to find out what you are really made of. □

(9) Lech Lecha: Two Kinds of Horror

The Teaching
from Shearit Menachem

The language "a great, dark" makes no sense. Can there be a great darkness and a tiny darkness? All darkness is equally dark.

The commentary *Torah Or* explains that the word *great* modifies *horror*. It was a "great horror" and not a "great darkness." And *horror* is appropriately modified by words like *tiny* and *great*. Such words must be meant to evoke an image of the great sorrow that Abraham beheld in his prophetic dream.

And this is according to the interpretation of Rashi: "And behold, a great, dark horror . . ." alludes to the sorrows and the darkness of exile" (cf. *Genesis Rabbah* 44:17).

Targum: English Translation
Genesis 15:10–15

10) **So he took [to himself] all these [aforementioned animals] and divided them, laying each half over against the other but he did not divide the birds. 11) Then birds of prey hovered over the carcasses but Abram drove them away. 12)** *And behold, a great, dark horror fell upon Abram* **when the sun was going down. 13) God said, "Know for sure that your offspring will be strangers in a land that is not theirs and they will serve them and be afflicted for 400 years. 14) But I will judge that nation that they will serve. Afterward, they will come out with great substance. 15) But you will go to your ancestors in peace; you will be buried in a good old age.** ☐

Scriptural Context

In this section of our Torah portion, Abram is promised an heir. The narrative of Abram's (and then Abraham's) spiritual journey takes place just before the covenant of the pieces and Abram's taking of Sarai's maidservant Hagar as a concubine in order that she would bear his children. ☐

From the Tradition

In Genesis 15:1, God tells Abram that God will be a shield to him. Thus, God is referred to as the "shield of Abraham," *Magen Avraham,* as in the first of the eighteen benedictions in the *Amidah.* ☐

Bava Metzia 83b, commenting on Psalm 104:20, which reads, "You bring on darkness and it is night . . . ," explains that "this refers to this world that is comparable to night."

Rabbi Moses Hayyim Luzzatto, in his book *Mesillat Yesharim* (chap. 3), drawing on this passage, goes on to suggest, therefore, that it might after all be possible to say that *great* does modify *darkness.* This world is likened to darkness. If this world is really like the →

Perush: Explaining the Teaching

This teaching, from the teachings of Menachem Mendl of Kotzk, collected by his disciples, points to what is an obvious question at first glance. Why would the text use the adjective *great* to modify the noun *darkness*? Is it to imply that there is also a tiny darkness? Taking his lead from the commentary *Torah Or,* Menachem Mendl suggests that *great* modifies the word *horror* and refers to the horror of exile we are all experiencing. This is to say that darkness is indeed horrible, for darkness implies a world (life) without Torah. For in darkness, one cannot see what is in front of one and might fall into error. In darkness, one would have trouble seeing the path of return. In the dark, one might even confuse the path of evil with the path of *teshuvah,* return, God forbid! ☐

Background In *Genesis Rabbah* 44:17, the rabbis assign each of the adjectives and phrases in the verse to one of the countries that con-

quered the ancient Jewish nation, including Babylon, Media, Greece, and Rome. ☐

The Teaching (*continued*)

night, then it is possible that in darkness, the eyes of a person could make two kinds of errors.

First, a person simply might not see what is in front of him or her. And second, in the darkness a person might confuse a pillar with a human being.

Thus, the physical, tangible reality of this world [of darkness] causes two kinds of errors. One is that a person simply does not see the stumbling blocks that are strewn in so many paths, and fools may be going along securely, when suddenly they fall and perish.

But the second error is even more grievous than the first. In this, people confuse what they see, so that the evil appears as if it actually were good! It is not enough for them that the evil that is right in front of their faces cannot be seen. They imagine for themselves that they behold great proofs and convincing justifications for their egregious opinions and evil ideas.

And just this is "the great darkness": the errors through which human beings stumble, as we have all seen after our many sins. □

(10) Va-Yera: Awakening Above from Below

The Teaching
from Davash Ve-Chalav

The Or Ha-Chayyim, noting a peculiarity of the Hebrew syntax, asks, why does the Torah put the one who sees before the One who is seen? One would expect the logical sequence to be [as the English translation customarily renders it] "And *Adonai* appeared to him. . . ."

It is possible to say, according to Maimonides in *The Guide to the Perplexed*, that one cannot ascribe to the Holy One any change, variation, or motion. Moreover, we find in the stories of the Bible, such as the one before us, "And *Adonai* appeared to him . . . ," and the like, that there is no intention to remove God from God's place [of being perfectly motionless], but rather that God's drawing near or God's revelation to human beings depends on *our* drawing near to God and not the other way around. →

Scriptural Context

As Abraham is resting in his tent, he notices three travelers have come upon him without warning. Rushing to be hospitable, Abraham bids them welcome. □

Targum: English Translation
Genesis 18:1–2

1) *And there appeared to him,* **Adonai,** *by the terebinths of Mamre as he sat near the opening of his tent, in the heat of the day.* 2) **When he looked up [from his rest] he noticed that three men were standing over him. He rushed to meet them at the flap to his tent, prostrating himself before them.** □

From the Tradition

The classic Jewish notion of *hachnasat orchim* (hospitality to wayfarers) takes its lead from this passage in the Bible. In ancient Israel, hospitality was a moral obligation, reflective of the nomadic life of the Israelite people. According to *Avot de Rabbi Natan 7*, Abraham (and Job) were said to have left all four sides of their tents open so that visitors might have easy access at all meals. Rabbi Huna (*Taanit* 20b) openly proclaimed, "*Kol dichfin yeitei ve-yeichal*" ("All who are hungry come and eat"), a phrase now prominent in our *seder* liturgy. This custom of R. Huna has found its way to the *seder* service. □

Perush: Explaining the Teaching

The Davash Ve-Chalav (Honey and Milk) is fascinated with the awkwardness of the Hebrew syntax. Since God, the "author" of Torah, does not waste words or use odd syntax for no reason, our commentary pursues the problem. We would expect the text to read, "And *Adonai* appeared to him," namely Abraham. Echoing the Rambam (Moses Maimonides), the Or Ha-Chayyim reasons, however, that if God were able to move, then God could neither be everywhere nor perfect. Indeed, only the ultimate perfection of God could allow God to be everywhere and thus unmoving. Therefore, it was Abraham, not God, who had to move. As elsewhere in the Bible, even where it initially appears that God is moving, it is actually the human protagonist who moves. It is we as human beings who must move to get closer to God since God cannot "move" to get closer to us.

The Or Ha-Chayyim wants more. He believes, like the kabbalists, that an inner world pulsates within all being. In and out change places. What is above and what is below mirror one another. Yet, we endure this paradox. Thus, the "there" of the text refers to psychospiritual space. □

Background Menachem Mendl Krengel (1847–1930) is the author of *Davash Ve-Chalav* as well as commentaries on other books of the Bible. He was a Polish rabbinical scholar and bibliographer. Especially important is his editing of H. J. D. Azulai's dictionary of scholars and their works. His position on a rather heated controversy with Cracow's rabbi, H. A. Horowitz, over Horowitz's *eruv* arrangements is contained in Krengel's *Torat Eruvim* (1888). □

The Teaching (*continued*)

For example, we notice the sequence of the loving in *Song of Songs* 6:3, "I am my beloved's and my beloved is mine," [which implies that first I give myself to my beloved, and only then does my beloved give himself to me]. This is really only another way of saying that it is according to a person's spiritual readiness and preparation that he will attain an awareness of God. [Only then] will ultimate awareness fill him with the ability to lovingly comprehend God. The same idea is also written in Proverbs 8:17: "Those who love Me, I love; and those who seek Me will find Me." [Again, note how first comes our love for God, which is only then followed by God's response.]

In the language of the kabbalistic maxim, "By means of the awakening below, comes the awakening on high." [Or, perhaps, "By means of the awakening on the outside, comes the awakening within."] And this explains the strange syntax of "And there appeared to him, *Adonai*. . . ." □

(11) Va-Yera: Body Parts

The Teaching
from Rabbi Meir of Peremyshlyany

Our sages have taught in *Yoma* 28b, "Abraham, our father, kept the whole Torah." But this only raises the obvious question of how he could know all the commandments? The Torah had not yet been given!

One explanation could be however that, as is known, there are 248 bones in the human body, which correspond to the 248 positive commandments, and 365 sinews, which correspond to the 365 →

Perush: Explaining the Teaching

There is a spiritual physiology in each and every one of us that is connected to the Torah. Likewise, this is connected to the universe. When we behave in a way we are meant to behave, we are in harmony with that universe. When we listen to our bodies, we will know how to behave. For example, our eyes are there to look at beautiful things. When we look at beautiful things, →

Targum: English Translation
Genesis 18:1-7

1) Abraham felt *Adonai*'s presence in the terebinths of Mamre. He [Abraham] had been sitting at the entranceway to his tent in the heat of the day. 2) When he looked up [from his semi-slumber], he saw three men standing over him. Fumbling to compose himself, he hurriedly bid them welcome, bowing to the ground. 3) *And he said, "My lords, if I have found favor in your eyes, please do not travel on past your servant. 4) Let a little water be brought, [you can] bathe your feet and rest under the tree. 5) Let me get you a little bread so that you might refresh yourselves. After that, you can continue your journey past your servant."* They said, "[We don't want you to go too much trouble], but whatever you want to do, go ahead." 6) Abraham looked into his tent and told Sarah, "Quickly prepare three cakes made from our best flour." 7) Then Abraham ran to his tent, took a first-quality tender calf, gave it to a young servant, who [understanding Abraham's urgency] hastened to prepare it. ☐

Scriptural Context

Following the establishment of circumcision as an affirmation of covenant (therefore *brit milah*) in the previous portion, Abram evolving into Abraham, this portion offers a brief interlude in Abraham's journey. While Abraham is recuperating from his circumcision, he is visited by three messengers of God. The visit is intended to reassure Abraham (and Sarah) that they will indeed bear children even at such an advanced age. When Abraham told Sarah of the Divine promise, she laughed. ☐

From the Tradition

Rabbinic tradition has set the number at 613 of those *mitzvot* given at Sinai, while authorities differ on the articulation of their *mitzvot*. The number is usually known by the Hebrew mnemonic *TaRYaG*. Most lists utilize one of several methods of enumeration. The most typical division is ascribed to Rabbi Simlai of the second century, who divided *mitzvot* into 248 positive →

Background Rabbi Meir ben Aaron Leib of Peremyshlyany (1780?–1850) was the grandson of Rabbi Meir of Peremyshlyany, a disciple of Israel ben Eliezer Baal Shem Tov. It is said that he assisted the Baal Shem Tov in his struggle against the Frankists. While he did not write down his teachings, they were collected and published in fragments by his students. ☐

The Teaching (*continued*)

negative commandments. And the limbs of a righteous one feel a physical yearning inside them to fulfill commandments. Indeed, in each limb resides the root of a different commandment. And conversely, the limbs recoil from doing evil.

In our story, therefore, Abraham must have felt his feet wanting to go and welcome the wayfarers, even though he was, as it were, standing on them. From this he must have learned that showing hospitality to wayfarers is greater than receiving the Presence of God. □

Perush: Explaining the Teaching (*continued*)

it feels good. That is a blessing.

There is also a notion in mystical circles that every part of our body is somehow connected to a *mitzvah*, designed for the special purpose of doing a special *mitzvah*.

Torah itself is a diagram for creation. When we do with a part of our body what it is supposed to do, we are repairing the universe. Our teacher explains that this is what Abraham is doing when he walks (with his feet) to greet strangers—doing great *mitzvot*. Even before the Torah was revealed, Abraham was fulfilling his obligation to the universe, responding to the feeling of his limbs to do *mitzvot*. □

From the Tradition (*continued*)

commandments, corresponding to the number of days in a solar year and 365 negative commandments, corresponding to what the rabbis thought were the number of bones in the human body. □

(12) Va-Yera: Satan on Jewish Survival

The Teaching
from Isaac of Vorki

The merit of Abraham, our ancestor, who bound Isaac, his son, on the altar, has sustained us from generation to generation. But what did Abraham really do that was so extraordinary? Wouldn't any Jew do the same? After all, if the Holy One of Being, in all God's awesome power, appears to you, you would do whatever God commanded.

The answer may be that when the Holy One said to Abraham, "Take your son . . . ," Satan also came to him and said, →

Perush: Explaining
the Teaching

How could Abraham be willing to sacrifice his son Isaac? Our teacher even increases the stakes. He teaches us that Abraham's simple response to the Divine command was even more profound in its simplicity. Satan came to Abraham – just after God – and tried to dissuade Abraham with rational arguments. Yet, Abraham dismisses all of the arguments and simply responds by saying, "I will do what *Adonai* has commanded me." For Isaac of Vorki, this is →

Scriptural Context

This portion focuses on the *Akeidah* – the binding of Isaac – and is read on the second day of Rosh Ha-Shanah (or in Reform congregations on the first day). According to tradition, it is the last of the ten trials that Abraham had to pass, whereby God might determine the extent of Abraham's faith. □

Targum: English Translation
Genesis 22:1-4

1) **After all of that had happened, *God tested Abraham,* saying to him, "Abraham," who responded, "*Hineini*" ["I am here"].** 2) **God said, "Take your special son whom you love and go to the land of Moriah. Offer him there as a sacrifice on one of the mountains, which I will point out for you." 3) And so, Abraham got up early the following morning, saddled his donkey, and took two servants with him, as well as his son Isaac. He had prepared wood for the offering and was all set to go to the place that God would show him. 4) On the third day [of their journey], Abraham noticed *the* place off in the distance.** □

From the
Tradition

Jewish tradition is filled with a variety of interpretations on the *Akeidah*. The *Mishnah* (*Taanit* 2:4) requires a reference to the *Akeidah* on public fast days, "May God who answered our ancestor Abraham on Mount Moriah answer you and respond to your outcry today." Ashes were to be placed in the ark (*Taanit* 2:1) and on the heads of the *nasi* and *av bet din* as a reminder of the ashes of Isaac (*Taanit* 16a). In the section of the liturgy for Rosh Hashanah called *Zichronot* (remembering), there is also an appeal to God to remember the *Akeidah*. Finally, one of the explanations for the sounding of the shofar on Rosh Ha-Shanah is as a reminder of the →

Background Isaac (Kalish) of Warka (1799–1848) was the founder of the Warka (or Vorki) chasidic dynasty in Poland. After officiating as rabbi in the villages of Gowanczow and then Ruda, he became a student of the Seer of Lublin (Jacob Isaac Ha-Chozeh), as well as Simchah Bunem of Przysucha. When Abraham Moses, Bunem's son, died, Isaac settled in Przysucha and became its chasidic leader. Later, Isaac moved to the town of Warka (within the Warsaw district), where he became an influential leader who helped in the abrogation of many government decrees hostile to the Jews (such as military conscription). He went so far as to solicit the help of Sir Moses Montefiore and the British government in order to persuade Czar Nicholas I to reverse several severe decrees (including the prohibition of wearing traditional hasidic garb). Tales about him have been collected in *Ohel Yitzchak* (Piotrkow, 1814) by Meir Walden and *Huzzak Hen* (1947) by Noah Weintraub. □

The Teaching (continued)

"Abraham, look at what you're about to do. Ishmael is already hopelessly distant from the ways of Judaism. That leaves only two Jewish men in the entire world: you and Isaac. So now make a simple calculation. You and Sarah are old; you will have no more children. If you go and slaughter your son, your only one, Isaac, won't you literally blot out Jewish men from the universe?"

But Abraham, our ancestor, would not accept any of these arguments. [Instead] he replied, "I am obligated to fulfill God's command. [God] told me that I should slaughter Isaac, my son; [therefore] whatever the case, I am obliged to slaughter him. All of those calculations that the world will be without Jews are not my concern. The world belongs to the Holy One and it is not for me to supply Jews for it."

And this is the greatness of Abraham: that despite the calculations, the arguments, and the reasons, which all appear correct, he was not dissuaded from the way of truth. □

Perush: Explaining the Teaching (continued)

the way of the highest holiness. Despite everything else, whether rational or emotional, we follow the Divine command.

The exciting thing that Isaac of Vorki has to teach us is what is contrary to a lot of voices in this generation. We hear many people saying that we have to save Jews. Our teacher is saying that we have an obligation to be a Jew. God will worry about whether or not there are Jews in the world. Our job is to worry about being a Jew. □

From the Tradition (continued)

substitution of the ram's horn for Isaac (Rosh Ha-Shanah 16a). □

24

(13) Chayyei Sarah: The Best Years of Life

The Teaching
from the Sefas Emes, Yehudah Aryeh Leib of Ger

Rashi: The word *years* is repeated and without number to indicate that they were all equally good.

But there must be differences, variations, and changes during the years of a person's lifetime. There are special times during a person's youth and special times during a person's old age. But the ones who are truly righteous find fulfillment in all their days. Now certainly, since things are not naturally this way, it must be a gift from God. And this is the meaning of [the words at the beginning of the next chapter]. "And *Adonai* had blessed Abraham in all ways" (Genesis 24:1) means with fulfillment, wholeness, completion, that it be found in every place and at every time. Thus we read in Rashi, "They were all equally good." □

Scriptural Context

Following the final test of Abraham (in the *Akeidah*) in the preceding chapter, the death of Sarah is recounted. The central part of the portion focuses on Abraham's acquisition of a burial place in Hebron: a cave in the field of Machpela. □

Targum: English Translation
Genesis 23:1–2

1) **This was Sarah's lifetime, *the years of the life of Sarah* [numbered] 127 [100 and 20 and 7]. 2) Sarah died in Kiryat Arba, now [known as] Hebron, in the land of Canaan; Abraham began his mourning and bereavement for her.** □

From the Tradition

According to the *midrash* to Proverbs 31, there are 232 women in the Bible deserving of being called a "woman of valor." Since Sarah is the greatest of these women, only her age is listed. □

Perush: Explaining the Teaching

Sensitive to the nuances of the text, the Sefas Emes is troubled by the fact that following the phrase *Chayyei Sarah*, literally, the [years of the] life [span] of Sarah, the word *years* (*shanah*) is repeated three times after each number 100, 20, and 7. Our teacher accepts Rashi's explanation but wonders how Rashi came to the understanding. He ties this phrase to the verse he reads just one chapter later. It is not merely that the years of Sarah's life were equally good. Rather, each and every one of them was good—even amid the seemingly regular disillusionments and disappointments we all must face. The Sefas Emes teaches us that we must live our lives trying to emulate Sarah. □

Background According to the *Midrash* (*Genesis Rabbah* 45:5), Sarah should have reached Abraham's age of 175 years, but 48 years were taken away because of her readiness to dispute with Abraham over Hagar. It seems that her years were reduced when she said, "Let *Adonai* judge between you and me." Rabbi Tanchuma in the name of Rabbi Chiyya the Elder and Rabbi Berekiah said in Rabbi Eleazar's name, "Whoever plunges eagerly into litigation does not escape from it unscathed." □

(14) Chayyei Sarah: Veil of Twins

The Teaching
from Divrei Yirmiyahu

According to *Genesis Rabbah* 60:15, there were two who covered themselves with a veil and who gave birth to twins: Rebecca and Tamar. What is the relationship of the veil to the twins?

Rebecca's twins, Jacob and Esau, were a portent of the war of one brother against another.

Tamar's twins, Peretz and Zerach (Genesis 38:29–30), are a hint of peace, for from them will come the Messiah, the prince of peace.

Both of these matters, the war of brothers and the messianic peace, are covered with a veil. No one knows when the first will end and the second will prevail. But one is bound to the other. When the Holy One removes the veil from one, the second will be revealed. □

Perush: Explaining the Teaching

This verse reminds our teacher of a similar one later in Genesis (38:27ff.) of another woman who gave birth to twins. Like Rebecca, this woman, Tamar, also veiled herself (Genesis 38:14), in order to disguise herself from Judah, and also bore twins. Thus, our teacher concludes that there might be some relationship between these two women and their twins. Why otherwise would Torah have bothered to tell us about the veil? It would have skipped over such a detail. Yet, the veil is really what hides Messiah from us. We do not know when Messiah will come, where Messiah will come. Everything regarding Messiah is veiled in a mystery for us, just as the births of both sets of twins were veiled in a mystery. Esau and Jacob's life was one of strife and struggle and the lives of Peretz and Zerach was pre-messianic. We don't understand why. Like the time of Messiah, it remains a mystery to us; it is veiled. □

Scriptural Context

Sarah has died and a new woman has to take her place. Abraham sends his servant (Eliezer?) to find a wife for Isaac. After Abraham gives the servant a specific set of things to look for in a woman, the servant sets out. At a well outside the city of Aram-naharaim, he meets up with Rebecca. She passes the test and the servant brings her back to meet Isaac. □

Targum: English Translation
Genesis 24: 62–65

62) Isaac had just come back from Beer-lahai-roi, since he lived in the Negev region. 63) In the evening, Isaac went out for a stroll in the field and noticed that camels were approaching. 64) Rebecca looked up [at the same time], saw Isaac get off [quickly] from the camel. 65) *And she said to the servant, "Who is this man coming in the field to meet us?" And the servant replied, "He is my master." So she took the veil and covered herself.* □

From the Tradition

Immediately preceding traditional (Ashkenazi) Jewish weddings, the bride is covered with the veil in a ceremony called *bedecken* (from the Yiddish, meaning "covering" the face of the bride). As this takes place, the rabbi or cantor utters the words from Genesis 24:60, "May you grow into thousands of myriads," the same words uttered by Laban (and perhaps Betuel) as Rebecca left her family to marry Isaac, whereupon bride and groom are separately led to the *chuppah*. □

Background Rebecca had said, "I will," in Genesis 24:58 without gaining her parents' permission. From this text, we derive the *halachah* that a child may make *aliyah* to Israel without the parents' permission – even if they object. □

(15) Chayyei Sarah: The Letter *Vav* as Ego

The Teaching
from Menachem Mendl of Kotzk

[The Hebrew vowel sound for "oo" can be written as either a *shooruk* or a *kubbutz*. A *shooruk* is written with a letter *vav*, which has a dot in its middle. Hebrew grammar refers to such a spelling as being *malei*, or "full." The vowel *kubbutz*, also indicating the "oo" sound, is written *without* the letter *vav* and instead only as three diagonal dots beneath the letter. Hebrew grammar →

Perush: Explaining the Teaching

Our teacher observed that in the two instances where Eliezer questioned whether Rebecca would come to him, when discussing his mission with Abraham, and then with Laban, the text spelled the word *perhaps* first with the full vowel structure and second with a "lacking" vowel structure. The Kotzker pondered what was reflected in the →

Background There is a sense of selflessness in real love, according to the mystics: a loss of self. When you really love some-

Scriptural Context

This section of the Torah portion focuses on the betrothal of Rebecca, as a wife for Isaac. This love story is set in the context of a polygamous, patriarchal society. The transition from singlehood to marriage was simple. Money (or personal services) was exchanged and the veiled bride was brought into the groom's tent as a marriage ceremony. This portion also concludes the saga of Abraham. □

From the Tradition

Shadchanut, the art of arranging a marriage, bringing union to individuals, has a long history in Judaism. According to the *Zohar* (I, 91b), "Each soul and spirit, prior to entering this world, consists of a male and female united into one being. When it descends on this earth, the two parts separate and animate two separate bodies. At the time of →

---

one, you are willing to put their pleasure and ego in front of yours, and mysteriously it means more to you as a result. □

Targum: English Translation
Genesis 24:2–6, 34–40

2) Abraham said to the senior servant in his house who had full responsibility for all he owned, "Place your hand under my thigh. 3) And swear by *Adonai*, God of heaven and earth, that you will not take a wife for my son from the Canaanites among whom I live. 4) But you will go to my land, where I was born, to find a wife for my son Isaac." 5) *And the servant said to [Abraham], "Perhaps the woman will not be willing to come after me to this land; shall I bring your son back to the land you came from?"* 6) Abraham responded to him, "Under no circumstances will you take my son back there."

34) So he began, "I am Abraham's servant. 35) *Adonai* has greatly blessed my master, by making him prosperous, giving him sheep, cattle, gold, servants, camels, and donkeys. 36) My master's wife, Sarah, gave birth to a son in her old age, and he [Abraham] has given him [Isaac] everything he owns. 37) My master made me swear that I would not take a wife for his son Isaac from 'among the Canaanite women in whose land I dwell,' 38) but go to my father's household to my kin, to get a wife for my son." 39) *And I said, "My master, perhaps the woman will not come after me."* 40) *And he said to me, 'The God before whom I have walked will send a messenger with you, and will prosper your way; and you will get a wife for my son from among my kin, from my father's clan.'"* □

27

(15) Chayyei Sarah: The Letter *Vav* as Ego

The Teaching (*continued*)

refers to this spelling as *chaseir*, or "lacking."]

"And the servant said to [Abraham], 'Perhaps [אולי, *ulai*, spelled, *malei* (full): *alef vav lamed yod*], the woman will not be willing to come after me to this land; shall I bring your son back to the land you came from?" (Genesis 24:5).

"And I [Eliezer, the servant] said to [Abraham], 'My master, perhaps [אלי, *ulai* spelled *chaseir* (lacking): *alef lamed yod*] the woman will not come after me.' And he said to me, 'The God before whom I have walked will send a messenger with you, and will prosper your way' " (Genesis 24:39–40).

Why, when Eliezer first asked Abraham himself the question, was the word *perhaps* (אולי) spelled *malei*, that is: *alef vav lamed yod*? Might it possibly be some kind of hint as to Eliezer's personal intention?

The explanation is that at the beginning of the story, Eliezer felt no connection with the matter. [He was a dutiful servant, but not a religious one. Who is Eliezer's real master here? At the onset of the narrative it is Abraham; by the end, he refers to Isaac as his master. Perhaps there is also an intentional shift from serving human masters to serving the Divine one.] It is like the case of a person who is occupied in a particular matter while his heart is directed off to one side or onto some other private motive. [He is filled with his own ego.] And this blinds him from seeing his own connection [to something larger] so that he remains convinced that he is traveling in the proper direction.

Thus, only afterward did Eliezer see that this whole matter came directly from God, that Rebecca was supposed to marry Isaac all along, and that his [unconscious] plan that Isaac marry his own daughter had corrupted his thinking. Only then did he fully realize that from the very beginning, when he first spoke to Abraham, " 'perhaps [אולי, *ulai* spelled *malei* with a *vav*] the woman will not be willing . . .' " he had had a personal interest in the matter and was really only seeking his own welfare.

For this reason, *perhaps* (אולי, *ulai*) is written *malei*, with a *vav* at the beginning of the *parashah*, but *chaseir* (without one) at the end. □

Perush: Explaining the Teaching (*continued*)

speaker that motivated the variation in spelling. He reasoned that at the beginning he was not preoccupied with self. Instead, he was willing to follow (God's directive through) Abraham. Later, when he discussed the mission with Laban, fearing that he would not allow Rebecca to accompany him, he was worried about himself. When one thinks only of self, thinking is lacking. Only when one acknowledges God's work in the world is one filled with the holy. □

From the Tradition (*continued*)

marriage, the Holy Blessed One, who knows all souls and spirits, unites them again as they were before, and they again constitute one body and one soul, forming the right and left side of the individual." With each child born, two souls are separated at birth. □

(16) Toledot: Son Fathers Child

The Teaching
from Yechiel of Alexander

Isaac never thought of himself as being much at all, other than "the son of Abraham"; everything depended on the merit of his father. Abraham, for his part, had never thought that he had done or accomplished much in the service of God or that he had earned any particular merit except for one thing: that he had raised up a worthy son. "Abraham fathered Isaac. . . ." It was a holy way that they did not see themselves as worthwhile in their own eyes; instead their merit came either through their parents or their children. □

Perush: Explaining the Teaching

Since the text here stresses Isaac by listing him first and giving him focus at this point in the narrative, Yechiel of Alexander reasons that there are times when we feel as if our identity is shaped through our parents. Perhaps the ultimate expression of respect for parents is liking who we are. At other times, our identity is colored by our children. We may feel inadequate but believe that our children are great, and we are reassured by virtue of that alone. There is always a constant tension. When we feel our "greatness" is a result of both our parents and our children, our sense of gratitude, fulfillment, and even holiness is heightened.

According to Malachi, in the messianic era, "I will send Elijah the prophet to you before the coming of the awesome day of *Adonai.* God will reconcile parents with children and children with parents—that when I do come, I will not strike the whole land with utter destruction" (Malachi 3:23–24). □

Targum: English Translation
Genesis 25:19–21

19) *This is the family line of Isaac, son of Abraham: Abraham fathered Isaac.* 20) Isaac was forty years old when he took Rebecca, daughter of Betuel the Aramean, of Padan-Aram, Laban the Aramean's sister, as his wife. 21) Isaac pleaded with *Adonai* on behalf of his wife since she was barren. And *Adonai* was persuaded. And [as a result] his wife, Rebecca, conceived. □

Scriptural Context

Following Abraham's death at the end of the last Torah portion and his burial in the cave of Machpelah, we are brought up to date in this portion with the succeeding generation of the ancestral line, through Isaac, Abraham's son. □

From the Tradition

The regular weekly Torah portion takes its name from the first unique word or phrase in the reading and sets the tone for the entire portion. This portion, named *Toledot,* means "generations or family history."

In Jewish tradition, *zechut avot* (the merit of our ancestors) is an important concept. We acquire merit on behalf of the good deeds of our ancestors. This unearned "gift" also urges us to live up to the legacy bequeathed to us. □

Background Yechiel of Alexander was part of a line of influential chasidic rabbis in Poland who were active from the second half of the nineteenth century. Yechiel was the son of Shraga Feivel Danziger, who founded the dynasty. He settled in Alexander (also called Aleksandrow) and made it the seat of the court. □

(17) Toledot: Deep Water

The Teaching
from Shem Mi-Shmuel

In the matter of the digging of the wells, my revered father, Rabbi Abraham of Suchtchov, spoke according to [Bachya ibn Pakuda's] *Duties of the Heart*, on Proverbs 20:5: "The designs of a person's heart are deep waters but a person of understanding can draw them out."

There actually are deep waters but they are concealed and hidden in the depths of the earth. A person of understanding is someone who [knows this and] removes whatever conceals them and then draws them up to the surface.

In the same way, there is also actually great wisdom in a person's mind and heart. One needs only remove the →

Scriptural Context

While the *parashah* begins by detailing the genealogy of Isaac following Sarah's death, as well as the birth of Jacob and Esau, our text focuses on the one brief chapter describing Isaac's adult life. In all other cases, the scant references made to Isaac refer to either his youth or his old age. This episode takes place in Gerar and resembles the experiences of Abraham in the same city (Genesis 20). While some scholars contend that both may be variants on the same story, both Abraham and Isaac claim that their companions are their sisters when they are, in fact, their wives. □

From the Tradition

Bachya (ben Joseph) ibn Pakuda, who lived in the second half of the eleventh century in Muslim Spain, probably at Saragossa, was a poet and philosopher, best known for his *Duties of the Heart* (c. 1080). It was a popular text that had influence on all later pietistic literature, and he made a distinction there between →

Targum: English Translation
Genesis 26: 17–18

17) As a result [of Abimelech's telling Isaac to leave, since the Philistines stopped up his wells—a grave offense in an area where water was precious], Isaac left and made camp in the wadi of Gerar, where he [eventually] settled. 18) *Isaac dug anew the wells that had been dug during Abraham's days [there], which the Philistines had stopped up following Abraham's death. He [Isaac] gave them [the wells] the same names that his father [Abraham] had given them.* □

Perush: Explaining the Teaching

Our teacher reminds us of the need for an individual to return to his or her roots, gaining a more mature understanding of the wisdom of one's parents. Isaac comes to understand and appreciate his father, →

Background This same generational reverence is described in a story about Bunem of Otvotchek-Vorki. After the death of Menachem Mendl of Vorki (on 16 *Sivan* 5628 [1887]), his *chasidim* appointed as successor, his son, Bunem of Otvotchek-Vorki, who ultimately emigrated to Israel. Bunem immediately set out for the court of Rabbi Yankeleh of Radzimin in order to receive formal confirmation of his new appointment.

But in Radzimin they did not even welcome him. So, stationing himself among the many there who had come seeking the *rebbe*'s help, he waited in line for an audience. When he was finally admitted to the chamber of the Radzi-miner, he was received with this statement: "We esteem the grandfather, and have even heard of the reputation of the father, but who are you?"

Whereupon Bunem of Otvotchek replied without hesitation: "We read in the Torah that Abraham dug wells and that so did Isaac, but we have no record of Jacob digging wells. This is because once Abraham, the father, and Isaac, the son, had dug wells of living water, Jacob, the grandson, was able to easily draw water right from the spring itself."

Upon hearing this, the rabbi of Radzimin immediately offered his hand and said, "*Shalom aleichem*, rabbi of Vorki!" □

The Teaching (continued)

clay that covers it and hides it.

This is the real meaning of the digging of the wells: it is a hint and metaphor for the lifework and influence of Isaac. For him the vulgar clay was not enough to conceal the holy wisdom in the heart of Israel. □

Perush: Explaining the Teaching (continued)

Abraham. Water, which frequently serves as metaphor for salvation, strikes a chord for Shmuel Bornstein, the author of *Shem Mi-Shmuel*. There is a redemptive quality about the wells. When Isaac digs them, he finally realizes what his father went through. Realizing his father's wisdom, Isaac now calls the wells by the very same names that Abraham had given them.

In so doing, Isaac comes to the profound realization that, despite our efforts to the contrary, we are our parents. We have become them. The middle-aged man looks in the mirror one morning while shaving and realizes that he looks just like his father–as he remembers him at that age. The struggle for Isaac (and for us) is like coming home. Spiritually mature adults realize that their parents are in them.

Isaac's digging is therefore a sacred task. We realize that as the narrative progresses in the Bible, he is a bridge between Abraham and Jacob. It is the same relationship we have to our parents and to our children. □

From the Tradition (continued)

those commandments that require physical action and those that are founded on more informal and private matters (hence, duties of the heart). Both kinds, he believes, are divinely commanded and contained in Torah, and duties of the heart are all rational. While it is a practical guide, he insists on a theoretical knowledge as a prerequisite for practice. Bachya's final goal in the book is love of God, which he defines as the soul's turning to God so that it may actually cleave to the Divine's upper light. The soul is a simple spiritual substance, implanted by God in the body, but it wants to free itself from the desires of the flesh in order to attain a spiritual state. Shunning asceticism as it is generally conceived, one's intentions must coincide with one's actions in working toward the service of God, realized in community, not in isolation. Humility, repentance, and self-examination are also essential. □

(18) Toledot: Freedom from Parenthood

The Teaching from Yalkut Yehudah

Genesis Rabbah 63:10 – Rabbi Levi offered a parable: They [Jacob and Esau] were like a myrtle and a wild rosebush growing side by side; when they matured and blossomed, one yielded its fragrance and the other its thorns. So for thirteen years both went to school and came home from school, [but] after this age, one went to the house of study and the other to idolatrous shrines. Rabbi Eleazar (ben Rabbi Simeon) said: A parent is responsible for his or her child until the age of thirteen; thereafter the parent must say: ברוך ‖ שפטרני מעונשו של זה, *Baruch sheptarani mei'ansho shel zeh*, "Blessed is the One who has now freed me from the responsibility of this child." →

Scriptural Context

This portion begins with the line of Isaac. Following Isaac's entreaty on behalf of his infertile wife, Rebecca, they are blessed with the birth of twins. Our text is taken just after Jacob and Esau were born. □

Targum: English Translation
Genesis 25:24–27

24) **And when she [Rebecca] came to term [she realized] there were twins in her belly.** 25) **The first one delivered was ruddy and hairy; he was called Esau.** 26) **Next, his brother was delivered with his hand holding Esau's heel; him they called Jacob. Isaac was sixty years old when she gave birth to them.** 27) *And the children grew up.* **Esau became a skillful hunter, an outdoorsman, and Jacob was a sedentary man, a homebody.** □

From the Tradition

According to Rashi, Jacob had prepared a mourner's meal when Esau sold him his birthright. It was the day of Abraham's death. Lentils are round, and mourning rolls from one person to another. Since they have no opening, during mourning we speak of no idle chatter. From this, we also derive the custom that eggs are served at the beginning of a mourner's meal. They roll and have no opening. □

Perush: Explaining the Teaching

Our teacher searches the text to determine what happened to Jacob and Esau as they grew into manhood. What do we know about their childhood? Did their parents recite the traditional blessing at their *bar mitzvah* (the contraction of time and place is, of course, of no consequence to classic rabbinic thought)? Our teacher is troubled that the parent should recite a blessing (and thereby rejoice) when he or she is freed from the responsibility of parenting. After all, parenthood itself is a blessing and a fulfillment of the *mitzvah peru urevu* (be fruitful and multiply). The structure of the blessing, which does not contain the expected formula *Baruch attah Adonai* (Praised are you *Adonai*), contains a hint that the blessing is not what you would expect it to be. And the blessing, therefore, should not be understood in the way people generally read it, as simply a sanctioned release from →

Background Mordechai ben Abraham Jaffe (c. 1535–1612) was born in Prague but studied in Poland under Solomon Luria and Moses Isserles. A great talmudist and kabbalist, he was a communal leader as well (later in Gradno and Lublin as well as Kremeniec, Prague, and Posen). He was also active in the Council of the Four Lands. He established a *yeshivah* in Prague in 1553, when he returned after his study of the *Kabbalah* with Mattathias ben Solomon Delacrut. In his *Levush Malchut* (which eventually became ten "books" compiled over fifty years), he presented Joseph Caro's *Bet Yosef* in abbreviated form. There he relied on the same three pillars of authority as had Caro, that is, Alfasi, Maimonides, and Asher ben Jehiel. In his later writings, he applied similar formulas to the work of Isserles. □

The Teaching (*continued*)

The reason the parent says ברוך שפטרני, "Blessed is the One who has now freed me . . ." is that up until this time the parent was punished whenever the child sinned, since [such behavior meant that] the parent had not properly educated the child.

However, in the *Levush* [Mordechai Jaffe, 16th century, Prague] it is written just the opposite: that until now the child was punished on account of the sin of the parent. As it says [in *Ketubot* 8b, citing Deuteronomy 32:19] " 'And *Adonai* saw and spurned, because of the provoking of God's sons and God's daughters.' [This means, in] a generation [in which] the parents spurn the Holy One, blessed be God, God is angry with their sons and their daughters and they die when you are young."

Thus also we read in *Midrash Sifrei* (alluding to Deuteronomy 24:16) " 'The parents shall not be put to death on account of the children, nor the children on account of the parents; each person shall be put to death for his or her own sin.' A person shall be put to death for his or her own sin; [nevertheless experience seems to teach that while] adults die for their own sin, children [do die] for the sin of their parents." If so, then a child ought to offer a blessing for being liberated from punishment incurred on account of his or her parents, since from now on the child no longer carries the iniquity of the parents.

So then why does the parent offer a blessing [at benei mitzvah]? The answer appears to be according to the *Levush*. For indeed, one ought to worry more that one not injure others than that oneself be injured. And the [author of] *Machatzit Ha-Shekel* conjectures according to the words of our sages, their memory is a blessing, in *Shabbat* 149b: Anyone through whom one's neighbor is punished is not permitted to enter within the barrier (precincts) of God. For this reason, the parent needs to rejoice especially, for from now on the parent can no longer injure his or her child nor could the parent cause the child to be punished on account of the parent's transgression. And that is why the parent makes the blessing. □

Perush: Explaining the Teaching (*continued*)

the obligation of parenting. Instead, this teaching suggests that the parents no longer have to worry that their wrong will potentially injure others. The parent can no longer cause a child to be punished on account of the parental transgression. It's like saying, "Thank God, I don't have to worry anymore about 'messing' up my child." It is this unique joy that is the release the parent feels. □

(19) Va-Yetze: Self-Annihilation

The Teaching
from *Tiferet Shelomoh*, Shelomoh of Radomsk

If the presence of the Holy One indeed dwells here, if I have invoked the holiness in this place, it must be because "My I, I did not know." I obliterated everything that was in me; my sense of self-awareness; any consciousness of ego; any trace of self-intention. Everything was now only for the sake of the Holy Name itself; for the sake of unifying the holiness within all being and its presence! □

Perush: Explaining the Teaching

The Hebrew syntax of the second part of the verse is unusual. The initial pronoun (*ve-anochi*) seems superfluous. In the past tense (*yadati*), the pronoun *I* is already included in the structure of the Hebrew verb. Yet, since there can be no redundancies in sacred text, we are challenged to search out its deeper meaning. Such →

Targum: English Translation
Genesis 28:10–17

10) Jacob left Beersheva and traveled in the direction of Haran. 11) As the sun was setting, he found *the* place to rest. Using stones as a pillow for his head, he lay himself down. 12) His dream: a ladder was standing straight up with its top rungs reaching heavenward. Angels were going up and down on it. 13) Suddenly, Jacob realized that *Adonai* was standing beside him [or on it] saying, "I am *Adonai*, the God of Abraham, your [grand] father, and the God of Isaac. I will give the land on which you rest to you and to your descendants. 14) I will also make sure that your descendants are numerous and spread them to the west, east, north, and south [all over the earth]. Through your descendants will all who inhabit the earth be blessed. 15) And don't worry, I will be with you wherever you go. I will bring you back to his land. I shall not leave you until I have fulfilled my promise to you." 16) Suddenly, Jacob arose from his rest and said to himself, "*Surely God is in this place and me, I did not know it.*" 17) Jacob was moved and thought to himself. "This place is awesome. It can be none other than God's dwellingplace and the gateway to heaven." □

Scriptural Context

In the preceding portion, with the complicity of his mother, Rebecca, Jacob deceived Isaac and stole his father's blessings originally(?) intended for Esau. In this portion, fearing retribution from Esau, Jacob fled, leaving Beersheva, traveling toward Haran. In a place later to be named Beth-el, Jacob rested and dreamed. Here, the text recounts the famous "Jacob's ladder" vision. □

From the Tradition

Hitlahavut (ecstacy), or the "inflaming" as Buber describes the word, reflects the rapture the individual feels as part of religious life. It does not merely reflect a mystical experience. Rather, when an individual attaches his life to God, this feeling envelopes him in the most menial of tasks. □

Background Shelemoh of Radomsk (also known as Solomon Ha-Kohen Rabinowich of Radomsko, 1803–1866) was appointed rabbi of Radomsk in 1834 and accepted as a chasidic leader beginning in 1843. He was well known for his wit. His *Tiferet Shelomoh* (1867–1869) is considered to be a classic work of Polish Chasidism. He was also the author of *Berit Avraham* (1819), a book of responsa. □

Perush: Explaining the Teaching (*continued*)

"extra" words must reveal something deeper. Here, the commentator, Shelemoh of Redomsk, brings us to the edge of language. By changing the usual translation of the verses, he suggests that we must get rid of our selves in order to know God. We must exit the self-reflective mode of consciousness for it impairs our ability to attain awareness of God's presence. In other words, we have to dance with so much of ourselves that when the music has stopped we realize that we were totally unaware that it was we who were dancing. □

(20) Va-Yetze: The Light of a Holy Place

The Teaching
from the Sefas Emes, Yehudah Aryeh Leib of Ger

Rashi: Our rabbis interpret it as if the verb meant "to pray," as we read in Jeremiah (7:16), ["Do not plead (תפגע, *tifgah*)] with Me...." We learn in *Berachot* 26b thereby that he established the evening prayer. The biblical text changes the word for praying and does not write the customary one, *va-yitpalalel*, in order to teach you that the earth shrank before his steps [cf. *chullin* 91b].

But this makes no sense, for what does the earth's shrinking have to do with establishing the evening prayer? Only perhaps that certainly through the force of will, a person is able to awaken the holiness of God in any place. And this is what Rashi says: Mount Moriah was uprooted and came to that place. Hence the interpretation that when Jacob, our father, →

Perush: Explaining the Teaching

Jacob comes (*va-yifgah*) to a place. By using the principle of *gezeirah shavah*, he hears in the word *yifgah*, "and he prayed." But Rashi says that he does not understand the relationship between the earth's shrinking and the evening prayer. Our teacher dismisses Rashi's criticism with a similar inquiry: "What indeed does one thing have to do with the other?"

Scriptural Context

On his way to Haran to visit relatives, Jacob stops to rest for the night. He places a stone under his head and dreams. □

Targum: English Translation
Genesis 28:10–11

10) So Jacob left Beersheva and headed toward Haran. 11) *And he came upon a place and spent the night there for the sun had [already]* **set. He took a stone from the area, placed it under his head, and lay down there.** □

From the Tradition

(1) The *gezeirah shavah* form of argument is a hermeneutic principle that allows the rabbis to compare similar expressions of the same word when it appears in two Torah texts. Thus, the law in one could be applied to the other. In order to control potential abuses, the rabbis determined that a rabbi could not reason a *gezeirah shavah* on his own. He had to have learned it from his teacher. Both passages must come from the Torah only (and not the Prophets or Writings sections of the Bible). And the word under scrutiny must not be superfluous; it must have a direct impact on the context of the sentence.

(2) According to mainstream Jewish tradition, although there is some difference of opinion among our teachers, the fixing of the three times for daily prayers can be traced back to the patriarchs: Abraham, "And Abraham got up early in the morning and stood before *Adonai*" (Genesis 19:27); Isaac, "And Isaac went out to meditate in the field at evening" (Genesis 24:63); and Jacob, "And he came upon a place and spent the night there for the sun had [already] set" (Genesis 28:11). □

Through the force of will, you can awaken God. So the Sefas Emes concludes that Rashi is smarter than even Rashi realizes himself. Mount Moriah came to where Jacob was. The Sefas Emes recognizes that light operates in two contexts: one physical and one metaphysical. Light is awareness and consciousness, and it is our responsibility to put these contexts together. Thus, for our teacher, the distinction of time and space ceases to exist here. For this lesson, he establishes a kind of time warp. If we want it enough, we can turn on the light anywhere. □

Background The ladder (or stairway, ramp), according to ancient belief, represents a cosmic bond between heaven and earth. □

The Teaching (*continued*)

had a strong desire to go to Mount Moriah, even though it was very far away, Mount Moriah jumped to where he was. This is the explanation of how he established the evening prayer, for certainly when it gets dark, there is no place where the light is revealed. For only by means of extraordinary desire can one awaken that light that is beyond natural order, for everything depends on a person's desire. And this is Rashi's meaning when he says, "to teach you that the earth jumped beneath him." The explanation is that from this we learn that for every person in Israel – with authentic reaching – there is no place where one is unable to feel the inner light. □

(21) Va-Yetze: The Great Truth of Reverence

The Teaching
from the Sefas Emes, Yehudah Aryeh Leib of Ger

Jacob dreamed and attained an awesome and incredible dream that under normal circumstances should have filled him with pride and strength, but instead fear and trembling overcame him: "And Jacob awoke from his sleep. Shaken, he said, 'How awesome is this place!'"

This is a sure sign of great truth. It contains so much. Every event that occasions reverence also participates in ultimate truth. And [when a person experiences] such an event with truth in it, then reverence overwhelms the person. Reverence: it is the beginning of everything and the end of everything. □

Perush: Explaining the Teaching

Instead of feeling special and arrogant about his dream, Jacob is humbled. The Sefas Emes senses this humility and suggests that feeling awe is an indication of truth. Reverence for the presence of God and ultimate truth go hand in hand. □

Scriptural Context

Jacob had fled Beersheva, heading toward Haran—trying to escape Esau's wrath. This portion begins with Jacob's dream—a ladder that binds heaven and earth. Awestruck he awoke and sensed God's presence in his midst. □

Targum: English Translation
Genesis 28:16–17

16) Jacob woke from his slumber. He said [to himself], "*Adonai* is in this place and I did not [even] know it." 17) *Shaken, he said, "How awesome is this place!"* **This is none other than God's place, the [very] gate to heaven."** □

From the Tradition

English is customarily printed with only one form of paragraph. The text of a *sefer Torah*, on the other hand, is broken into two kinds, which are distinguished by the shape of the "white space" that follows them. "Open" paragraphs end with a space that runs uninterrupted into the white space of the margins, as in English printing. "Closed" paragraphs end with enough white space for only a word or two, whereupon the first word of the next paragraph begins without commencing a new line. This creates an area of white space entirely "enclosed" by text.

In *Parashah Va-Yetze*, unlike any other *parashah* in the Torah, there are no paragraph spaces at all, neither open nor →

Background According to the alternative comment on the same text by the Sefas Emes, Jacob, our father, presumed that the holiness of the revelation was because of the holiness of the place. But our sages, their memory is a blessing, said that Mount Moriah jumped up and came to him. There is no contradiction here; both are true.

Jacob, from his great piety and humility, felt that the place was the cause of the revelation whereas actually everything was because of Jacob's merit.

Things are this way because of the kindness of God. God sees to it that those who love God are spared from having any of their good deeds contaminated with even the slightest bit of arrogance. In this way the upright do not stumble. □

From the Tradition *(continued)*

closed. This is the way it has been handed down by Masoretic tradition. (See Minchat Shai and Maimonides' commentary to chapter 8 on *Hilchot Sefer Torah.*)

According to the Sefas Emes, the Torah implies by this that Jacob, our father, never took his thoughts off the Land of Israel during his two-decade long journey. Even going far away from Israel never distracted him. As we read at the end of the *parashah*, "Laban left on his journey homeward. Jacob went on his way, and angels of God encountered him" (Genesis 32:1–2).

This is what Rebecca said when she sent Jacob fleeing off to Haran to stay with her brother Laban: "Stay with him a few days . . ." (Genesis 27:44). All those years were like just a few days for Jacob because he was one with its Source. Perhaps this is the intended meaning of the Torah: that all those years were like just a few days on account of his love for her (Israel or Rebecca?), for by means of this love he was able to be one with God.

And this is the main intention behind his vow just after he had the dream of the ladder: "If God will be [one] with me . . ." (Genesis 28:20), that he not be separated from being one with God and with his root.

(22) Va-Yishlach: Engraved on a Throne

The Teaching
from the Sefas Emes, Yehudah Aryeh Leib of Ger

In *Chullin* 91 we learn that dust from their wrestling ascended all the way to the Throne of Glory itself. "This in turn might mean that, since [according to tradition] the form of Jacob was engraved on the Throne of Glory, then the force of the struggle with the Other Side must extend all the way to the throne itself. Consider the *Maftir* of *Parashah Be-Shallach:*

"Then *Adonai* said to Moses, 'Inscribe this in a →

Perush: Explaining the Teaching

In this rather complicated and clever series of wordplays, the Sefas Emes brings us to the notion that Messiah is not possible unless the inclination to do evil is completely destroyed. Let us follow his reasoning. From the word *and he wrestled,* בְּהֵאָבְקוֹ, he hears a homonym for dust *(avak).* And so he calls our attention to a text from *Chullin* that suggests that the dust of the struggle reached the Throne of Glory (an image of Ezekiel's vision and a paradigm for →

Scriptural Context

Here at the beginning of this portion, Jacob is near the end of his exile. He has not seen his brother for over two decades. While preparing to meet him, at night, alone, and terrified on the other side of the river Jabbok, a man wrestles with him. When the struggle is over, Jacob emerges with a new name, Israel. □

Targum: English Translation
Genesis 32:23–29

23) On the same night [that Jacob prepared to meet Esau] he arose, taking with him his two wives, their maidservants, and eleven children; together they all crossed the Jabbok ford. 24) After crossing them all through the river, he sent over all his possessions. 25) And while Jacob was alone, he struggled with a man until dawn. 26) When he [the man] saw that he had not prevailed, *he wrenched his [Jacob's] hip at the socket so that it would be sore as they wrestled.* 27) Then he said, "Let me go for dawn is breaking." And he [Jacob] said, "I will not set you free until you bless me." 28) And he [the man] responded, "What is your name?" And he said, "Jacob." 29) And he [the man] said, "No longer will you be called Jacob. You are now [to be known as] Israel, since you have striven with divine and human beings and prevailed. □

From the Tradition

The Baal Shem Tov taught that Rashi's explanation raises two further problems. If Jacob was already so wealthy that he could afford to send Esau many flocks as a gift, why would he bother risking his life by returning for a few little things? And furthermore, why would the patron of Esau wrestle with Jacob here [of all places] when he was on such a trivial errand?

The explanation is that every now and then, a person needs to put himself or herself in danger in order to save "just a little thing," a clay pot that has become ritually defiled by its contents and must now be retrieved for atonement.

The evil patron of Esau does →

Background Rashi taught that the reason Jacob went back alone to the other side of the river, after taking his family and possessions across, was that he had forgotten a few little things and returned for them.

According to Nachalat Chamishah, our sages have taught that the angel was the patron of Esau. And, in the *Zohar* I, 155, we learn that this is none other than "the Adversary himself," our own evil impulse. Indeed, the *gematria*, the Hebrew numerical equivalent for "a few little things, [*Pachim ketanim,* פכים קטנים, →

40

The Teaching (continued)

document as a reminder, and read it aloud to Joshua: I will utterly blot out the memory of Amalek from under heaven!' And Moses built an altar and named it Adonai-nissi [*Adonai* is my banner]. He said, "It means 'Power extending unto the throne of *Adonai*!' *Adonai* will be at war with Amalek throughout the ages" (Exodus 17:14–16).

The implication here seems to be that even the Throne cannot be complete until the name of Amalek is blotted out. But could one, God forbid, ascribe a blemish to the Throne of Glory? Perhaps our text means to teach that the revelation of God's glory in the world cannot occur as long as Amalek endures. Thus, in the same way, the expansion of the power of Jacob and the revelation of his form must remain incomplete until Amalek's memory is eradicated.

As we read in *Genesis Rabbah* 77:1: " 'There is none like unto God, O Jeshurun [Jacob]' (Deuteronomy 33:26) . . . Rabbi Berekiah interpreted this in the name of Rabbi Simon: There is none like God; yet who is like God? Jeshurun, which means Israel [Jacob] the Patriarch. Notice that just as it is written of God, 'And the Lord alone shall be exalted' (Isaiah 2:11), so too is it written of Jacob, 'And Jacob was left alone.'" [Both Jacob and God are] unable to fully reveal themselves until sometime yet in the future. □

Perush: Explaining the Teaching (continued)

mystical encounters). Yet, the Sefas Emes knows from other rabbinic tradition that Jacob's image is also engraved on the throne. If Jacob is now no longer a perfect form, since he was crippled in the struggle, how could his form be on the Throne of Glory, which should be perfect in all aspects? After all, this is where God sits.

This teaches us that the struggle we have with the dark side of our personalities (with Amalek and the peoples of the world who seek our destruction and our own darker side) extends all the way to and ultimately affects God – that is why the image of Jacob is on the Throne. □

From the Tradition (continued)

everything within his power to perpetuate states of defilement [even] for clay pots and struggles with Jacob who wants to save them. But if Jacob persists again and again to save even "little things," even placing himself in danger to restore them to the purity of their former state, certainly the Holy One would come to his help. □

Background (continued)

40 + 10 + 50 + 9 + 100, 40 + 10 + 20 + 80 = 359] and the Adversary" [Satan, שטן, 50 + 9 + 300 = 359] are identical.

There is a hint here, through using "a few little things" (*pachim ketanim*, which has the same numerical equivalent as "the Adversary"), that in such a way the Evil Impulse first seduces a person with "a few little things" [just trivial matters, little by little, imperceptibly] until it finally says, "Now go and [do the most horrendous imaginable act:] worship idols!

But Jacob, our father, showed the way for generations yet to come. By returning even for a few little things, he showed that by their power one is able to do battle with "the Adversary," the Evil Impulse.

"And a person wrestled with him until the break of dawn," until, that is, the dawning of the truth. As our sages have taught in *Sukkah* 52a: "In the time to come, the Holy One will slaughter the evil impulse, obliterating it entirely from creation." □

(23) Va-Yishlach: Esau's Head

The Teaching
from Joshua of Kutno

Initially it seems surprising that Jacob, who was accustomed to angels, should ask for the name of an angel. Indeed, it appears that Jacob thought it was a human being.

How could he have made such an error? The idea here is that the name of a thing contains its essential being. Rabbi Meir was always meticulous about the name.

Now this angel was a patron saint of Esau, an angel from the highest heavens. But nevertheless Jacob detected in it the Source of Evil, the spirit from which Esau drew nourishment. And it was astonishing to Jacob. And that is why the angel replied, "Why do you ask my name?"

Scriptural Context

Following the intense spiritual struggle that Jacob endures through the night, he inquires of the name of his adversary. The response he receives is also a question. At that point, he recognizes that he is on holy ground and is spiritually transformed. □

Targum: English Translation
Genesis 32:30–31

30) *Jacob asked and said, "Please tell me your name."* **But he answered, "Why do you ask my name?" And he left.** 31) **So Jacob named the place Peniel, meaning "I have seen God face-to-face and my life has been preserved."** □

From the Tradition

According to *Zohar* I, 250b, as long as Jacob lived in Canaan, a heavenly light shone on the cave at Machpelah. When Jacob entered it, the fragrance of paradise was ever apparent. All this ceased when Jacob went down to Egypt and did not return until his dead body was brought back to Canaan. □

The essential being of Esau is a mixture of good and evil, but [note that during the skirmish that broke out during the burial of Jacob, when Esau appeared, claiming the sepulcher was his, he was decapitated, so that] the head of Esau [rolled down into the tomb and] is buried in the cave at Machpelah. □

Perush: Explaining the Teaching

Like so many of our teachers, Joshua of Kutno is intrigued by Jacob's wrestling with God. He is surprised that Jacob, who was already accustomed to angels, would ask the wrestler his name. Since the author of Torah included Jacob's question for a reason, it must be to teach us that Jacob thought that the angel with whom he was wrestling was really a human being. But this angel was not an ordinary angel. While it was an angel on high, it was the patron of Esau. This astonished Jacob – and so he pressed the angel to see if the angel was indeed somehow connected to Esau (whom Jacob was getting ready to meet). The angel, in turn, is surprised at Jacob's request, and instead of telling him, the angel replies, "Why do you ask my name?"

Our teacher concludes this teaching by reminding us that Esau too was a mixture of good and evil. We are reminded of a bizarre legend in *Sotah* 13a that Esau got involved in a fight [read, wrestled] when Jacob was buried at Machpelah. Esau said he deserved the burial place among his ancestors. He was decapitated, so the story goes, and thus his head was buried at Machpelah. □

Background According to *Leviticus Rabbah* 32:5, one of the causes of the Israelites' eventual deliverance from bondage is that they did not change their names. The ancients believed that one's essence was inextricably bound to one's name. If you changed your name, you were, in effect, changing who you were. In a modern sense, we understand this as well. The European immigrants who quickly Americanized their names strove to discard their heritage, who they were. And those of the Diaspora who Hebraized their names upon immigrating to Israel also wanted to shed the baggage of their past. □

42

(24) Va-Yishlach: What's It to You?

The Teaching
from Y. L. Hasman

Our sages have taught that this un-named wrestler was the patron saint of Esau, Satan, the Impulse to Evil. And this is why he answered Jacob that his name was למה זה תשאל לשמי (Why do you ask my name?).

Every name conveys something of the essential nature of the one who bears it. And the essential nature of the Im-pulse to Evil is למה זה תשאל לשמי (Why do you ask my name?). In other words, "Why should you search and examine?"

This is because all its (Evil Impulse) power derives from lack of under-standing and illu-sion. But it pos-sesses no intrinsic substance or importance by itself. It is all breath on the mirror and bad breath at that.

And so it is with the objects of all worldly desires. They are only illusions that portray for a person the sweetness of what is desired, but once a desired object is attained, it is transformed from illusion to reality. Then in bright sunlight, the person beholds what has seized him and what he has really gained. □

Scriptural Context

The struggle now over, Jacob has a new name: Israel. Now Jacob wants his adver-sary to disclose his identity. Jacob reasons that if he knows his name, he might be able to understand the essence of his strug-gle. But he does not get the answer he seeks and therefore must seek the answer to his struggle on his own. □

Targum: English Translation
Genesis 32:30–33

30) *Jacob, asked, and said, "Please tell me your name." But he answered, "Why do you ask my name?" And he left.* 31) **So Jacob named the place Peniel, meaning "I have seen God face-to-face and my life has been preserved."** 32) **The sun rose as he was traversing Peniel limp-ing on his hip.** 33) **As a result, Israelites may not to this day eat the thigh muscle that is on the hip socket, since Jacob's hip socket was wrenched at the thigh muscle.** □

From the Tradition

Since the tradi-tion of not eating thigh meat was ap-parently so widely observed, it is not specifically men-tioned in the biblical dietary codes. The actual removal of the sciatic nerve and the accompanying forbidden fat is called porging (in Yiddish, *treibuering*; in Hebrew, *nikor*). It is a difficult procedure and only financially worthwhile in communities where meat is very scarce. For this reason, in most communities Jews simply refrain from eating the hindquarters. □

Perush: Explaining the Teaching

Our teacher Y. L. Hasman deliberately misreads what appears to be a question in answer to Jacob's question, as indeed an answer. Since one's name conveys one's essential nature, and the essential nature of evil is illusory, and since this question is in response to Jacob's request for the wrestler's name, we learn that the wrestler is none other than the Evil Impulse. This wrestler is an illusion just like all worldly possessions. Only God and truth are transcendent. In the light of dawn, the wrestler would be seen by Jacob for what he really was, and so he sought his escape.

Likewise when we scrutinize what we have gained in worldly pursuit by the light of dawn (read, God), we see that such gains are not illusory. □

Background Jacob was renamed Israel. And all his descendants became the ancestors of the Jewish people. Thus, the spiritual struggle he endured became symbolic of the later history and tribulation of the entire Jewish people. The spiritual life of each Jew, in a sense, mirrors Jacob's life. We struggle with the Divine and emerge transformed. □

(25) Va-Yeshev: What Are You Looking For?

The Teaching
from Menachem Mendl of Kotzk

The angel [the unnamed person] taught Joseph here that whenever he finds himself wandering on life's paths, when his soul weeps inside him from despair and doubt, he should remember first to become clear about what he really wants and yearns for. Then he will be able to return to his task; his vision and his path now will be the same. □

Scriptural Context

This portion begins Joseph's career as a dreamer. Jacob's sons were supposed to be tending the flocks in Shechem. Jacob sent Joseph after them in order to bring back word of how they were doing. When Joseph reaches Shechem, he does not find his brothers. They had already left Shechem for Dothan. Joseph discovers this when an unnamed person in Shechem informs Jacob that his brothers were now pasturing in Dothan. □

Perush: Explaining the Teaching

Like generations of rabbinic commentators before him, the Kotzker is intrigued by the unnamed person Joseph came upon when he sought his brothers in Shechem. We have no knowledge of where he came from or what he was doing in the field. Like the nameless person with whom Jacob wrestled, this person, perhaps an angel, comes to teach Joseph a lesson about life. When what you seek on the path →

Targum: English Translation
Genesis 37:12–17

12) Once when his [Joseph's] brothers were tending their flocks in Shechem, 13) Israel said to Joseph, "Your brothers are pasturing in Shechem. Come here and I will send you to them." He [Joseph] told him, "*Hineini* – I am ready [to go]." 14) And so he [Israel] said to him, "Go and see how they are doing. Bring me back word." So he sent him from the valley of Hebron. He reached Shechem, 15) *And a person found him and beheld he was wandering in the field and the person asked him, "What do you want?"* 16) And he replied, "I seek my brothers. Might you tell me where they are pasturing?" 17) The person told him, "They have gone from here. I heard them say; 'Let's go to Dothan.'" So Joseph left and followed his brothers to Dothan. □

From the Tradition

In order to emphasize Joseph's readiness to assume the task, Rabbi Chana bar Chanina taught: "When Jacob recalled these things, he winced, 'You know your brothers hated you and yet you said to me *Hineini*: Here I am.'" Even early in his life, Joseph knew that God had a plan for him, his life, that he must follow. Joseph knew that his brothers hated him, and yet he went to them at his father's request.

Background As this story of the Kotzker also suggests, one has to be clear about what one is looking for in life. As a young man the Kotzker made a pilgrimage on foot to see his rebbe in a distant town. It was wintertime. The journey was tiring and the weather grim.

Suddenly, a rich man from his town came by in a sumptuous carriage drawn by four horses, with two extra horses in the rear. When he saw Reb Mendl trudging along, his bundle on his shoulders, he ordered his coachman to stop and asked, "Where are you going?"

Reb Mendl told him.

"Well," said the rich man, "get in. I will take you there."

"Why not?" said Reb Mendl.

Sitting in the carriage was a genuine pleasure. There was no lack of warm, woolen blankets. The rich man even asked whether he would like something to drink.

Reb Mendl warmed himself with some tea and ate a piece of cake as well. Then he took a piece of roast goose and another sip of tea. He felt most comfortable. →

44

Perush: Explaining the Teaching *(continued)*

of life eludes you, and you are confused about what you seek, reach deep inside yourself and God will help you clarify the truth you seek. □

Background *(continued)*

Suddenly he turned to his host. "Tell me please, what are your worldly pleasures?"

The man looked at him in astonishment. "Can't you see? The carriage and horses, the expensive food I can have even on the road. Do you mean to say that all of this is not enough for a fellow like you?"

"No," teased Reb Mendl, "these are your heavenly pleasures, the acme of your pleasures, but where are you with worldly pleasures?" □

(26) Va-Yeshev: The Wisdom of Reverence

The Teaching
from the Sefas Emes, Yehudah Aryeh Leib of Ger

It seems, on first reading, as though he refused without any reason. As our sages have said (in *Midrash Sifrei* on *Parashat Kedoshim*), "A person should not say I don't want to eat pork, because, indeed, I'd like to. But precisely because I would, the reason I behave as I do is because God wants it so!"

It is by means of just such reverence toward being alive that one is blessed to understand the real reasons for choosing good and rejecting evil. And so it is →

Perush: Explaining the Teaching

The Sefas Emes is trying to explain the nature of religious refusal to enjoy things that are probably (or obviously) pleasurable. He argues that, for instance, we do not abstain from eating pork by saying to ourselves, "I don't eat pork because I hate it anyway." Instead, we say, "I (presumably) would love the taste of pork but still I won't eat it since it is forbidden." We keep kosher (and observe the *mitzvot*) because of God's reasons (usually unknown to us), not because of our own.

Joseph's refusal results not from any lack of sensual interest but only from God's prohibition against promiscuity. The Sefas Emes's focus is on reverence for God. Such reverence predisposes us to do good. When we serve God in this way, we are elevated above urges that would normally bring us down. It is a higher expression of self to serve the Source of self, moving our regular self out of the way. God is that ultimate expression of self. Such is the difference between just living and being alive. →

Scriptural Context

The Joseph narrative continues in this portion, with the slight interruption of the story of Tamar. Joseph arrives in Egypt and is placed in the household of Potiphar, the captain of Pharaoh's guard, where he is elevated to chief of Potiphar's household staff. There, Joseph gets into trouble – he refuses the sexual overtures made by Potiphar's wife. ☐

Targum: English Translation
Genesis 39:7:10

7) **After these things [that happened to Joseph] his master's wife was attracted to Joseph and said to him, "Lie with me." 8)** *And he [Joseph] refused and said* **to his master's wife, "Listen, since my master doesn't really know what he has, he has put me in charge of it all. 9) He does not consider himself greater in the home than I am. He has kept nothing from me except you; you are his wife. [Knowing how trusting he has been to me], how could I do such a despicable thing, for it would be a sin to God. 10) It came to pass that he refused her daily advances and did not lie with her or respond to her [at all].** ☐

From the Tradition

The *shalshelet* (literally, "chain"), one of the musical notes used for chanting the Torah (the system is called *trope* in Yiddish or *taamei ha-mikrah* in Hebrew), looks like a stylized lightning bolt and appears only four times in the Torah. Thus, when it appears, the word *Va-Yema'ein* – and he [Joseph] refused (Genesis 39:8), it implies a difficult, prolonged refusal, a struggle of conscience. We can hear in its lengthy oscillations Joseph's inner struggle as he refuses the amorous advances of Potiphar's wife. ☐

Background The story of Potiphar's wife serves as a paradigm for the rabbis to remind their students of the temptations of the flesh. In *Sotah* 36b, we read that Joseph was indeed on the verge of succumbing to her temptation, when the image of his parents appeared before him and cooled his passion, thus preventing him from sinning. ☐

The Teaching (*continued*)

that by means of "And he refused" [without offering any reasons] that he was rewarded with the reason. For mere human intelligence is able to mislead and go astray. Whereas only wisdom that comes from reverence toward being alive is accurate and correct.

This is what our sages meant in *Pirke Avot* 3:9: "Anyone whose fear of sin comes before his wisdom, his wisdom will endure." And likewise in Proverbs 15:33: "The fear of God is the discipline of wisdom," which means that real wisdom comes only from the power of the reverence toward being alive. □

Perush: Explaining the Teaching (*continued*)

The basis of religious life is releasing of sacred power and a reverence for life–serving the Source of life. In this way we become immortal. Knowing that God made us is the beginning of clarity. And sin is an estrangement from our Source. □

(27) Va-Yeshev: Being There

The Teaching
from the Sefas Emes, Yehudah Aryeh Leib of Ger

We have already read in 39:2, "And he was in the house of his master, the Egyptian." And also, in 39:7, "And it was after these things. . . ." The verb *to be* here is used to convey the idea of "remaining in existence" or "not susceptible to change." As our sages have explained in *Pesachim* 23a, " 'And they will be' means 'and they will be in existence.' "

This is because Joseph did not change who he was in any of the different places he dwelt; he remained the same Joseph whether he was Joseph the shepherd or Joseph, deputy pharaoh. "And Joseph was →

Perush: Explaining the Teaching

The Sefas Emes is sensitive to the various uses of the verb *to be*. If Joseph's

Scriptural Context

Here we are in the midst of the Joseph story. Joseph's life reads like a roller coaster. At this point, he has been sold into slavery by his brothers, purchased by Potiphar and placed in charge of his household. As a "reward" for refusing the amorous advances of Potiphar's wife – although Joseph said no, the wife accused him of doing what she wanted – Potiphar puts Joseph in jail. □

From the Tradition

What does someone do to withstand exile? You must constantly be aware of who you are and how you got there. This sense of purpose will allow you to stand firm. Know your history, your source, your essence. That's really what it means that "Joseph was there." □

Targum: English Translation
Genesis 39:19-23

19) **When his [Joseph's] boss [Potiphar] heard his wife's story, which she told him [providing all the details], he said, "After all I did for him, he knifes me in the back." 20)** *And Joseph's master took him and put him in jail, a place where the prisoners of Pharaoh were incarcerated; and he was there in jail.* **21) But** *Adonai* **stayed with Joseph and acted kindly toward him and left a good impression with the prison warden. 22) And the warden named Joseph superior over all the other prisoners and their activities. 23) Since the warden gave Joseph a free hand, [and] since** *Adonai* **was with Joseph, all he did,** *Adonai* **made [to] prosper.** □

master put Joseph in jail, why does the Torah repeat he was there in jail? – we already know he is there. Our teacher suggests that *to be* refers to more than a location; it implies a state of being and that is why it is repeated in our text.

Throughout Joseph's life, the phrase *to be* is used to indicate not "where" Joseph is but rather that in each place, he remained the same; the essential Joseph unchanged at all. Not one of his life's many disastrous events altered this unique ability to remain who he was. Even when Joseph was in Egypt [a state of mind for the Jewish people transcending time and place], he remained Joseph. Whenever we are in exile as a people, or whenever we are exiled as individuals from our true selves, the Holy One intends it. It is a cleansing journey. Even though we do not always understand the rationale, if we remain true to ourselves, our mission will be blessed. And our true self will once again be revealed to us. □

Background The rabbis teach us in *Torah Sheleimah* 39:18 that with humans, friends can always be found when you are successful. When you are in trouble, these friends may not be so easily found. However, God was with Joseph when he was a slave, when he was in prison, and when he was vizier. □

The Teaching (*continued*)

in Egypt" means that, as we read in Proverbs 10:25, "the *tzaddik*, the righteous one, is the foundation of the universe," which is the characteristic of Joseph [the foundation of all the *Sefirot*].

And so the Holy One was revealed to him, for Joseph stood in his time and his power like a Jew. He was sent first to Egypt to prepare the way for all the children of Israel.

This is because the principal test of exile is to withstand every attempt to change the essence and the very being of what it means to be a Jew. For this reason every Jew needs to know and to believe that even when he or she descends into Egypt, into the dungeon itself, it is all divine providence and not a chance event. It is an errand for the Creator. And no matter where the Holy One wishes to send a person, that person needs to accept the mission and the will of the Holy One. □

(28) Mi-Ketz: Dream World

The Teaching
from Mayir Aynei Yesharim

When a man comes to the end of his days, to the time of his old age (ופרעה, u-pharaoh), and Pharaoh can be misread as פרוע הוא, paruah hu, "he is confused," for it is revealed to him that it was all a dream, which is to say that he realizes that his whole life has been nothing more than a dream.

"And behold, standing on the edge of the river . . . ," he sees that still he has not repaired anything in the world. And not this alone, for not only has he not crossed the river, he has not even yet entered it. □

Perush: Explaining
the Teaching

In a reflective, almost existential moment, our teacher shares an insight into the meaning of life in old age. Perhaps he sees himself or an aging parent in the passage. But he also sees all of humanity. Using a wordplay on "and Pharaoh" (u-pharaoh) that could be read "he was confused" (paruah hu), our teacher instructs us about the paradox of the human condition. We go through life thinking we are great and that we have accomplished something great when, in fact, our lives are merely illusory (dreams). More than that, like Pharaoh, even when we think we are just about there (ready to cross the river), we aren't even close! We have to be willing to enter the river before we can try to cross it. □

Scriptural Context

This Torah portion begins with Joseph still in jail – and now it is Pharaoh's turn to dream. And Joseph, the master dream interpreter, is released from jail in order to interpret Pharaoh's dreams. As a result of his ability, this Hebrew prisoner is eventually elevated to the second highest office in Egypt. □

Targum: English Translation
Genesis 41:1–4

1) *At the end of two years time Pharaoh dreamed and behold, standing on the edge of the river.* 2) **When out of the Nile came seven cows, handsome and sturdy, and they grazed among the grasses.** 3) **Behold, seven more cows followed closely behind, also coming up from the river, skinny and ugly, and they stood beside the cows on the bank of the river.** 4) **But the skinny and ugly cows devoured the seven handsome and sturdy cows. Then [suddenly] Pharaoh woke up.** □

From the
Tradition

As impossible as it is for stalks of grain to be free of straw, so is it impossible for a dream to be entirely without worthless elements. The interpretation of a dream sometimes determines the actual event. If we interpret a dream beneficently, good may result. A dream is a prophecy in miniature. A fast helps counteract an evil dream, and it should be observed on the very day, even if it is the Sabbath (based on *Berachot* 55b and *Shabbat* 11a). □

Background On Yom Kippur, we symbolically rehearse our deaths by not eating, not drinking, not engaging in sexual activity. Yom Kippur is also a day of ego death. On the path of *teshuvah*, it is our opportunity to start afresh with a new self, washed clean and pure. □

(29) Mi-Ketz Clean Thoughts

The Teaching
from Tzidkat Ha-Tzaddik, Tzadok Ha-Kohen of Lublin

The power of imagination is one of the great powers God has given people; even prophecy itself has its root in this power.

Nevertheless, it is not the same as the prophetic vision whose true source is ultimately →

Perush: Explaining the Teaching

Our teacher is fascinated by the subtle difference between dreams that have their source in the human imagination and prophetic visions that have their source in God. (It is not clear in the dreams of Pharaoh because they are interpreted by Joseph and indeed come true, thus making them essentially prophetic.) Only when we purge our minds of fantasies, however, is prophetic vision possible. And this becomes a sacred vessel for God's plan. □

Targum: English Translation
Genesis 41:8-16

8) The next morning [after Pharaoh awoke from his dream], he was out of sorts, so he sent for all the magicians of Egypt, all its sages. Pharaoh recounted his dream for all of them but they could not interpret it. 9) The chief cupbearer spoke up and told Pharaoh, "I must recall for you my offense." 10) Once [you] Pharaoh were angry with your servants and placed me in the custody of the chief steward, along with the chief baker. 11) We each had dreams that one night, he and I, with individual meanings. 12) A young Hebrew was there, a servant of the chief steward, and when we told him our dreams, he interpreted them for us. 13) Just as he explained to us, so did it happen, I was returned to my position and the other was impaled. 14) So Pharaoh sent word for Joseph and he was hurried out of the dungeon. His hair was cut and he was shaved. He changed his clothes and was brought before Pharaoh. 15) Pharaoh said to Joseph, "I had a dream that no one can interpret. *Now I have heard it said about you, that for you to hear a dream is to interpret it.*" 16) Joseph answered Pharaoh, "Not me, God will see to Pharaoh's well-being." □

Scriptural Context

Pharaoh's chief cupbearer, whose dream Joseph had interpreted while they were still both incarcerated, recommended Joseph as a dream interpreter for Pharaoh, so Pharaoh sends for Joseph – still in jail. □

From the Tradition

In his humility, Joseph told Pharaoh that he was not an interpreter of dreams. Instead, he was merely a vessel through which God's wisdom flowed into the world. Rashi wrote in the case of Joseph, "God will put in my mouth an answer that will be for Pharaoh's welfare." □

Background A complicated, creative, and even fierce man, Tzadok Ha-Kohen of Lublin (1823-1900) was a chasidic *tzaddik* who was born in Kreuzburg (Krustpils) Courland. A disciple of Mordecai Joseph Leiner of Izbica, he had a special interest in historiography. While his knowledge of *halachah* informed his chasidic teachings, he enriched *halachah* with *Kabbalah* and other mystical elements. Besides *Zidkat Ha-Kohen* (1902), his writings include *Dover Tzaddik* (1911), *Mahashavat Charutz* (1912), and *Resisei Lailah* (1913). His sermons are collected under the title *Peri Tzaddik* (1901-1934), issued in five volumes. □

The Teaching (continued)

in the mind of God. [Prophetic visions enter the mind of the prophet] in the same way that fantasies enter the heart of a human being [except that, instead of emanating from the mind of God, imaginative fantasies have] their foundation in fantasizing about things that a person's soul loves.

And whenever a person is purified from evil qualities, such as lust, anger, pride, and quarrelsomeness, so that all the person's fantasies are disconnected from each one of those contaminations, the person ascends to the level of prophecy.

Dreams and fantasies are beyond the control of a person to cleanse. Nevertheless, they possess a kernel of truth, for dreams and fantasies are one-sixtieth prophecy (*Berachot* 57b).

And only one whose body is not preoccupied with vain fantasies will be able to penetrate into the very midst of the dream and to separate the good from the evil, the vision of prophecy from the fantasy of falsehood.

Therefore, Joseph was made ready, so that he could keep away from sexual lust [with Potiphar's wife] and remain innocent, and Daniel, in order to distinguish his innocence from the craving for food, so both might become interpreters of dreams. For the root of every distracting thought is in desiring, for the heart desires to meditate on them. □

(30) Mi-Ketz: Fancy Dresser

The Teaching
from Bunem of Przysucha

Ordinarily a person who is righteous and pious is dressed in special clothing, but they are not extravagant or disorderly.

But here Pharaoh sees before him "a person in whom is the spirit of God," who has neatly combed hair and painted eyebrows, outwardly dressed very well indeed.

For this reason Pharaoh [is surprised and] says, "Can we find like this one a person in whom is the spirit of God?" [It is not a simple question but an expression of his astonishment.] Is it also therefore possible that God would dwell in a human being dressed like this? □

Perush: Explaining the Teaching

Simchah Bunem believed that one's piety was reflected in the way one dressed. He wanted to understand what Pharaoh meant when Pharaoh asked where to find a "person in whom is the spirit of God." Simchah Bunem suggests that it was not a question. Instead, it was a statement of astonishment. Looking at the fancy way Joseph was dressed, he was amazed that the spirit of God could rest in him. □

Scriptural Context

Joseph was taken from prison and brought before Pharaoh to interpret his dreams. Pleased at the way Joseph interpreted the dreams and the suggestion that someone be found to be put in charge of food collection and eventual rationing, Pharaoh selected Joseph himself. □

Targum: English Translation
Genesis 41: 37–40

37) **The plan [of Joseph] pleased Pharaoh and all of his servants.** 38) *And Pharaoh said to his servants, "Can we find like this one a person in whom is the spirit of God?"* 39) **So Pharaoh said to Joseph, "Since God has made all this known to you, there is none so discerning and wise as you. 40) You shall be in charge of my court, and by your command shall all my people be directed, only in regard to the household shall I be superior to you.** □

From the Tradition

A dream that is not interpreted is like a letter that is not read. . . .

Neither a good dream nor a bad dream is ever entirely fulfilled. . . .

Just as there can be no wheat without some straw, there can be no dream without some nonsense.

While a part of a dream may be fulfilled, the entire dream never is. . . .

A person should wait for a good dream to be fulfilled for as long as twenty-two years. . . .

Three kinds of dreams come true: a dream you have in the early morning, a dream a friend has about you, and a dream that is interpreted in the middle of another dream. Some add a dream that is repeated. . . .

A person sees in his dreams only what is suggested by his own thoughts (*Berachot*, 55a–b).

Background Midrashic tradition imagines that Joseph was preoccupied with how well he dressed and looked. The Przysucha school of Chasidism, founded by Simchah Bunem, is a reaction against the "rabbinic elegance and pomp" that characterized many contemporary chasidic *rebbes*. □

(31) Va-Yigash: Draw Near to Yourself

The Teaching
from Menachem Mendl of Kotzk

At first glance, it seems that the words "to him" (אליו) are superfluous.

It is possible to explain this apparent redundancy, however, if we read the words "to him" (אליו) as referring [not to Joseph, the apparent object, but to the subject, the speaker] to Judah himself.

Judah reiterated his words a second time in Joseph's presence. He did so because in the retelling he spoke them with extra feeling from the depths of his heart. ☐

Perush: Explaining the Teaching

Puzzled by the ostensibly redundant phrase "to him," the Kotzker reasons that it is not to be read "And Judah drew near to him." Rather Judah drew near to himself because Judah's plea emerged from the very depth of his being. He cast aside any illusions and when he was himself, he was able to speak persuasively. ☐

Scriptural Context

This portion is the third of the four comprising the Joseph story. Joseph has become vizier. There is famine in the land of Canaan and Joseph's brothers have come to Egypt seeking grain. But they do not know that the "man" from whom they are buying grain is actually Joseph. Joseph sets his brothers up so that it appears that in the midst of his generosity, Benjamin had stolen his goblet. The portion begins with Judah's eloquent plea to take responsibility for Benjamin and finally to do what he should have done when Joseph was sold into slavery. ☐

Targum: English Translation
Genesis 44:18

18) *Then Judah drew near to him and said, "Please, sir, let your [humble] servant appeal to my lord; do not be impatient with your servant, you who are Pharaoh's equal."* ☐

From the Tradition

Rashi: The fact that Judah said, "Don't be angry," [we know he] means that he spoke to the man on the throne in harsh words. ☐

Background According to Alshich, at first Judah thought that all these misfortunes had been on account of the sin of selling Joseph into slavery, measure for measure. All of them would be slaves, so he said, "What can we say, how can we demand justice, God has uncovered the sin of your servant" (Genesis 44:16). By using the word *sin* he was referring to the sale of Joseph.

But when he saw that the brothers were to be allowed to go free and that, of all of them, Benjamin, who had nothing to do with the sale of Joseph, was to be taken into slavery, then he understood that what was happening was not on account of the sale of Joseph, but some other act. Then he began to speak harshly. ☐

(32) Va-Yigash: *Teshuvah* as Rewriting the Past

The Teaching
from the Sefas Emes, Yehudah Aryeh Leib of Ger

Our sages have said in *Genesis Rabbah* 21:6, "Every use of 'and now' [ועתה] implies *teshuvah*."

Indeed, even at first Joseph's brothers turned in *teshuvah*, as it is said in Genesis 42:21, "Alas, we are guilty. . . ." But this kind of *teshuvah* is only from fear of retribution, whereas in the present situation, they have turned in love and this has transformed their previous sin into a merit. This is just what Joseph says to them: "For it was in order to save life that God sent me ahead of you" (Genesis 45:5). Indeed, every cause issues from the →

Perush: Explaining the Teaching

According to *Genesis Rabbah*, "And now" (*Ve-ata*) is always associated with *teshuvah*, making repentance. Knowing this, our teacher anticipates that Joseph's brothers will be repentant when they approach Joseph. However, the Sefas Emes knows also that the brothers have already made *teshuvah*, because we read in a previous chapter of Genesis (42:21), "Alas, we are →

Targum: English Translation
Genesis 45:3–8

3) Joseph said to his brothers, "I am your brother Joseph. Is our father still alive?" Joseph's brothers were dumbfounded, and couldn't say a word. 4) Joseph continued to speak, "Please come near me," which they did. "I am really your brother Joseph, the one you sold to Egypt. 5) *And now, do not be sad or reproach yourselves because you sold me down here; for it was to save life that God sent me ahead of you.* 6) There have already been two years of famine here and there are five more years yet to come. 7) God sent me here to give you what food is left, to keep you alive so that God can [later] deliver you. 8) So believe me, it was God who sent me here, not you. God made me a father figure to Pharaoh, to oversee all his holdings, to rule over all of Egypt." □

Scriptural Context

This is the third of four Torah portions that comprise the saga of Joseph. Famine had hit the land of Canaan, but Joseph had stored up grain in Egypt during its years of plenty in order to prepare for this period of hunger. This portion begins as Judah draws near to Joseph in a heartrending gesture of moral responsibility. This makes it possible for Joseph to reveal his identity and, instead of reproaching his brothers for the events that led to his sojourn in Egypt, tell his brother that God had an ultimate plan for him (and us all) that led to the brothers' ostensibly evil actions. Our text focuses on the scene when Joseph finally reveals his identity to his brothers. □

From the Tradition

We are obliged to go to our neighbors, especially before Yom Kippur, and tell them if they have offended us. We are taught in Leviticus 19:17 among the laws of holiness that separates Israel from the nations of the world, "You should not hate your neighbor in your heart. Reprove your neighbor but incur no guilt on his account." The Rambam writes in his *Mishneh Torah, Sefer Mada,* →

Background Yehudah Aryeh Leib (Alter) 1847–1905, was orphaned as a child and raised by his grandfather. He succeeded Hanoch of Aleksandrow, successor to founder Isaac Meir Rothenberg, as leader of the Ger *chasidim*, one of the most celebrated of dynasties and largest in the modern state of Israel. He led his community to become the most influential of all *chasidim* in Poland. A modest individual and distinguished scholar, his writings were collected under the title *Sefas Emes* (5 vols. 1905–1908). □

The Teaching (*continued*)

Source of All Causes.

Nevertheless, the one who sins pays for his sin. But when he turns in *teshuvah* from love [as you have done] every sin is transformed into an actual merit. As our verse reads, "So now [ועתה] it was not you who sent me here but God" (Genesis 45:8). This is just the way things were meant to be from the very beginning. They sold me into slavery. But now, *teshuvah* has transformed [and revealed] everything to be just the way God intended it. And all because you made *teshuvah* in love. So [whatever you do,] don't be forlorn. □

Perush: Explaining the Teaching (*continued*)

guilty" – indicating the admission of guilt, the first step on the road to repentance. Then in the last chapter (44:30), "And now" (*Ve-ata*) – indicating repentance – was used directly in connection with the brothers' return to Joseph. Our teacher, therefore, concludes that there must be two levels of *teshuvah*: one out of fear and one out of love. When one makes *teshuvah* out of fear of punishment, it resembles a child forced into apologizing, resentfully muttering "I'm sorry" because he knows that if he doesn't, his parents will punish him. The second form of *teshuvah* comes from love. This is when one is truly sorry for what one has done and yearns for a renewal of love. *Teshuvah* done out of love actually transforms the prior transgression into merit by placing it in a new and larger constellation of meaning. Reflecting back on the original transgression, we may even laugh at our original sin, realizing now that it has become the reason for a new and even greater intimacy and friendship. After *teshuvah* from love, our relationship can actually be purified. The worst of enemies can become friends and even cherish the event(s) that once drove them apart. One cannot change the reality of an act, but by repenting out of love, one can change the reality.

There is another theme addressed that appears to be secondary but, in fact, permeates Jewish spirituality. While it might seem paradoxical, the Sefas Emes suggests here that God is the source of all that happens. Nothing is coincidental; we simply do not always fully comprehend all the events. In the sequence of the Joseph narratives, it appears that Joseph's brothers are in control, but later we learn, "For it was in order to save life that *God* sent me ahead of you" (Genesis 45:5). □

From the Tradition (*continued*)

Hilchot Teshuvah: "When an individual sins against another, the injured party should not hate the offender and keep silent. But it is his duty to inform the offender. If the offender repents and pleads for forgiveness, he should be forgiven." Yom Kippur frequently finds people hugging and crying in the hallway outside of the sanctuary before the commencement of *Kol Nidre*.

"Better a person who has done *teshuvah* than one who is perfectly righteous (*tzaddik gamor*)." In our *parashah*, Judah does *teshuvah* for his crime against Joseph – and Joseph forgives him. □

(33) Va-Yigash: Don't Quarrel with the Way

The Teaching
from Menachem Mendl of Kotzk

Rashi [citing *Genesis Rabbah* 94:2]: Don't take long strides in order to enter a town while it is still daylight so that you don't have to travel by night.

Joseph understood well that his brothers would naturally want to hasten their steps—so much so that they might not even rest at night-time—in order to bring the wonderful news to their father: Joseph was still alive.

For this reason Joseph said to them, "The hour of your arrival at your destination has been appointed by Heaven. And if you hurry on the way, you will only be delayed by some other reason. So 'don't quarrel with the way' that has been appointed for you." □

Perush: Explaining the Teaching

The Kotzker reminds us that the preposition ב does not always mean "in." Sometimes, it can be translated as "with." Therefore, *ba-derech* can be read as "with the way." As a result, he enters another mode of reverence that acknowledges a divine way set before us, which we are supposed to accomplish. The route is just as important as the destination. □

Scriptural Context

Now vizier in Egypt, Joseph is in control of the destiny of his brothers, those who had earlier sold him into slavery. But Joseph is not vindictive. He gives them their food and sends them back to Canaan to bring to Egypt their aged father, whom Joseph had not seen for many years. As they leave, Joseph offers them brotherly advice, "Don't quarrel with one another during your journey home." □

From the Tradition

Traditionally, when one starts on a journey, the *Tefillat Ha-Derech* (traveler's prayer) is recited: "May it be in accordance with your plans for me and for the world, *Adonai* my God and God of my ancestors, that I may set out on my journey peacefully. Guard me from perils along the way and bring me safely to my destination. Help me to complete my journey unscathed so that I may return home, joyfully alive and at peace with myself."

It is a good idea to use this prayer to begin the day, as well, setting out on your daily journey in life. □

Targum: English Translation
Genesis 45:24–26

24) *And he [Joseph] sent his brothers off and as they left he said to them, "Don't quarrel on the way."* 25) So **they went up from Egypt and came to their father, Jacob, in the land of Canaan.** 26) **And told him thus, "Joseph is still alive; he is a ruler over the land of Egypt." His [Jacob's] heart fluttered because he couldn't believe them.** □

Background Another way of understanding what is going on in this comment comes to us from Y. Y. Trunk in the name of Menachem Mendl of Kotzk. He asked, "Could such behavior be appropriate for Joseph, the *tzaddik*? Isn't it the way of righteousness to first make oneself known to one's brother? While tears of great feeling ran down their faces, how could he not make mention of the great sin they committed against him!" This is the explanation: "I am the same Joseph, as I was when you were separated from me when I was sold into Egypt. I have not changed in this filthy and perverted place. And you do not have to worry that you caused me any injury. I am [the same] Joseph, your brother—fit to be your brother, son of Jacob, just as I was at the time when you sold me into Egypt." □

(34) Ve-Yechi: Exile of the Spirit

The Teaching
from the Sefas Emes, Yehudah Aryeh Leib of Ger

Rashi: Why is this *parashah* closed, that is, why is this the only *parashah* that begins in the middle of a paragraph of Torah text? Because as soon as Jacob, our father, died, the eyes and hearts of the Jewish people were closed by Egyptian slavery.

We find a further difficulty in *Exodus Rabbah* 1:8, " 'And Joseph died, and all his brothers, and all that generation' (Exodus 1:6). This teaches that as long as one of those →

Perush: Explaining the Teaching

Sensitive to the graphic layout of the Hebrew text itself in the Torah, the Sefas Emes calls our attention to Rashi's observation that *Parashat Va-Yechi* is the only one

Scriptural Context

This portion begins just before Jacob dies, as he blesses his grandsons Ephraim and Manasseh and adopts them. He then assembles his children and offers them a final testament, a sort of ethical will. Joseph's death at the very end of Genesis serves almost as an epilogue. □

Targum: English Translation
Genesis 47:28–31

28) *And Jacob lived in the land of Egypt for 17 years, so that Jacob's life span came to 147 years.* 29) When the time came for Israel to die, he called his son Joseph and said to him, "If I have found [any] favor in your eyes, pay attention, and place your hand under my thigh [to swear an oath] and show me a [final] loving act of kindness: do not bury me in Egypt. 30) When I lie down with my ancestors, take me from Egypt and bury me in their burial place." And he [Joseph] said, "I will do as you wish." 31) And he [Jacob] said, "Swear to me." So he [Joseph] swore to him. Then Israel bowed at the foot of his bed. □

From the Tradition

It is a sacred custom to bless one's children on *Shabbat* eve, a reference to the blessing in Genesis 48 that Jacob gave to Ephraim and Manasseh.

The strange but traditional language of the blessing is, "To sons: May God make you like Ephraim and Manasseh; and to daughters: May God make you like Sarah, Rebecca, Rachel, and Leah." □

that begins in the middle of a paragraph, rather than at the beginning. While Jacob was alive, the Jewish people continued to thrive. When he died, Jewish history changed. The Israelites entered spiritual slavery. Then when Joseph died (as noted in *Exodus Rabbah* 1:8), Jewish history changed as well. The Israelites entered physical slavery. When their eyes and hearts were closed to the Torah of God's way, they became slaves; that was their real exile. They could only see and feel the world around them, not the ultimate reality as taught in Torah. When we are in personal exile, estranged from ourselves, enslaved by the Egypts of our world, our eyes and hearts are closed as well. □

Background The Sefas Emes provides a further explanation to the one he already offered concerning the way the text actually appears in the Torah. He claimed that Jacob sought to reveal to his children the date of the End of Days when Israel's exile would finally end, but the vision was concealed ("closed") to him. [Rashi, on Genesis 49:1, suggests the reason was that the Divine presence departed from him and he began to speak of other things.]

And why was a reckoning of the end of exile withheld from Jacob? Because the exile came to cleanse Israel of their sins in order that things might ultimately go well for them. And if they knew the time of the end, they would feel none of the unhappiness of the exile. This is because any unhappiness that has a known end is not serious. □

The Teaching (*continued*)

who originally went down into Egypt was alive, the Egyptians did not enslave Israel."

From this we infer that the slavery began a short time after the death of Jacob. It is also probable that the actual physical slavery did not begin immediately whereas the spiritual slavery did begin with the death of Jacob.

The Jewish people were unaware; they did not see or feel how Egyptian culture began to penetrate and influence them. What was really going on was not evident. [In Rashi's words, mentioned above:] "The eyes and hearts of the Jewish people were closed," until finally their eyes were unable to see and their hearts unable to feel anything but superficiality. And this is the core experience of exile. □

(35) Va-Yechi: Revealing the End

The Teaching
from Menachem Mendl of Kotzk

Rashi: He wanted to reveal to them the end of Israel's exile but the Divine Presence departed from him, and he began to ramble on about other things.

This comment by Rashi is a little surprising. No matter what you will say, if the Holy One had revealed to Jacob the mystery of the End of Days, why was it now closed from him when he wanted to reveal it to his sons? And if it were forbidden for him to reveal the secret of the End even to his sons, just how did he know this?

The answer is that Jacob himself did not know the secret; he prayed to God that it would be revealed to him in order that he would be able to transmit it to his sons. →

Perush: Explaining the Teaching

At the end of Jacob's life, for his children, he wanted to apply his wisdom to seeing the future. Menachem Mendl of Kotzk is incredulous as to Rashi's traditional interpretation of the text. Jacob was about to tell his children about the end of their exile but the Divine Presence left him and with it, knowledge about the end. Menachem Mendl wonders why this happened. If Jacob was prevented from telling his sons, why had God let him know in the first place? How had Jacob come to this knowledge? The Kotzker suggests that Jacob had called his children together so that as he prayed for the knowledge he sought, he might be able to share it with them. But Rashi may have misunderstood. God wanted Jacob to yearn for the knowledge with great longing, telling his children to live their lives in anticipation of the end of their exile, but that they would not know when it might come—until it came. The message is the same for the exile of every Israelite, as well. □

Scriptural Context

At the end of Jacob's life, he calls all of his sons together to bless them and offer them what has come to be called an ethical will. It is both the prophetic utterance of a dying father and a collection of tribal memories seen through the life of Jacob. □

Targum: English Translation
Genesis 49:1–2

1) *And Jacob called his sons and said, "Come together and I will tell you what will happen to you in the end of days.* 2) **Assemble and listen you sons of Jacob. Hearken to Israel your father."** □

From the Tradition

Just as *galut* becomes an expression of personal estrangement, reflective of what it means for the Jewish people to be in exile (literally, *galut*) from the land of Israel, its spiritual home, *kibbutz galuyyot* serves to refer to the reorientation of the self, as it does for the collective self of the people of Israel to be gathered (reoriented) to the land of Israel. While the term is found only in rabbinic literature, it is held that such an ingathering occurs time and time again—especially as seen in the prophesies of Jeremiah, Isaiah, and Ezekiel. First mentioned in Deuteronomy (30:3–4), the promise is given that *"Adonai* your God, will turn your home captivity and have compassion on you and will return and gather you from all the peoples where *Adonai* your God has scattered you."* □

Background The number seventeen, according to gematria, is equivalent to the Hebrew word, טוב, *tov.* [ט, *tet,* the ninth letter + ו, *vav,* the sixth letter + ב, *bet,* the second letter = 17.] This teaches you that Jacob clarified the confusion, for the main idea of the Egyptian exile was that we should learn how to clarify our confu-

sion between good and evil. This is the reason that our time in Egypt is referred to as "the iron furnace" (Deuteronomy 4:20).

Jacob, however, said that the angel, the one who redeems me from all evil, even in Egypt will not allow any evil to befall me. And this was sufficient preparation for redemption. □

The Teaching *(continued)*

"The Divine Presence departed from him."

God hinted to him from the heavens that Jacob did not really want to know. Better that he not know the end or the beginning of the redemption but that [his sons should] yearn for this knowledge with a great longing. □

(36) Va-Yechi: Returning to Your Source

The Teaching
from Yad Yosef

It is part of the nature of everything to draw near and to cleave itself to its root and its source. For this reason the time of death of the righteous ones is described as a "drawing near," as if they had a desire to return to their root and to draw themselves near to their source.

Our parents and their parents before them had a great yearning to be brought near to the Land of Israel, for there was the root and the source of where they were formed.

As our sages said in Deuteronomy 32:43, "And [God] will make atonement for God's land, God's people." From the place of our creation is our atonement. □

Scriptural Context

We come to the end of Jacob's life and to the end of Joseph's, as well. And so, Jacob blesses all his sons and offers two special blessings to two of his grandchildren: Ephraim and Manasseh. □

Targum: English Translation
Genesis 47:28–30

28) Jacob lived 17 years in the land of Egypt, so that the span of Jacob's life came to 147 years. 29) *And when Israel's time drew near to die,* he summoned his son Joseph and said to him, "If I have found favor in your eyes, place your hand under my thigh as a sign of your unswerving commitment [*chesed shel emet*] and do not bury me in Egypt. 30) When I lie down with my ancestors, take me up from Egypt and bury me in their burial place." He replied, "I will do as you have said." □

From the
Tradition:

Free burial societies are often called *chesed shel emet*. Such a *mitzvah* is a true *mitzvah* because there is no chance that it is done in anticipation of a reward from its recipient. □

Perush: Explaining the Teaching

Our teacher pierces the text in order to understand this unusual construction of words. Why would Jacob draw near to death as the syntax and words imply? Yad Yosef explains that righteous people are anxious to return to their roots, the Source of all life itself. But he takes his lesson one step further and explains that Jacob, now Israel, yearns to return to the roots of our people in the land of Israel, for this return makes atonement for the sins that caused our exile. □

Background The Sefas Emes taught that Jacob survived in Egypt by means of the truth, as it says in Micah 7:20, "You will give truth to Jacob." By means of the truth, one is able to withstand and endure sorrow and distress, even in the land of Egypt.

This is because the Hebrew word for falsehood, שקר (*sheker*) has no feet, whereas the word for truth, אמת (*emet*), stands forever.

[Each of the three letters of the Hebrew word for falsehood (שקר, *sheker*: shin, ש; kof, ק; resh, ר) have pointed bases, whereas the letters of the Hebrew word for truth (אמת, *emet*: alef, א; mem, מ; tav, ת) have flat bases, or two "feet." Furthermore, the word שקר (*sheker*) itself balances precariously on the single point of the letter *kof*, which descends below the baseline, whereas the word אמת (*emet*) stands firm on the line with a wide base.]

When one leaves to truth there is no pain, no sorrow. And this is an inheritance that transcends the bitterness of Egypt. □

EXODUS

(37) Shemot: The Seed of Redemption

The Teaching
from *Otzar Ha-Hasidut*, Isaac Meir Rothenberg Alter of Ger, citing Menachem Mendl of Kotzk

In Kotzk they used to say that one needs to study these *parshiyot* of slavery and redemption with the same meticulous attention normally reserved for matters of *halachah* [Jewish law].

Furthermore the Kotzker used to teach that the experience of going into slavery is recorded in only one *parashah* alone, while the redemption is recounted in many *parshiyot*, indeed, the whole Torah.

And therefore, for this reason, we realize that redemption is to be found in the midst of slavery. It is the very seed of redemption itself, merely concealed. And when the redemption comes, its real source will be revealed. □

Perush: Explaining the Teaching

"Exile" and "redemption" are psycho-spiritual categories. Exile may be understood as alienation or estrangement from self and from God. Redemption, on the other hand, refers to "getting cashed in" for what you are really worth, as in redeeming a savings bond. At the Red Sea, God redeemed worthless slaves for free men and women. □

Scriptural Context

This portion, and the verse from which our text comes, commences the Book of Exodus, and with it the Exodus from Egypt – a paradigm of the ultimate political and personal redemption. The first two chapters of the book tell of our people's enslavement following the deaths of Jacob and Joseph. □

Targum: English Translation
Exodus 1:1–7

1) *These are the names of the children of Israel who came down to Egypt with Jacob, each coming with his household.* 2) *Reuben, Simeon, Levi, and Judah;* 3) *Issachar, Zebulun, and Benjamin.* 4) *Dan and Naphtali, Gad, and Asher.* 5) *The total number of Jacob's offspring came to seventy people, with Joseph already in Egypt.* 6) *Joseph died [as well as] all his brothers: that entire generation.* 7) *But the Israelites were fertile and multiplied; they grew [in number] and increased significantly so that the land was full of them.* □

From the Tradition

According to Menachem Mendl of Kotzk, recalling *Exodus Rabbah* 1:5: "All the names by which the tribes are called hint at redemption: 'Reuben' – 'I have surely seen [punning *raah*, 'to see,'] the affliction of my people' (Exodus 3:7); 'Simeon' – 'And God heard [punning on *Shema*, 'to hear,'] their groaning' (Exodus 2:24)." This implies that with exile come the signs of redemption. And similarly our sages teach that the Messiah (the ultimate redemption) will be born on Tishah B'Av (which commemorates the destruction of the Temple). □

Background Once a disciple asked the Kotzker *rebbe*, "Since you separate yourself from worldly affairs, how are you able to give advice?" Menachem Mendl of Kotzk answered, "Sometimes an outsider sees more clearly than the one who stands on the inside." □

The Teaching
from Joshua Horowitz, Dzikow *rebbe*

Rashi: Of what importance am I that I should speak with kings?

The difficulty here [in this logical reading of the text] is with God's reply in the next verse: "For I will be with you; and this shall be a sign for you that it was I who sent you. And when you have freed the people from Egypt, you shall worship God at this mountain" (Exodus 3: 12).

What kind of answer is that? Moses wasn't looking for a sign; he was merely expressing his humility. →

Perush: Explaining the Teaching

Our teacher is not puzzled by Moses' humility. Rather, he is intrigued by God's unusual response to Moses' expression of this humility. God offers Moses the promise of a sign in order to build up his self-esteem. From this we learn that while humility is important, especially in reference to one's relationship with God, it is equally →

Scriptural Context

In the first chapters of Exodus, the Torah relates the state of slavery in which the Israelites found themselves. With each episode, their enslavement became more unbearable. Finally, Moses appears, and though raised in the household of Pharaoh, he goes out to his kinsmen. God summons him to tell Pharaoh to "let My people go." But Moses is reticent. □

From the Tradition

In *Binah Le-Eitim*, it is written: "And he said, 'Who made you chief and ruler over us? Do you mean to kill me as you killed the Egyptian?' Moses was frightened and said, 'Surely the matter is known.'"

At the beginning of the *parashah* it is said, "And Moses grew and went out to his brothers" (Exodus 2:11). He wanted to emulate their ways, to learn and explore their customs and practices.

"He saw an Egyptian beating a Hebrew, he turned this way and that and seeing no man around . . ." →

Targum: English Translation
Exodus 3:7–12

7) And *Adonai* continued [speaking to Moses], "I have taken note of the plight of My people in Egypt and have responded to their outcry [under the burden placed upon them] by their taskmasters. [Indeed], I know their pain. 8) I have come down to rescue them from the stranglehold of the Egyptians, to bring them out of that land to a good and spacious land, a land flowing with milk and honey to the home of the Canaanites, the Hittites, the Amorites, the Perizzites, the Hivites, and the Jebusites. 9) And now, the screams of the Israelites have reached me [alternately, touched me]. I have seen [with my own eyes, so to speak] how the Egyptians abuse them. 10) Come [forward] so that I may send you to Pharaoh; you will set my people, the Israelites, free from Egypt. 11) *And Moses said to God, "Who am I that I should go to Pharaoh and free the Israelites from Egypt?"* 12) And [God] said, *"For I will be with you; and this shall be a sign for you that it was I who sent you. And when you have freed the people from Egypt, you shall worship God at this mountain."* □

Background Menachem Mendl at Kotzk taught that the first step toward freedom is the [inner] revolt against slavery. The redemption was not planned until [they reached such a low point that] they no longer hated exile. Moses [then] brought the good news to Israel that the Holy One would bring out from inside of them the patience [סבלנות, *savlanoot*] – burdens [סבלות, *sivlot*] punning on the word patience [סבלנות, *savlanoot*] – to serve Egypt and her abominations, because [now] they would be unable to endure them any further. Just this is the foundation from which redemption sprouts. □

The Teaching (*continued*)

Perhaps sometimes a person simply needs to rescue his self-confidence, as we read of Jehoshaphat in 2 Chronicles 17:6, "His mind was elevated in the ways of *Adonai. . . .*" And as it is written in Psalm 121:1, "I lift up my eyes to the mountains." [The verb here is משה, meaning "to draw out or rescue"; it is also the standard biblical root and folk etymology of Moses' name, "one who draws out, rescues." The pun cannot be accidental. For the Torah, it is possible that each person's name can also be a verb, which in turn is an action primary to that person's purpose and fulfillment.]

Indeed, the Torah was given on a low mountain to teach us humility. But in that case then why wasn't the Torah just given on a flat field? Perhaps to teach that sometimes even against your will, there is a need for a little bit of self-esteem in serving God.

We know already that Moses had mastered the attribute of humility: "Who am I?" God's answer implies that he needed a little bit of self-confidence here: "For I will be with you."

Moreover, while in *Sotah* 5a we learn that God says of anyone who glorifies himself that "I and he cannot both dwell in the same world," nevertheless [here we read that] "I will be with you [increasing your self-confidence and esteem]."

And the proof will be "when you have freed the people from Egypt, you shall worship God at this mountain." On a mountain, and not in a flat field, to remind us that sometimes a person needs just a little pride. And especially now, when Israel needed freedom, it is not the time for humility. □

Perush: Explaining the Teaching (*continued*)

important to have a well-integrated ego (that is, a little self-confidence). Furthermore, while humility is often an appropriate posture, when the situation demands self-confidence, humility may then be inappropriate. □

From the Tradition (*continued*)

(Exodus 2:12) means that there was no Jew who would save the oppressed from the hand of the oppressor.

He thought, it is possible that on account of the severity of the slavery, they do not have the strength to fight back.

When he went out the next day, he looked and behold two Hebrews were fighting and wrestling with one another, and when one of them said to him, "as you killed the Egyptian" (Exodus 2:14), he realized that he [the wrestler] considered his act to be evil.

Moses said, "Surely the matter is known," not from the severity of the slavery or from lack of strength to fight back, for behold their heart is like the heart of a lion to fight with one another.

But they lack the sense of right and justice, of mutuality, of helping the weak. And thereby they understood the reason for the delay of the exile. "Surely the matter is known." □

(39) Shemot: How Good It Will Be

The Teaching
from Yaakov Mosheh Hiyyah, chief rabbi of Poland

The explanation here is that [by paying close attention to the tense, we learn that] the mystery of the redemption is mainly something that is yet to be revealed. Anything good in the present will by comparison, seem like nothing, when set beside the incredible goodness of the redemption [yet to come].

For this reason, our present mind-set is incapable of comprehending it. →

Perush: Explaining the Teaching

In perhaps one of the most puzzling phrases of the entire Torah, our teacher Yaakov Mosheh Hiyyah helps us to understand the seemingly aloof way in which God told Moses the Divine name when Moses asked it. God's name and essence is inextricably bound to ultimate redemption, but we are so far from it (and have so much personal and collective work to do before we get there) that even if God had told Moses a more readily understood name, he still would not have understood it. So God simply said, the mystery of my name will be clear to you when you are ready to understand it. When you have readied yourself for redemption, I will be all that I can be for you. □

Scriptural Context

The dialogue at the "Burning Bush" continues. Moses is still not quite sure of the mission or who is sending him on it. God tells him to go to Pharaoh, that God will be there with him the whole time. God identifies Godself as *Ehyeh Asher Ehyeh*. The instructions for the mission are detailed one by one. □

Targum: English Translation
Exodus 3:13–15

13) Moses said to God, "Look, when I come to the Israelites and tell them that the God of your ancestors sent me to you, and they say to me, 'What's this God's name?', what should I tell them? 14) *And God said to Moses, "Ehyeh Asher Ehyeh – I will be who I will be." God continued, "This you shall say to the Israelites: 'I will be' has sent me to you."* 15) **And God said further to Moses, "This you shall say to the Israelites, 'Adonai, the God of your ancestors, the God of Abraham, the God of Isaac, and the God of Jacob has sent me to you.' This is my eternal name and shall be my reputation from generation to generation [forever]."** □

From the Tradition

Rabbi Larry Kushner teaches in his *River of Light*:

1. Ani: I
On the first level, there is only consciousness. Person who is alive and eating. Corresponding to Ani, "I." No god, autism. To such a person apply the words, "One who is full of oneself has no room for God."

2. Elohim: god; Shaddai: power
Then there is becoming aware of oneself in contradistinction to other selves. There are powers in the universe other and sometimes greater than my own. There are people around us who define our childhood. This is also the god called *Shaddai* or *Elohim*. A strange kind of limiting that is the touchstone for all religion. And while it often seems to cripple, devastate, or frighten – creating a consciousness that is closed off, obeisant, broken, rebellious – it usually initiates a sense of awe, wonder, and mystery. The →

Background Yaakov Yitzchak of Przysucha, "The Holy Yehudi," taught: Why is the name of the Holy One "I will be who I will be"? Because this name teaches something about turning [or, repentance]. When a person regrets [what he or she has done] and vows, "From now on I will be good," the Holy One immediately responds; "And I too will be with you and My presence will dwell upon you." □

The Teaching (*continued*)

And thus, all attempts even to describe the form of the redemption must necessarily be limited to our present reality. And this is the real reason that the Name of the God [who speaks to us] of the redemption is "I will be," as if to say that such a reality cannot exist now, but only in the future yet to come. □

From the Tradition (*continued*)

beginning of search. Beginning of therapy. There is someone more than me here.

3. YHWH *Adonai*: The Lord of Being

Now on a higher level is the realization of one's own consciousness. Sense of self. The Lord *Yod Hey Vav Hey*. The one of Being. The therapist, teacher, friend holds up a mirror and we behold who we are. Neither all the universe like child, nor frightened and anxious on account of it, but one human being within it. One human being with other beings.

4. Ehyeh: I am not yet

Above this level no one may ascend by will or perseverance alone. A gift from above, an undeserved favor must be granted. Here at last is the ability to imagine that we might become other than we now are. *Ehyeh asher Ehyeh*: I am not yet. This is done from within when we (the students) discover that the next thing to do, after studying the reply of the teacher (whose silence shows us who we are), is to find within ourselves our own mirrors. One mirror "looking" at another mirror.

5. Echad: One

There is no longer confusion. While the reciprocated images are the same on each "glass," each side, each discrete mirror is precious and indispensable. This is the meaning of *Echad* unity. That the image on the mirrors is the same even though each mirror remains unique unto itself. "Hear O Israel, the Lord your God, the Lord is One" (Deut. 6: 4).

6. Ayin: Nothingness

Until at last, in giving up the struggle for individuality, we know that our unique gifts cannot be withheld. Now there can be *Ayin*. Nothingness. For the Lord of this consciousness is the *Ayn Sof*, the One without end. The apparent world of differences, fallen away, gives way to a return to a self no longer at odds with brothers and sisters or its infinite source. The ultimate self-reference loop. The eye beholds itself. No more silver on the back of the mirror – only glass. The one who set out in search of a distant mountain has found, on the way, that he is the mountain. And Moses gazed over the whole land. No longer any difference between fantasy and life. Repression melts. Something logically impossible, unthinkable, indeed, something truly messianic happens. The river of light now flows upon the surface of the land.

7. Ani: I

As the three letters of the Hebrew word *Ayin* – *Ayin, Yod, Nun*: "Nothingness" – rearrange themselves again (and again) into the primary *Ani, Ayin, Nun, Yod*, "I," and I who was nothing return again (and again) to I who am only I. It has been "I" all along. The one reading/writing these words. Caught up in the net of using, selling, working, forgetting is the One. Is this not the great mystery of religious consciousness? That the one who began as the fool has ascended through the heights of heaven. Through all the rungs of consciousness and divinity. Back to this ordinary person who feels somehow blessed to simply awaken each morning. What loftier goal could there be for any therapy? (All we can do, warned Freud, is transform your hysterical misery into common unhappiness.) The "I" that set out is different from the very same "I" that has returned. What seems to be a perfect circle, upon a change of vantage, is revealed now to have been a spiral.

And what other goal for religion could there be? To see the Holy Ancient One face to face. Or through scripture to reimagine the story and thus be reminded of its ever- →

From the Tradition (*continued*)

present possibility. Or through ritual, whose sacred script compels us to act as if we were dreaming, to relive it.

Go on. Bring the dream into waking. Join each one of its discrete words into one long name of God. Endure the silence in which it is heard, there at the foot of the mountain. Feel that subtle consciousness form the very protoplasm of our collective body. Return through that body to the light of creation itself. Allow that light to dissolve the "letters" of ego into Nothing. And be reborn.

See once again, gently pulsing beneath all being, a river of light. Permit it to rise to the surface. Realize that the one gazing at the river and the river are one. We are the light. □

(40) Va-Era: Patient Slavery

The Teaching
from Simchah Bunem of Przysucha

"The burdens of Egypt." Even though the slavery was hard and crushing, nevertheless they became accustomed to the bitterness and bore the burden and the distress patiently [punning on the similarity of the words for patience (סבלנות, *savlanoot*) and burdens (סבלת, *sivlot*)]. They regarded their situation as natural. Said the Holy One, "Since already they are not healthy nor do they sense the bitterness of their lot, the danger would be great to detain the redemption any longer." "Therefore speak to the children of Israel.... And I will bring you out from under the burdens of Egypt." □

Perush: Explaining the Teaching

Like so many of our teachers, Simchah Bunem wonders why this particular time was chosen by God to deliver Israel from Egypt. There must be a method and logic to the Divine plan – even if it is beyond human understanding. Sensitive even to the aural quality of the words themselves, the word for "burdens," (*sivlot*) sounds to him like "patience" (*savlanoot*). Thus, he reasons that God feared that the Israelites had become too patient under their burdens. They had grown accustomed to their slavery as routine. It was only then that God intervened, because God feared that to wait any longer would affect redemption. □

Scriptural Context

The Torah continues the tale of our people's redemption from slavery. First it gives a review and then adds a genealogy for Aaron and Moses, apparently in order to bolster their leadership status. Moses and Aaron are sent back to Pharaoh for the rod and serpent episode. Our text is taken from this second revelation, when God reveals the Divine names to Moses. □

Targum: English Translation
Exodus 6:2-8

2) **God spoke to Moses and said to him, "I am** *Adonai.* **3) I appeared to Abraham, Isaac, and Jacob as** *El Shaddai* **but I did not inform them that I am YHWH [read:** *Adonai*]. **4) I also established my covenant with them, to give them the land of Canaan, the land in which they lived as sojourners. 5) I have heard the Israelites' outcry, a result of their slavery in Egypt; I remember our covenant. 6)** *Therefore say to the Israelites, I* **Adonai** *will bring you out from under the burdens of Egypt.* **7) And I will take you to be my people and I will be your God so that you will know that** *Adonai,* **your God, redeemed you from under your burden in Egypt. 8) And I will bring you to the land I promised to Abraham, Isaac, and Jacob, with an outstretched hand. I will give it to you as an inheritance, I am** *Adonai.* □

From the Tradition

God is known to the Jewish people by many names, but the personal name of God, YHWH, is the most common and least understood. It expresses the personal relationship between God and the people of Israel as a collective, but also with the individual Jew. The tradition takes the vowels from *Adonai* and places them under the consonants YHVH. Thus one does not pronounce this four-letter name or tetragrammaton) – replacing it with *"Adonai"* instead. Never to be pronounced, it implies the more personal attributes of the God of Israel, rather than the powerful energy unleashed by the descriptive term of *Elohim,* the God of the world. □

Background Simchah Bunem taught, "You must imagine the evil spirit as a thing hovering over you with a raised hatchet, ready to chop off your head." "What if I can't imagine it?" asked a disciple. "That's a sure sign that he has already chopped it off," answered the *rebbe.* □

(41) Va-Era: Strong Leadership

The Teaching
from the Sefas Emes, Yehudah Aryeh Leib of Ger

If the children of Israel refuse to listen to their leaders, there can be no leaders who are able to speak, who can become a mouth for them, which could be of "impeded speech" [in the first place]. As it is written in Psalm 50:7, "Pay heed my people, and I will speak. . . ." As long as there are those who will listen, then there can be those who speak, because the power of the leader issues from the people.

For this →

Perush: Explaining the Teaching

While Moses is usually portrayed as one who simply stutters, Aryeh Leib of Ger searches the text for some deeper significance of this impediment. He realizes that God is teaching us something, not just about →

Scriptural Context

In this ongoing dialogue of revelation between God and Moses, Moses expresses his concern about his ability to speak to Pharaoh on behalf of the Israelites. He reasons that if the Israelites won't listen to him, how could he possibly persuade Pharaoh to even think about releasing the Israelites. □

Targum: English Translation
Exodus 6:10–13

10) *Adonai* spoke to Moses saying, 11) "Go to Pharaoh, King of Egypt, and tell him to let the Israelites leave his land." 12) *But Moses appealed to* Adonai *saying, "[If] the Israelites would not listen to me, why would Pharaoh respond to me, a man of impeded speech?"* 13) So *Adonai* spoke to Moses and Aaron and instructed them regarding the Israelites and Pharaoh, king of Egypt, to deliver the Israelites from the land of Egypt. □

From the Tradition

The sages said the following regarding the conduct for speaking, especially in the content of our argument: (*Pirke Avot* 5:7) (1) Don't speak before one who is greater in wisdom; (2) Do not interrupt the speech of another; (3) Do not be hasty in answering; (4) Ask only relevant questions; (5) Answer appropriately; (6) Speak on the first point first and the last point last; (7) Acknowledge the truth. □

Background The Sefas Emes, Yehudah Aryeh Leib of Ger, taught: My father, his memory is a blessing, taught that they were not able to endure the abominations of Egypt. And this indeed is the purpose of the redemption, that the children of Israel should come out from the "iron furnace" from Egypt. And all the holy sparks that were found there would ascend, and the restrictions and waste from the *Sitra Achra*, "the Other Side," would not cleave to them. That is how a Jew must be, that no evil can cleave to him.

And that is how they prepare for and come to resemble the Land of Israel, as it says about her: "So let not the land spew you out for defiling her" (Leviticus 18:28) – because the Land of Israel cannot endure any abomination

And this is brought out in the holy *Zohar*, that the children of Israel resemble a heart that cannot accept waste, only the part that is cleansed and purified from defects. Just as any food entering the person's body is separated and purified, the waste purged from the rest of the sustenance, and the blood transformed [now fit] to be included in the person's soul, so it needs to be in a spiritual dimension, because the person raises and purifies the holy element and cleaves to it while the waste is purged.

All of this is with the help of God. And this is as it is written, "And know you that I, the Lord, am the one who brings you out from the burdens of Egypt (Exodus 6:7)." And our sages, their memory is a blessing, said, "Without spiritual awareness, from where would the separation come?" (*J. Berachot* 5:2). □

The Teaching *(continued)*

reason, if the children of Israel listen to Moses, his mouth would be opened, his speech would be fluent, and his words would reach Pharaoh. But if they don't want to listen to him, he would be effectively made into one "of impeded speech" – and "how then should Pharaoh heed me?" □

Perush: Explaining the Teaching *(continued)*

Moses, but about leadership as well. If Moses succeeds as a spokesperson for the Israelites then, in effect, his speech is effectively not impeded. Thus, it is in the power of the Israelites (and in our power as well) to impede our leaders or to put such an impediment in their speech. □

(42) Va-Era: If He Only Had a Heart

The Teaching
from Yalkut Shimoni

A parable: Once upon a time a lion, the king of beasts, and a fox set out on a voyage by ship. A jackass came and tried to collect the cost of the passage. Said he, "Pay me the fare."

Replied the fox to the jackass, "What are you, crazy? Don't you know that the king of beasts is with us, and you're worried about collecting the fare!"

The jackass only answered, "I take what I please from the king and have access to his treasuries."

Now the lion was furious and roared, "Enough! Bring me the ship." He went and tore apart →

Perush: Explaining
the Teaching

Most readers of the exchange between Moses and Pharaoh are perplexed by what the Torah refers to as a hardening of Pharaoh's heart. Why would God harden Pharaoh's heart–and, by extension, permit the further suffering of the Israelites? Perhaps God merely allowed Pharaoh's predisposition toward a hardened heart to be realized and did not change the natural course of events. God wanted to demonstrate to Moses and the Israelites who was really in charge.

Scriptural Context

This portion reviews the genealogy of Moses and Aaron in order to validate their leadership. The centerpiece is the revelation of the name YHWH to Moses. The struggle between Pharaoh and God ensues. Our text is taken just prior to the commencement of the plagues. Moses has been unable to persuade Pharaoh to release the Israelites and God uses the opportunity to show Divine strength to the unbelieving. □

Targum: English Translation
Exodus 7:14–17

14) *And* Adonai *said to Moses,* *"Pharaoh's heart is stubborn, he refuses to let the people go.* 15) Go to Pharaoh in the morning, as he is coming out of the water, and station yourself before him at the edge of the Nile, taking with you the rod that turned into a snake. 16) And say to him, *'Adonai,* the God of the Hebrews, sent me to you to say, "Let My people go so that they can worship Me in the wilderness" but you paid no heed until now.' 17) Thus says *Adonai,* 'By this you will know that I am *Adonai.'* " □

From the
Tradition

Pharaoh's hardened heart has always puzzled our teachers. Perhaps Pharaoh's heart was predisposed to insensitivity (hardening) and God simply allowed Pharaoh (without intervening) to show the Israelites his essential self. Some may even argue that God could have intervened and prevented the suffering, but instead wanted to show Divine wonders and miracles to all of Israel and all of Egypt so that no one would question the God of Israel in the future–especially with the long journey through the desert and through history still ahead of them. □

This graphic parable, not the kind we are accustomed to in rabbinic literature, tells the story well: If you fool around with God's people, you will incur God's wrath and the fury of God's power. The jackass was warned (as was Pharaoh), even given a chance (as was Pharaoh with the early plagues). Ultimately it was Pharaoh's heartlessness that did him in. □

Background The *Yalkut Shimoni* is perhaps the best known and most comprehensive of all the *midrashim* since it covers the entire Bible. While it is traditionally ascribed to one Simeon of Frankfurt, it is not entirely clear who the real author is. The *Yalkut* draws on various rabbinic collections and is the only known source for many of them. □

The Teaching (*continued*)

the jackass and gave his carcass to the fox with these instructions: "Arrange the limbs of this fool."

So the fox cut them into pieces and splayed them. When he came to the heart of the jackass, he took it and ate it. The lion returned, saw the splayed carcass and asked, "Where is the fool's heart?"

Replied the fox, "My lord, King, the animal had no heart, for if he had a heart, he surely wouldn't have tried to collect a fare from the king!"

So too with the wicked Pharaoh, if he had a heart, he surely wouldn't have said to the King of Kings, give me a gift!" □

(43) Bo: Your Humble Servant

The Teaching
from *Likkutei Yehudah* citing the Sefas Emes, Yehudah Aryeh Leib of Ger

Rashi: As it is rendered in the Aramaic translation, אתכנעא, "to surrender oneself."

Rabbi Abraham Mordechai of Ger commented on this verse. He told of how his father, the Sefas Emes [Rabbi Aryeh Leib of Ger] had said that by uttering the phrase from Psalms "*Ana Adonai* ['Please God']. . ." one is able to accomplish anything. His congregation thought he was referring to the verse from →

Perush: Explaining the Teaching

In the midst of this comment, you have a kind of supercommentary (for the purpose of clarification) on the insight offered by the Sefas Emes as

Scriptural Context

Once again, Moses and Aaron have been sent by God to demand of Pharaoh, "Let My people go." This modest one-line communication sets the stage for the remaining plagues – before the final blow. It is the last stage of the confrontation between Moses and Pharaoh before Pharaoh enters into negotiations with him. □

Targum: English Translation
Exodus 10:1–3

1) So *Adonai* said to Moses, "Go to Pharaoh for I have hardened his heart and the heart of his servants in order to show these signs of Mine right in front of them [literally, "in their midst"] 2) and so that you may relate to your son and grandson what I have done to Egypt, all of My signs. [I did all this so] that you may know that I [am serious. I] am *Adonai*. 3) *So Moses and Aaron went to Pharaoh and said to him, "Thus says* **Adonai**, *the God of the Hebrews, 'How long will you refuse to humble yourself before Me?* Let My people go so that they may serve Me.' " □

From the Tradition

For the Jew, *Ana Adonai* is a kind of meditative mantra. It is found in the *Hallel* psalms and has a leitmotiv aural quality to it. Moreover, members of the ancient school of *merkavah* (chariot) mysticism, seekers of Ezekiel's chariot vision, would often deprive themselves of food for days at a time, remove themselves from society, and endlessly repeat such phrases until they attained their goal. □

taught by his son. The disciple corroborates his understanding of the verse by quoting Rashi (who calls to our attention a translation from *Targum Onkelos*). Thus, in isolating one verse, one episode, which precipitated the Exodus from Egypt, not only do we gain an insight into the creative tension our teachers perceived in the style of leadership offered by Moses and Aaron, and their relationship with God, but also we listen as our teachers sweep through Jewish literary history. They have all come to teach us about Jewish spirituality. We learn here that there are two ways of understanding our relationship with God. The former corresponds to Psalm 118:25, "*Ana Adonai* ['Please God'], save us now . . . ," and the latter to Psalm 116:16, "*Ana Adonai* ['Please, God'], for I am Your servant. . . ."

"Please God, save us" sees us as helpless and hopelessly distant from God. Our only chance is to coax and plead for God's help. God is in heaven; we are on earth. God runs everything from a celestial throne, and if we are "good little children," God will listen to us and do what we want. It is third-grade theology. →

Background Menachem Mendl of Kotzk taught that there are times when the leader must display dignity in order that the people have the proper respect for him. However, this pride must be like an outer garment; it must not subdue the humility of his inner heart. Pride has its place only on the outside, never within. □

76

The Teaching (*continued*)

Psalm 118:25, "*Ana Adonai* ["Please, God"], save us now. . . ." I, however, explained Rabbi Abraham Mordechai, felt he meant the verse from Psalm 116:16, "*Ana Adonai* ["Please, God"], for I am your servant . . . ," since through humility [which Pharaoh did not have] one is able to accomplish anything.

We learn here that there are two ways of understanding our relationship with God. The former corresponds to Psalm 118:25, "*Ana Adonai* ["Please God"], save us now . . . ," and the latter to Psalm 116:16, "*Ana Adonai* ["Please, God"], for I am your servant. . . ." □

Perush: Explaining the Teaching (*continued*)

The second verse, on the surface, does not seem to provide a significant alternative. The choice between coaxing and being obsequious isn't much. But we must remember that the Sefas Emes said that, with the second, you are "able to accomplish anything!" Perhaps there is more to being a "humble servant" than we realize. To be a servant is more than being servile; it is carrying out the will of an "Other." It is being the agent, the instrument *through which* what is supposed to happen, happens. A good servant is always aware of the importance of his act, and this gives heightened meaning to his life.

And just this is one of the great spiritual insights of all time. We are *agents, instruments* of God's intentions. We are not at odds with the Self of the Universe or with God's world; we are part of it; we are made of it, and to be so aware is to give our lives ultimate meaning and purpose. To realize that we are servants–through everything that we do, with or without consent, with the very stuff of our bodies–is to be able to do anything. It is our empowerment and fulfillment.

Everything we do, and everything we do it with, and everywhere we do it is filled with the Presence of God. We are free to choose whether or not we will be aware of it, whether we will be servants. That is Jewish spirituality. □

(44) Bo: From Rosh Ha-Shanah to Pesach

The Teaching
from the Sefas Emes, Yehudah Aryeh Leib of Ger

How could *Nisan* also be Rosh Ha-Shanah? We have an argument in *Rosh Hashanah* 10b–11a as to whether the world was created in *Nisan* or *Tishri*.

Rabbi Eliezer says that in *Tishri* the world was created.... On Rosh Ha-Shanah the slavery of our ancestors in Egypt ceased [six months before the redemption]; in *Nisan* they were redeemed and in *Nisan* they will be redeemed in the time to come. Rabbi Joshua says that in *Nisan* the world was created.

They're both right. The head of the year in *Nisan* is for the kings of Israel, which is to say that the children of Israel are called the children of kings, for they are free people, free at last from serving the Other Side (*Sitra Achra*), no longer under the control of the laws of nature.

Now *Tishri* is the New Year with regard to stern judgment and the fear of heaven. And *Nisan* is the New Year with regard to compassion and the love of heaven, and this is the reason that our text says that "this month shall be [only] for you."

According to *Midrash Rabbah, Parashat Bo,* 15:25, we understand "this month shall be for you" in the light of Psalm 147:19, "He issued His commands to Jacob, His statutes and judgments to Israel." "His commands to Jacob . . ." refers to the Torah; "His statutes →

Scriptural Context

Part of the narrative highlighting the Exodus from Egypt, this portion focuses on the last stage of the confrontation between Moses and Pharaoh. In the midst of the retelling of the last plague, Passover is described in anticipation of deliverance. Our text is taken from this section of the portion. □

Targum: English Translation
Exodus 12:1–2

1) Adonai said to Moses and Aaron in the land of Egypt 2) *"This month shall be for you the head of the months; it shall be the first for you of the months of the year."* □

From the Tradition

"There are four New Years. On the first of *Nisan* is the New Year for kings and for festivals; on the first of *Elul* is the New Year for the tithe of animals; Rabbi Eliezer and Rabbi Simon say, the first of *Tishri* is the New Year for the years, for Sabbatical years, for Jubilee years, for planting and for vegetables; and on the first of *Shevat* is the New Year for trees, according to the view of the School of Shammai, but the School of Hillel, says on the fifteenth of *Shevat*" (*Mishnah Rosh Ha-Shanah* 1:1). □

Perush: Explaining the Teaching

Reading this passage from Exodus, the Sefas Emes wonders how *Nisan* (the month during which Pesach is observed) can also be Rosh Hashanah (which is observed during *Tishri*). He cites a passage from the Talmud that partially explains the verse. The world was created during *Tishri*; thus, Rosh Ha-Shanah is observed at that time. On Rosh Ha-Shanah, the beginning of the Hebrew calendar year, the Israelites were redeemed from slavery in Egypt. The head of the year in *Nisan* is for the Israelites who are called Kings of Israel—now a free people. But the head of the year in *Tishri* is when the Israelites stand before God as they are being judged. Our teacher supports this assertion with statements from the *Midrash*, Psalms, and the *Zohar*, closing the circle regarding judgments and a dispensation from it on Pesach. □

Background The Lizensker *rebbe* argued that there are those who are distant from God the entire year but on the first day of *Elul* begin to devote a portion of their time to God. They are like cattle. They have no sense to remember God until the Day of Judgment approaches. □

The Teaching *(continued)*

and judgments . . ." refers to the sanctifications of the months that involve statutes and judgments.

After God chose Israel, God set the new month of redemption. For also in Tishri is a time for judgment, but this is a special, intimate judgment just for God. □

(45) Bo: Light at the End of the Tunnel

The Teaching
from Menachem Mendl of Kotzk

In Genesis 1:4 we read that "God saw the Light that it was good and made a separation."

Rashi, citing *Chagigah* 12a, interprets this to mean that the wicked were unworthy to use [the Light]; God therefore set it apart, reserving it for the righteous in the world to come.

Indeed, during the plague of darkness, since the wicked were unable to use the light in any way at all, it must obviously have been possible for Israel to make use of the primordial, hidden light.

And this is what our sages taught: that Israel was able to see all the hidden treasure of Egypt. For in this primordial, hidden light, nothing was concealed from them. And just this was the light enjoyed by Israel in their dwellings. □

Perush: Explaining the Teaching

What was this plague of darkness? Menachem Mendl teaches us that during the plague of darkness, the Israelites were able to use the primordial light that had been hidden since creation. If it had been reserved for the world to use, why would the Israelites, albeit righteous, be able to use it now? Redemption had come; they were now able to see things that had been there all along, now able to leave the slavery of Egypt. □

Scriptural Context

This portion begins with the last four plagues and the final blow: the death of the firstborn. These introduce the Passover theme of liberation, and here we see a demonstration of God's power in greater detail. □

Targum: English Translation
Exodus 10:21–23

21) **Then *Adonai* said to Moses, "Hold out your arm toward the sky so that darkness may fall on the land of Egypt, a darkness that can be touched." 22) Moses held out his arm toward the sky and thick darkness descended on the land of Egypt for three days. 23)** *People could not see one another, and for three days no one could get up from where he was, but all the Israelites enjoyed light in their dwellings.* □

From the Tradition

Since the first thing God made was light, but the sun, moon, stars, and heavenly luminaries were not created until the fourth day, we conclude that there were two different kinds of light. The ordinary light that we see by was created on day four, but the light of day one was the light of ultimate awareness. It was light so powerful that, in it, a person could see from one end of space to the other, from the beginning to the end of time. *Havdalah*, the ceremony that marks the transition from sacred to normal everyday, *Shabbat* to the other six days, holy days to workdays, brings this light into the dwellings of Israel. With it we are able to carry the light of *Shabbat* with us throughout the week. □

Background Dov Baer of Mezerich taught that in order to offer proper prayer, we must feel ourselves encompassed by the light of the spirit. □

(46) Be-Shallach: Miracle without Song

The Teaching
from Rabbi A. Chein

["The waters coming down from upstream piled up in a single heap a great way off. So the people crossed near Jericho. The priests who bore the Ark of *Adonai*'s covenant stood on dry land exactly in the middle of the Jordan, while all Israel crossed over on dry land, until the entire nation had finished crossing the Jordan" (Joshua 3:16–17).]

The miracle of the splitting of the Red Sea endures in the memory of the people on account of the song that they sang at the sea. →

Perush: Explaining the Teaching

Our teacher is moved by the power of music and its ability not only to move us but to make an indelible imprint on the mind. To prove his point, he compares the splitting of the Jordan in Joshua 3:16–17 – which is almost an "identical miracle" – with the splitting of the Re(e)d Sea. This is a simple lesson with profound implications and an incredible insight into the human psyche. □

Scriptural Context

Finally, the Israelites leave Egypt. The Pharaoh changes his mind once again and sends his armies after them. God allows the Israelites to walk into the "midst of the sea on dry ground," unscathed by the waters – but the Egyptians drown. In thanksgiving, the Israelites sing "the Song of the Sea." □

Targum: English Translation
Exodus 14:28–15:1a

28) **And the waters returned, covered the chariots and the horsemen, the entire army that Pharaoh had sent after them [the Israelites] into the waters. 29) But the Israelites walked upon dry land in the midst of the sea and the waters were like a wall on their right and left. 30) Thus** *Adonai* **saved Israel that day, just beyond the grasp of the Egyptians. And Israel saw the Egyptians scattered dead on the seashore. 31) Moreover, Israel saw the great work that** *Adonai* **did in Egypt, so much so that they revered God and believed in** *Adonai*, **and in the servant Moses. 15:1)** *Then Moses and the Israelites sang this song to* **Adonai. . . .** □

From the Tradition

Shirat Ha-Yam (Song of the Sea) is the name given to Exodus 15:1–18, sung by Moses and the Israelites after the miracle of the parting of the Red Sea. It retells the miracle (from Exodus 14:28). It is written in the Torah scroll in a graphically unique way, resembling "half bricks set over whole bricks" (*Megillah 16b*). It is even chanted in a special way; the Talmud offers three different methods of rendering it (*Sotah* 30b). The *Shabbat* on which it is read is called *Shabbat Shirah*. Since it is read on the seventh day of Passover, some *chasidim* hold a special ceremony at midnight in order to chant it. It is also found in →

Background David of Kotzk taught: We read in Psalm 68:26, "First come singers, then musicians. . . ." When Israel emerged from the Red Sea, the angels right away came forward in song before God. But God said to them, "Let My children go first," as we read, "Now let Moses and the children of Israel sing. . . ."

Literally, Exodus 15:1 does not read in the past tense, "Then Moses sang," but future, "Then he will sing." This is because God said, as we read in *Exodus Rabbah*, 23:7, "First, let Moses and the children of Israel sing."

Now why should Israel be awarded permission to sing first? Because the angels are eternally and at a moment's notice prepared to offer songs of praise, but not so the children of Israel. They are only capable of song when the desire and the feeling are spontaneously awakened within them. God feared that unless they were permitted to sing immediately, their desire would pass. □

The Teaching *(continued)*

The miracle of the splitting of the Jordan has not survived in our memory. There was no song. □

From the Tradition *(continued)*

Pesukei Dezimrah and is read in some communities during the *brit milah*.

During the song, Miriam took the women and led them in dance. This is the precedent that the rabbis have taken for traditionally separating the sexes (*Midrash Mechilta, Shirah* 10, 44a; *Midrash Lekach Tov* to Exodus 15–20). □

(47) Be-Shallach: The Very First *Shabbos*

The Teaching
from the Sefas Emes, Yehudah Aryeh Leib of Ger

Shabbat 118b: "Rab Judah said in Rab's name: Had Israel kept the first *Shabbat*, no nation or language would have had dominion over them. As it is said, 'And it came to pass on the seventh day, that there went out some of the people to gather,' which is followed by, 'Then came Amalek' (Exodus 17:8). [This refers to the manna, in connection with which *Shabbat* is mentioned explicitly for the first →

Perush: Explaining the Teaching

Shabbat for all of us provides the path for *(te)shuvah*, that opportunity to turn to God. Since *Shabbat Shuvah* is the first *Shabbat* of the year, following Rosh Ha-Shanah (which reflects creation), it provides each of us with an opportunity to do *teshuvah*. (Here →

Scriptural Context

Free from the pursuit of the Egyptians, the Israelites now begin their journey toward the Promised Land. From now on, the desert shapes the character of the people as it is forged into a free people. □

Targum: English Translation
Exodus 16:21–27

21) **So they gathered it every morning, each person according to personal food needs since when the sun grew hot, it [all] melted.** 22) **On the sixth day, they gathered twice as much food, two *omer* portions each. Then all of the tribal leaders came and told Moses.** 23) **Moses said to them, "This is what *Adonai* intended: Tomorrow is a day of rest, a holy Sabbath to *Adonai*. Cook or bake whatever [you need] and put aside everything remaining until morning."** 24) **So they put it aside until morning just as Moses had instructed them. It had not turned foul and no maggots were found in it.** 25) **Next Moses told them, "Today you should eat for it is a Sabbath to *Adonai*; today you will not find it [manna] on the plain.** 26) **For six days you may gather it but the seventh day [is] a Sabbath and there will be none [there].** 27) *And it came to pass on the seventh day, that there went out some of the people to gather but they did not find anything.* □

From the Tradition

On the eve of the Sabbath two ministering angels accompany a person from the synagogue to his home, one a good angel, the other a bad one.

If, when he arrives, he finds the lamp lit, the table set, and the bed covered with a spread, the good angel says, "May it be this way on another Sabbath, too." And the evil angel unwillingly answers, "Amen."

But if the house is messy and gloomy, the evil angel says, "May it be this way on another Sabbath, too." And the good angel is forced to say, "Amen" (*Shabbat* 119b). □

Background The Sefas Emes, Yehudah Aryeh Leib of Ger, taught that *Shabbat* helps with *teshuvah*, for as our sages say in *Berachot* 34b, "A *tzaddik*, a completely righteous person, is unable to stand in the place of a *baal teshuvah*, a master of (re)turning."

For the righteous ones [only] sustain the world, as it is said in Proverbs 10:25, "A *tzaddik*, a completely righteous person, is an everlasting foundation, [literally, the foundation of the world]." Whereas the path of *baalei teshuvah*, the

masters of turning, both precedes creation and transcends it, as is told in *Pesachim* 54a: "*Teshuvah* was one of the seven things created before the creation of the world."

Shabbat likewise partakes of that supernal light that is beyond the seven days of the week. She is a fountain of paradise. This is explained in *Genesis Rabbah* 22:13: "Adam once met Cain and asked him, 'Whatever happened with your sentence?' He replied, 'I made *teshuvah* and I was acquitted.' Adam began slapping himself, 'If →

The Teaching *(continued)*

time. It is also interesting to note that both here, with the first national defiling of the *Shabbat* and in Eden with Adam's son, the crime was eating.]

Rabbi Yochanan said in the name of Rabbi Simeon ben Yochai: If Israel were to keep two *Shabbatot* according to the laws thereof, they would be redeemed immediately, for it is said, 'Thus says *Adonai* concerning the eunuchs that keep My *Shabbatot*' (Isaiah 56:4) which is followed by, 'even them will I bring to My holy mountain . . .' (Isaiah 56:7).ʸ

There are those who are encouraged on *Shabbat Shuvah* because it is the first *Shabbat* of the year. As we read in the *Gemara:* "Had Israel kept the first *Shabbat*, no nation or language would have had dominion over them."

And on Rosh Ha-Shanah a new order is made over all the days of the year. If the day of the first *Shabbat* is repaired, the entire year is repaired!

And just this was the sin of the first man. For man was created on the sixth day in order that he should immediately enter the Garden of Eden. But, alas, he sinned before *Shabbat* came. For this reason, on *Shabbat*, it is possible to repair everything. □

Perush: Explaining the Teaching *(continued)*

we see the connection between *Shabbat Shuvah*, the Sabbath of return, from the same word as *teshuvah*, "repentance and return.") Since we have the opportunity to repair the world on *Shabbat*, according to Jewish tradition, on this first *Shabbat* we can repair the entire year. Thus, it is imperative that we all observe *Shabbat* in an effort to restore the world to its primordial state. □

Background *(continued)*

I had only known *teshuvah* had such power!' Whereupon Adam arose and sang the words of Psalm 92:1–2: "A song in praise of the *Shabbat*. It is good to give thanks [make confession] unto *Adonai*, to sing hymns to Your Name, O Most High," for *Shabbat* helps *teshuvah*. □

(48) Be-Shallach: Something New Every Day

The Teaching
from the Sefas Emes, Yehudah Aryeh Leib of Ger

Here is the main idea. The Torah is perpetually self-renewing, even though we read in Ecclesiastes 1:9, "There is nothing new under the sun." This is because the Torah is above the sun.

Indeed we read in the prayer book that God "renews daily the work of creation" [which also seems to contradict Ecclesiastes]. This teaches us therefore that one is always able to find a little novelty in this world. For this reason, perhaps the real meaning of Ecclesiastes is "Not everything is new under the sun," implying that there is a little renewal.

Just as one [must learn to] raise nature from its source and awaken a little novelty [each day], so one merits afterwards [to discover new insights] in Torah.

For this reason our sages ordained that in the daily and Sabbath liturgy, the blessings of creation (*Yotzer Or* and *Maariv Aravim*), which speak of the perpetual renewal of nature, should come before the blessings of love (*Ahavah Rabbah* and *Ahavat Olam*), which speak of Torah [as a symbol of love].

And thus the phrase "each day that day's portion" alludes to the perpetual renewal in nature, for the Holy One performs renewal every day; and the phrase "in order that I may test them, to see if they follow My Torah or not" alludes to the preparation for Torah. □

Scriptural Context

Beginning with the crossing of the Red Sea, this portion follows the Israelites as they begin their desert journey. Now free from Egyptian slavery and the pursuit of Pharaoh's armies, the Israelites still struggle. This struggle, however, while often played out in the physical world (What shall we eat?), seems to be more a spiritual one with self and God. □

Targum: English Translation
Exodus 16:1–4

1) **Setting out from Elim, the whole Israelite community came to the wilderness of Sin, which is between Elim and Sinai, on the fifteenth day of the second month after their departure from the land of Egypt. 2) In the wilderness, the whole Israelite community grumbled against Moses and Aaron. 3) The Israelites said to them, "If only we had died by the hand of** *Adonai* **in the land of Egypt, when we sat by the fleshpots, when we ate our fill of bread! For you have brought us into this wilderness to starve the whole congregation to death!" 4)** *And* **Adonai** *said to Moses, "I will rain down bread for you from the heaven and the people shall go out and collect each day that day's portion in order that I may test them, to see if they will follow My Torah or not."* □

From the Tradition

Manna was collected by the Israelites each day as it rained down from heaven in the Israelite encampment. They could not save what was left after twenty-four hours because it rotted—except for the manna that fell on the sixth day, prior to *Shabbat*. That double portion kept for forty-eight hours so that the Israelites would not have to go about collecting it during *Shabbat*. According to *Yoma* 76a, receiving the manna each day prompted the Israelites to turn to God for their daily bread. □

Perush: Explaining the Teaching

From sensitizing ourselves to the subtle novelty of each day (and its gifts of manna), we rise to being able to find new insights each time we study Torah.

Background Jewish tradition teaches that one actually awakens in the morning with a renewed soul. During sleep, we are actually transformed, awakening each day with the potential to return to God and do good. □

(49) Yitro: Godtalk

The Teaching
from Joshua of Kutno

Berachot 45a says it means "in Moses' voice," that is, God's Presence was speaking from the throat of Moses; the voice was Moses' voice. □

Scriptural Context

This is the central experience of the Jewish people, the revelation of Torah to the people through Moses. In our text, Moses speaks and God answers him. □

Perush: Explaining the Teaching

Our teacher comes to explain something that is ostensibly already explained by the Talmud. A quick read might render simple authority to Moses — that he was speaking on behalf of God. Still struggling with the notion of God communicating directly at Sinai, as well as the use of an intermediary, Joshua of Kutno is saying that whatever was heard, it was nevertheless God speaking. Moses had been filled with the presence of God. Would that we could all be filled with the presence of God so that the words we speak might be God's, even if heard in our voice. □

Targum: English Translation
Exodus 19:19

19) The blare of the horn [*shofar*] grew increasingly. *Moses spoke, and God answered in a voice.* □

From the Tradition

When God gave the Torah, no bird sang and no fowl flew, no ox bellowed, no angel stirred a wing. The *seraphim* did not say, "Holy, Holy," the sea did not roar, and no creature spoke.

The whole world stood hushed into breathless silence, and the voice went forth and proclaimed, "I am *Adonai* your God" (*Exodus Rabbah* 29:9). □

Background Joshua Isaac ben Yechiel Shapira (d. 1873) was a rabbi and talmudist known as *Eitzel Charif* (literally, "sharp") because of his keen intellect. He was an outstanding pilpulist and *av bet din* at Kalvarija, Kutno, Tiktin, and Slonim. He is the author of numerous commentaries on *halachah* and *aggadah* as well as books of homilies. □

(50) Yitro: The Distance between Heaven and Earth

The Teaching
from *Daat Soferim*

From this apparent contradiction we can learn that at the moment of the giving of the Torah, everything reverted to the primordial state of creation before the Holy One had made a separation between the heavens and the earth. For at this hour the earth was joined with the heavens, the distance between them, removed. □

Scriptural Context

The drama atop Mount Sinai continues. The Decalogue is revealed to the Jewish people and the eternal covenant between God and Israel is sealed. □

From the Tradition

A philosopher once said to Rabban Gamaliel, "God found good materials, which God used in the creation of the world: *Tohu, Vohu,* darkness, water, wood and the deep." Gamaliel replied, "Woe to that man! The term 'creation' is explicitly used of them" (*Genesis Rabbah* 1:9). Gamaliel refutes both the existence of primordial matter and the gnostic notion that God was not the sole creator of the world. □

Perush: Explaining the Teaching

Having read ahead in the next chapter, our teacher realizes that the venue changes. Knowing that there can be be no real contradictions in the Torah, only apparent ones, he helps us to understand why we might think that God is on Mount Sinai in Exodus 19:20, but when God refers to this communication (later, in Exodus 20:19), God suggests that the conversation had taken place from heaven. At the moment of revelation, at the giving of Torah at Sinai, the world was, in a sense, just as it was before creation. Heaven and earth were one. For the Torah really created the world anew. □

Targum: English Translation
Exodus 19:20; 20:19

19:20) *And* **Adonai** *descended on Mount Sinai.* 20:19) **Adonai said to Moses, "Thus, you shall tell the Israelites,** *'You saw for yourselves that I spoke to you from the heavens.'"* □

Background A certain caravan merchant once said to Rabbah bar Channah, "Come, I will show you the place where heaven and earth touch so closely it appears that they are kissing" (*Bava Batra* 74a). □

(51) Yitro: Coveting's Promise

The Teaching
from Jehiel Michael of Zloczow

It is a widely known problem: How is it possible to caution someone to refrain from something that is not in his power? Even if he didn't want to covet, would not coveting come into his heart anyway? [The answer] "You shall not covet" is [not only a commandment] but also a promise; as a person who is careful to observe the [preceding] nine holy utterances, it is certain that we will not covet. □

Perush: Explaining the Teaching

Our teacher offers a profound explanation of one utterance that is probably the most frequently violated (I see it; I want it). He does so by offering a unique perspective on the structure of the Dacalogue. The observance of the other nine commandments holds the tenth one in check. Thus, this tenth commandment is not a commandment at all. Rather, it is God's promise to us that if we observe God's other instructions, we will not [be motivated at all] to covet. □

Scriptural Context

Our text is taken from the tenth utterance at Mount Sinai. □

From the Tradition

Jacob Zvi Mecklenberg taught in his *Ha-Ketav Ve-Ha-Kabbalah*: Many are surprised by this commandment. How is it possible for a person not to covet a beautiful thing in his heart? Doesn't the heart covet by itself, contrary to a person's wishes? The answer seems to be as the author of *Sheni Luchot Ha-Beit*, Isaiah Horowitz wrote concerning the verse "And you shall love the Lord, your God, with all your heart. . . ." What would the scriptural text be lacking if it were simply written, "And you shall love the Lord, your God, with your heart" [it would have been sufficient]? What could be the purpose of adding the words "with all"? The answer is simply that the intention of the text is that your heart be filled with the love of God. In other words, that there be in your heart nothing other than the exclusive love of God, for there cannot be both the love of God and the love of anything else. And if your heart be filled to overflowing with the love of God, it is impossible that it would covet anything from among all the beautiful things of this world, for then there is no place in the heart that would desire or covet anything at all. It is like a full cup, unable to receive anymore. □

> ### Targum: English Translation
> ### Exodus 20:14
> 14) *You shall not covet your neighbor's house; you shall not covet your neighbor's wife, or his ox or his ass or anything that is your neighbor's.* □

Background Jehiel Michael of Zloczow (Zlotchow, c. 1731–1786) was one of the earliest *chasidim* in Galicia. When the Baal Shem Tov died, Yechiel was one of the few disciples who accepted the authority of Dov Baer, the *Maggid* of Mezerich. Yechiel was highly regarded as a teller of miracle tales and strongly opposed by the *mitnaggedim*. According to *Likkutei Yekarim* 31b, written by one of his disciples: "It little mattered whether he had before him a *Gemara* or a kabbalistic text, for Yechiel saw in them only the means of serving God." □

(52) Mishpatim: Hearing What You Do

The Teaching
from Menachem Mendl of Kotzk

There are so many wise men, scholars, and philosophers in the world, all of them pondering, investigating, and delving into the mystery of God. And why do they misuse their wisdom? They only misuse it because they are limited by their intellectual level and perceptual capacity.

But the people of Israel are a holy people. They possess special instruments that elevate their perceptual capacity and enable them to transcend the level of their intellect and attain the level of the ministering →

Perush: Explaining the Teaching

Menachem Mendl of Kotzk ponders the classic response of the Israelites when they agreed to their responsibilities of the covenant as stipulated. Literally, the text reads, "We will do and we will hear." The Kotzker faces the obvious question: How can we do something before we hear it? By encapsulating →

Scriptural Context

In the previous portion, the covenant, the revelation of God to Moses on Sinai, begins. In this portion, we get the details. It begins with the rules on slavery and serfdom, then laws on property and injury, and directives for moral behavior and Israelite cultic ordinances. Since Moses is invited to come up the mountain, while he is supposed to already be there, the sequence has long puzzled scholars. The portion concludes with the Israelites' acceptance of the requirements and responsibilities of the covenant. □

From the Tradition

Rabbi Yishmael was accustomed to saying, "The one who studies in order to teach will be enabled to study and to teach. The one who studies in order to practice will be enabled to study and to teach, to observe and to practice (*Pirke Avot* 4:5). □

Targum: English Translation
Exodus 24:4–8

4) Moses wrote down all of *Adonai's* directions. He arose early and built an altar at the base of the mountain, with twelve pillars corresponding to the twelve Israelite tribes. 5) There he [Moses] instructed young Israelites to offer burnt offerings and sacrifices as peace-offerings to *Adonai*. 6) Next Moses took half of the blood [from the sacrifices] and placed it into basins. He sprinkled the rest [the other half] of the blood [all] over the altar. 7) He [Moses] then took the Book of the Covenant and read it in earshot of the people; in response [to the reading] they said, "All that *Adonai* spoke *we will do and we will hear*." 8) Moses took the [remaining] blood and sprinkled it on the people while saying, "This is covenantal blood, sealing the details of the agreement that *Adonai* made with you." □

Background While the Kotzker *rebbe* (1987–1859) is a relatively unknown figure in the history of Western civilization, he is often compared to the philosopher Søren Kierkegaard. They lived worlds apart (the Kotzer in Guray, Poland, and Kierkegaard in Copenhagen, Denmark) and never met. By the time Kierkegaard (1813–1855) published his first book, *Either/Or*, in 1843, the Kotzker had already removed himself from the world and lived in virtual isolation (perhaps a psychotic break). While their ways of life were obviously worlds apart, their theological concerns express a remarkable similarity. They both searched for a way to determine how one lives one's life in accordance with a personal religious creed and commitment. Neither left their students answers, only a limitless challenge. For the Kotzker, the one who thinks he is finished *is* finished. Hence, their struggle urges us on in our struggle. □

The Teaching (*continued*)

angels themselves. And these are their instruments: the performance of *mitzvot*.

This is just what Israel said when they stood at Mount Sinai, "We will do and we will hear." Through the power of the *mitzvot* we perform, we are able to understand. □

Perush: Explaining the Teaching (*continued*)

the Jewish way of life, Menachem Mendl answers his own query by reasoning that through *doing mitzvot*, we will *hear* (understand God and the Divine mystery of the world.) Here, the Kotzker ritualizes all behavior so that everything we do is connected in some way to God. Through the process of doing God's *mitzvot*, we come to understand God. □

(53) Mishpatim: Being Where You Are

The Teaching
from Menachem Mendl of Kotzk

There is an apparent difficulty here. If Moses came up on the mountain, he would already be there, so why would God also bother to specify, "and be there?"

But from this apparent redundancy we find proof that even one who strains himself to ascend onto a high mountaintop, and is indeed able to reach the summit, it is nevertheless possible that he is still not there. Even though he may be standing on the very peak itself, his head may be somewhere else.

The goal, you see, is not merely to ascend but also to be there, to be actually present there, and nowhere else – and not to be going up and down at the same time. □

Scriptural Context

After their sojourn in the desert, the people arrive at the foot of Mount Sinai and God tells Moses to come up to the mountain so that he may receive the Divine instruction on behalf of the entire people.

This portion, which contains what is now called the covenant code, is filled with specific laws and statutes that the Israelites are asked to fulfill. Thus, their acceptance and affirmation is requested before Moses goes up the mountain (and will again be asked and acted upon later after the Torah is given). □

Targum: English Translation
Exodus 24:12–14

12) *And God said to Moses, "Come up to Me on the mountain and be there. I will give you the stone tablets, as well as the law [literally, Torah] and the instructions [literally, mitzvot)] that I have composed, so that you might teach them."* 13) *Moses arose, along with his minister Joshua, and Moses went up the mountain.* 14) *To the elders, he [Moses] said, "Stay put until we return. Look [don't worry], Aaron and Hur are with you. If anyone has any problem whatsoever, let him bring it to them."* □

From the Tradition

Let a person always learn from the Creator, for here the Holy Blessed One forsook all of the mountains and high hills and caused the Divine presence to rest on lowly Mount Sinai. (*Sotah* 5a). □

Perush: Explaining the Teaching

Menachem Mendl of Kotzk, the Kotzker, is struck by an obvious redundancy in the text. If Moses were to follow God's instruction and come up to the mountain, then he would already *be there*. Why then does the text add "and be there"? Where else could Moses be? The Kotzker concludes that "being there" is not merely geographical, and thus even if Moses were "there" on the mountaintop, he may not yet "be fully present." Furthermore, if God is everywhere, then why would Moses have to ascend the mountain in the first place? Had God told Moses he did not have to go anywhere to "be there," perhaps Moses would not have believed God. Moses, like all of us, needed to feel that physically going somewhere would help to get to where he was spiritually going. →

Background Menachem Mendl of Kotzk (1787–1859) was a disciple of the Seer of Lublin (Jacob Isaac Ha-Chozeh) and Jacob Isaac (the Holy *Yehudi*) of Przysucha. Later, he also studied with Simchah Bunem of Przysucha. He was considered to be revolutionary among *chasidim*. He was zealous and harsh in his pursuit of truth. The Kotzker said that every day prayer must be created anew. Every day, one must try to find the truth as if the individual had not known it before.

The Kotzker had such a reputation as a fanatic for the truth that *chasidim*, frustrated by the intensity of their fellow students, have been known to yell, "You can go live in Kotzk." □

Perush: Explaining the Teaching *(continued)*

Thus, the ascent itself may be a metaphor. You can achieve it right where you are. The call of the Divine is not somewhere else – providing you are brave enough to hear it. The search for the Divine is actually a spiral that results in the individual coming back to the self, a feeling similar to the childlike wonderment of waking up in the morning. □

(54) Mishpatim: Creation's Prejudgment

The Teaching
from Simchah Bunem of Przysucha in *Kol Simchah*

The statutes and the judgments were legislated for the nations of the world and fixed by sages and people of understanding, those who knew about religion and justice. Those lawgivers actually preceded the statutes and the judgments themselves.

But it is the other way around with the judgments of Israel, the statutes of the Torah. According to the *Zohar*, the Torah was created an aeon before the creation of the world. As we read in Proverbs 29:4, "With judgments a King founds the earth," and all creation, all of it, is based upon the Lord of judgment.

And just this is the meaning of "which you shall set before them. . . ." Do not read it spatially but temporally: before them in time! Judgment comes before all being, for God gives us the law. □

Scriptural Context

As part of the revelation, various laws are given to the Israelites. These include civil and criminal laws and cultic provisions, ending with details concerning the concluding of the covenantal agreement. Our text introduces this portion and the rules that follow. □

Targum: English Translation
Exodus 21:1

1) *And these are the judgments that you shall set before them*: □

From the Tradition

Life is in the details. The covenant between God and the people of Israel is not a simple agreement – blind faith and then ultimate and eternal salvation. The covenant entered into at Sinai involves a commitment and follow-up on the part of both parties. The Torah, understood through the lens of the rabbis, provides us with the follow-up (*mitzvot*), what it is we have to do in order to reach God and bring the holy into our lives. The mystical tradition illuminates that follow-up by providing us with "metameaning" for the *mitzvot*. □

Perush: Explaining the Teaching

Our teacher, Simchah Bunem, is struck by the expression "before them." What is meant by the expression "before" – since it is usually associated with space, that is, literally placed in front of them? But Simchah Bunem argues that "before" here is temporal, that the judgments (Torah) actually preceded the Israelites and the creation of the world. This is what makes God's judgments, and Israel, unique. □

Background The *Zohar*, the *Book of Splendor*, is the central work of the kabbalists, the Jewish mystics. It is a collection of several sections which purport to be a long *midrash* on the Five Books of Moses. It is customarily printed in three volumes. The material is ascribed to Shimon bar Yochai, but there are many anonymous sections, as well. Most scholars now believe it to be the work of Moses de Leon, who lived in thirteenth-century Spain. □

(55) Terumah: Self Set Apart

The Teaching
from Simchah Bunem of Przysucha

Rashi: According to Onkelos's Aramaic translation, *terumah* means "something set apart."

At least at the time when you are occupied with doing commandments, separate yourselves and your souls entirely for God. A person should not set about doing sacred business with a heart full of avarice, caught up in the material world. Rather, let him purify his heart and his thoughts for what is holy.

And this is the meaning of "and you shall take," that is, "when you take yourselves". "For Me" refers to "for My sake, for the sake of fulfilling My commandments." "*Terumah*," as Rashi and Onkelos suggest, means "you shall be separate and set apart from the vanities of this world." □

Scriptural Context

Now that the various statutes and ordinances have been given to the Israelites, it is time to turn to the sanctuary and its service. And so, our text introduces the instructions for furnishing the tabernacle. □

Targum: English Translation
Exodus 25:1-7

1) **Adonai spoke thus to Moses, 2) "Tell the Israelites '*And you shall take for Me* terumah *[gifts]* from everyone who is moved to do so [literally, "whose heart speaks to him"].' 3) And these are the *terumah* that you should accept from them: gold, silver, and copper 4) blue, purple, and crimson yarns, fine linen, goat's hair, 5) tanned ram skin, dolphin skin, and acacia wood, 6) oil for lighting, spices for the anointing oil and for the good-smelling incense, 7) lapis lazuli and other stones for setting, for the *ephod* and breastpiece."** □

From the Tradition

Targum Onkelos is an Aramaic translation of the Hebrew Bible by Onkelos (a proselyte). It often appears side by side with the original (in *Mikraot Gedolot* – the so-called *Rabbis' Bible*). It dates from the second century of the common era and for those who know both languages, it serves as a commentary and interpretation for the Hebrew. Onkelos is often confused with Akila, who lived at the same time in the same place and translated the Bible into Greek. □

Perush: Explaining the Teaching

Sensitized to the nuance of the text by Rashi, who in turn has called our attention to *Targum Onkelos* (the Aramaic translation by Onkelos), our teacher explores further the notion that *terumah* is something "set apart." Simchah Bunem suggests that *terumah* is a not a gift, as it is generally considered. Offering *terumah* is when you literally take *yourself* as a set-apart, consecrated gift to the tabernacle. In this way, you give yourself to God. □

Background Following his marriage to Rebecca of Bendin, Simchah Bunem became attracted to Chasidism. After years as a timber merchant and traveling to visit various *rebbes*, he became a pharmacist in Lvov. He finally became a disciple of the Seer of Lublin. When the Seer died, Simchah Bunem became his heir apparent. But some were unable to forget his business background. Responding to the criticism of Rabbi Meir of Opatow, Simchah Bunem responded, "Rabbi Meir does not know what sin is and he does not know how to sin. I can understand temptation and can help people to withstand it." (J. Levinstein, *Si'ach Sarfei Kodesh*, Lodz, 1928, vol. III, p. 14.) □

(56) Terumah: The Proper Order

The Teaching
from Simcha Bunem of Przysucha

Rashi: Also in future generations (cf. *Sanhedrin* 16b).

The Torah specifies in each paragraph the order of the work to be done on the Tabernacle and its utensils, what comes earlier and what comes later. First is the ark, then the curtains, after that the cherubim, and so on. From this we can conclude that since the Torah brothers to mention the sequence of what is to be done and says, "So you shall do," it must mean for future generations also.

Even those children in generations still to come, when your turn comes to do holy work, follow the example of the building of the wilderness tabernacle. Go from one level to the next, each at its proper time. Don't put what is supposed to go at the beginning at the end, nor put what is supposed to go at the end at the beginning. □

Perush: Explaining the Teaching

The phrase "so you shall do," while not redundant in the usual sense (although the instructions for building have appeared in Exodus 25:8), has an emphatic aspect to it. Thus, our teacher believes that it makes the time-bound instruction of building the Tabernacle for the wilderness generation into an eternal instruction for all generations. Simchah Bunem teaches us that the plan for building and furnishing the Tabernacle should serve as a model for us and for all generations. Part of properly performing holy tasks lies in performing them in the order they are prescribed. It is the same way with everything sacred in life. □

Scriptural Context

The Tabernacle was to be built according to the painstaking detail delineated in the Torah text. This portion focuses on the ark, lampstand, tent, and altar. Even with the great detail, it is hard to imagine the majesty of the Israelites' completed work. □

Targum: English Translation
Exodus 25:8-9

8) **And let them make Me a sanctuary so that I may dwell among them.** 9) *According to everything that I show you, the plan for the Tabernacle and the plan for all its utensils, so shall you do.* □

From the Tradition

The touchstone for Jewish spirituality is Torah. A verse of Torah is the grounding for commonplace conversation. When we study Torah, we activate a different mode of understanding. This is the psychospiritual tradition in Judaism. God has ultimate truth and reveals it to people through Torah. Here the Jewish people is born. The division of Torah into fifty-four *parshiyot* to be read weekly (some portions are joined together, doubled, depending on the calendar, especially when festivals fall on *Shabbat* and actually displace regular weekly Torah portions). Each Torah portion is a rubric for Jewish spirituality. □

Background Simchah Bunem was once asked, "Why should a *tzaddik* be called a good Jew? If he prays well, he should be called a good worshiper. If he learns well, he should be called a good student." Bunem replied, "A good Jew thinks, eats, sleeps goodness. Goodness appears in everything he does." □

(57) Terumah: The *Menorah* Makes Itself

The Teaching from the Sefas Emes, Yehudah Aryeh Leib of Ger

Rashi: The passive voice is used here [in contradistinction to the active voice used throughout the rest of the section. This implies that the *menorah* will be made] of itself (*mei'ahleha*, מאליה) [without any help from people]. Which explains why Moses was puzzled by it. (The assignment was too hard to understand.) In verse 40, we read, "Watch and make [them] →

Perush: Explaining the Teaching

Sensitive to the various voices used in the text, our teacher begins by quoting Rashi, who offers his explanation as to why the text chooses a passive voice where in the other elements of construction for the Tabernacle, the text speaks in an active voice. Moses was puzzled. How could the *menorah* be erected if it was to be made "of itself" without the aid of people? Rashi →

Targum: English Translation
Exodus 25:31–40

31) *You shall make a* menorah *of pure gold; the* menorah *shall be hammered work*, its base and its shaft, its cups, calyxes [outer part of the flower], and petals shall be one piece. 32) Six branches shall issue from its sides: three branches from one side of the *menorah* and three branches from the other side. 33) On one branch there should be three cups shaped like almond blossoms, each with calyx and petals, the same for all six branches that extend out from the *menorah*. 34) On the *menorah* itself should be four cups shaped like almond blossoms, each with calyx and petals: 35) a piece of the calyx under a pair of branches and one piece of the calyx under the second pair of branches and one piece of the calyx under the last pair of branches, the same for all six branches that extend out from the *menorah*. 36) The calyxes and stems should be a part of it [the *menorah*], all should be one single hammered piece of pure gold 37). Make its seven lamps so mounted so that light emanates from its front side. 38) Its tongs and fire pans [should also be made] of pure gold. 39) The whole thing should be made from a talent [measurement] of pure gold. 40) Carefully follow the pattern that you see on the mountain. □

Scriptural Context

This portion, which focuses on the erection of the Tabernacle, is given careful attention in the Bible as well as by later commentators and the sages. Special attention is given to the ark, *menorah*, tent, and altar. □

From the Tradition

The *menorah* (distinguished from a Chanukah *menorah* or *Chanukiyah*), which predates the six-pointed "Star of David" as the symbol of Judaism, may reflect an artistic representation of a plant as it grows in Israel, a type of sage called *salvia* (*moriah* in Hebrew). Perhaps it was a stylized sacred tree used for cultic purposes. The *menorah* was often referred to as the *ner tamid* because of the established routine that attended to its daily lighting. While there was only one *menorah* in Solomon's Temple, in the Second Temple (the one taken by the Romans and represented in the Arch of Titus), →

Background Rashi (Solomon ben Isaac), 1040–1105, who was born in Troyes, and lived in Worms, France, is considered the leading commentator on the Bible and Talmud. While he adds little of his own insight to any text under discussion, his encyclopedic recall of the tradition makes his commentary extremely important. Most of his commentary is based on midrashic sources, often abridging the text rather than reproducing it in its entirety. →

The Teaching (*continued*)

according to their patterns. . . ." About this verse Rashi says, "This teaches that Moses was puzzled about how to make the *menorah* until the Holy One showed him the pattern of it in a *menorah* of fire.

If the *menorah* was made "by itself, automatically," why did God show him a *menorah* of fire?

The contradiction can be resolved in this way: Obviously, human beings are unable to completely fulfill the will of God. But by means of a person's innermost yearning to fulfill the will of the Holy One, help is given from on High, that the yearning might be realized.

The yearning of a person influences a given undertaking so that it can actually complete itself. Now Moses couldn't understand the will of God with regard to the *menorah*, so God showed him a *menorah* of fire. And, since he yearned to do what God wanted, even though this is beyond the strength of human beings to accomplish [as Rashi explains], "it was made by itself!" □

Perush: Explaining the Teaching (*continued*)

concludes that God simply showed Moses a pattern for the *menorah* in fire. And since Rashi generally repeated what he had learned as accepted tradition (rather than adding his own insight), he was satisfied. But our teacher Aryeh Leib of Ger, was not content with that explanation. The Gerer *rebbe* reasoned that if indeed the *menorah* was to be made "of itself," then why did the Holy One even bother to show Moses a pattern for the *menorah*? He reasons that since the Divine creation of the *menorah* was literally beyond the competency of human beings, although Moses yearned to help in its building, God met Moses halfway by helping him through showing him a pattern for the *menorah* in an unusual way. Moses' yearning was a sufficient catalyst for the action to be completed, so to speak, on its own. Through his vision, he was given the strength to complete the task, which was beyond him. Likewise, a person's yearning enables him or her to transcend normal physical limitations. □

From the Tradition (*continued*)

three lights were continuously burning, while the remaining lights were kindled each night. According to rabbinic legend, when the First Temple was about to be destroyed, the *menorah* was hidden away and brought back to the Second Temple by exiles who had returned from Babylonian captivity to Jerusalem.

For the kabbalists, the seven branches of the *menorah* represent the lower seven *Sefirot*, each part of the *menorah* playing a part in the mystical scheme of the world. For example, the oil placed in the branches in the force for the light of the *menorah*, which signifies the dynamic stream influenced by the *Ein Sof*. □

Background (*continued*)

What little he adds is primarily philological. Yet it is a compromise between the literal and midrashic commentary on the text. One simply does not study *Chumash* without Rashi. His aim is to make the text lucid, more easily and readily understood. □

(58) Tetzaveh: Jump Start

The Teaching
from the Sefas Emes, Yehudah Aryeh Leib of Ger

Rashi says it means that [the priest] must enkindle it until the flame ascends by itself. [Rami ben Hama, in a discussion about the wicks and oils appropriate for *Shabbat* and temple lights] interpreted *le-haalot* in our verse, which literally means "to cause to go up," as teaching that the flame must ascend by itself [without frequent attention] and not through something else (*Shabbat* 21a; also, Sifra on Leviticus 24:2). →

Perush: Explaining the Teaching

As is common, the Sefas Emes is concerned by what appears to be a redundant phrase in the text. The Israelites are instructed to take "the pure oil of beaten olives for *lighting*, to cause a *continual flame (le-haalot)* to ascend." He reasons that there are two kinds of flames. Hence the redundant use of the image for lighting. One flame has trouble igniting; the second ignites quickly without any trouble. From this observation, he sees an analogy between fire and a religious act. A religious act demands more than just physical strength. It requires religious faith and commitment as well – which he regards as spiritual power. We could perform a religious act for a while, but we could not keep it up without God, without the requisite spiritual strength necessary to perform a holy act. Thus, we perform religious acts for reasons beyond ourselves. The religious act or gesture is self-transcendent. As such, we are agents for something more than we are.

The mode of religious behavior is such that we can only do it as agents for someone else. Sometimes we do not want to do these things, but we do them anyway. We know →

Scriptural Context

The preceding portion began the focus on the furnishings of the Tabernacle. This portion continues with instructions for kindling the *ner tamid*, the eternal light. Aaron and his sons are introduced as priests, and their priestly garments are detailed. □

Targum: English Translation
Exodus 27:20–21

20) *And you shall command the children of Israel and they shall take for you the pure oil of beaten olives for lighting, to cause a continual flame to ascend.* 21) **[The lamp should be placed] in the Ohel Mo'ed outside of the parochet [veiled curtain] that is set before the testimony. Aaron and his sons are [responsible] to keep it in order so that it will burn from evening to morning before Adonai. It is an everlasting statute [which shall be kept] throughout time on behalf of the generations of Israel.** □

From the Tradition

The *ner tamid* in the synagogue reminds us, as it is intended, of the *menorah* that burned continually in the Temple. Originally it was placed in a niche in the western wall of the synagogue to represent the position of the *menorah* in the Temple. Later, it was placed directly in front of the ark, usually suspended from the ceiling. The *ner tamid* is said to be symbolic of God's presence (*Shabbat* 22b) as well as the spiritual light that emanates from the ancient Temple (*Exodus Rabbah* 36:1). □

Background The city of Ger (Yiddish; known in Hebrew as Gur) was known to the world as Gora Kalwaria – known popularly as Nowy Jeruzalem – and located approximately twenty miles from Warsaw, Poland. While Jews settled there following its deliverance into Prussian hands in 1795, its population, which had grown to 3,500 just prior to World War II, became a concentration-camp site for the nearby communities of Lodz, Pabiance, and Aleksandrow (or Alexander) – to eventually die at the hands of the Nazis along with Warsaw Jewry. □

The Teaching *(continued)*

The explanation here is that religious acts cannot be accomplished by personal strength alone but rather, through the power of performing a religious act some spiritual power is awakened. So it is with everything a person does.

This is because the Holy One of Being sets in the soul of each Jew a holy spark, and by means of devotion and service, like attracts like. [The spiritual power in the deed and the spiritual power in the Jew] are roused and the inner power awakens. Just this is what Rashi means when he says that "the flame must ascend by itself"; it is all a matter of endurance.

Anything accomplished by the power of a human being sooner or later must stop. But when the power of the Holy One is awakened, this kind of power continues forever. This is the meaning of the next verse, "Aaron and his sons shall arrange it" (Exodus 27:21). The whole idea behind performing religious deeds is to arrange things and set them in their proper places, until they are joined to their root and their source: "To cause an eternal flame to ascend," for by means of ascending to its holy root, it endures forever. □

Perush: Explaining the Teaching *(continued)*

that if we don't do them, we will be distressed. As a result, the religious system gains its own momentum.

To be a serious Jew, we have to behave in a serious way. Thus, we tie the flame to something above. Flame is a metaphor for the intention behind a *mitzvah*, a holy act – in response to a divine request. □

The Teaching
from *Otzar Ha-Chasidut,* Israel Baal Shem Tov

Memory is the source of redemption; exile comes from forgetting.

And therefore it is also written with regard to the war with Amalek, that it is the commencement of redemption: "Write this in a scroll as a reminder, and read it aloud to Joshua, 'I will utterly blot out the memory of Amalek from under heaven'" (Exodus 17:14; *maftir* of *Beshallach*). →

Perush: Explaining the Teaching

While our teacher lived before World War II, his statement "Memory is the source of redemption" is inscribed over the entrance to Yad VaShem, Israel's memorial to those who perished in the Holocaust. Nevertheless, he teaches us the lesson of Jewish history. The historical memory of the Jewish people binds us one to another, throughout the generations. This memory will ultimately lead us to our redemption. Without memory, such redemption will have no meaning. You cannot realize your full potential unless you remember how far down you have been. □

Scriptural Context

This Torah portion continues the theme established previously: the building of the Tabernacle and its furnishings. In this portion, the eternal light (*ner tamid*) is described, as are the priests and their garments. The short paragraph that separates the eternal light from the remainder of the *parashah* serves as a literary bridge between the sacred objects and the people who use them. □

Targum: English Translation
Exodus 28:29–30

29) *Aaron shall carry the names of the children of Israel on the breastplate of decision over his heart, when he enters the sanctuary, for remembrance before* **Adonai** *at all times.* 30) **Place the** *urim* **and** *tummim* **inside the breastplate of decision so that they are over Aaron's heart when he comes before** *Adonai.* **This way, Aaron will always carry the instrument of decision for the Israelites over his heart before** *Adonai.* □

From the Tradition

On the high priest's apronlike garment called an *ephod* was a breastplate. This pouchlike structure was inlaid with twelve precious stones, one each for the tribes of Israel. This breastplate held the *urim* and *tummim.* By wearing this *urim/ tummim* device, the priest was able to inquire of *Adonai* on behalf of the ruler. This breastplate was therefore called *choshen mishpat* (breastplate of decision). According to *Yoma* 73b, *urim* was interpreted to mean "those whose words give light," while *tummim* were defined as "those whose words are fulfilled." The rabbis explained that the oracle was effected by rays of light shining on →

Background In *Sanhedrin* 98a we read: Rabbi Joshua ben Levi met Elijah standing by the entrance to the cave of Rabbi Simon bar Yochai. . . . He asked him, "When will the Messiah come?" Elijah replied, "Go and ask him." "And where is he sitting [asked Rabbi Joshua]?" "At the entrance to the city of Rome [came the reply]." "And by what sign might he be recognized [came the next query]?" "He is sitting among the poor lepers. But where they untie their bandages all at once and tie them back together, he unties and ties them back separately, thinking 'Perhaps I will be summoned.

Let me not be delayed.'"

Rabbi Joshua went to the Messiah and said to him: "Peace upon you, my master and teacher." "Peace be upon you, son of Levi," he answered. Joshua then asked: "When will you come, Master?" He answered, "Today!"

Rabbi Joshua returned to Elijah who asked, "What did he say to you?" . . . He replied, "He lied to me. He said that he would come *today*; yet he has not come." Elijah answered, "This is what He said to you—'*Today*, if you would but hearken to God's voice'" (Psalm 95:7). □

The Teaching (*continued*)

King David also said in Psalm 102:13-14a, "But You, O *Adonai*, dwell in eternity, Your remembering is forever and ever. You will surely arise and take pity on Zion." Notice here that this remembering is connected with the rebuilding of Zion and Jerusalem.

And thus also in Psalm 137:7, "Remember, O *Adonai*, against the children of Edom, the day of Jerusalem . . ." [for Edom is only another way of saying Amalek, the mythic enemy of the Jewish people throughout all history]. □

From the Tradition (*continued*)

the letters forming themselves into groups so the priests could read them. Only priests – who had the holy spirit through the *Shechinah* rest upon them – could invoke them. The one who made the inquiry directed his face to the high priest and the priest directed himself to the *Shechinah*. □

(60) Tetzaveh: The Job of the *Tzaddik*

The Teaching
from Abraham Isaac Kook

One who is a *tzaddik* stands eternally poised between heaven and earth. He joins the world of darkness to the utterance and light of God. All the senses of the authentic *tzaddik* are devoted to making the Divine connection with all the worlds. His yearning, his desires, his inclinations, his meditations, his deeds, his conversations, his habits, his movements, his sorrows, his grief, his joys, all of them, without exception, are in accord with the holy music. For the vitality of God flows throughout all these worlds giving to people their voice, the voice of strength. Souls

Scriptural Context

This portion begins with the specific instructions to kindle the *ner tamid*. It serves as a literary bridge between the objects to be used in the sanctuary and the people who will use them. Our text is taken from the section of the Torah portion that describes the priestly garments and the headdress that was worn by the officiants. □

From the Tradition

According to the rabbis, a *tzaddik* can actually annul the decrees of God (*Mo'ed Katan* 16b).

And God will not destroy the world as long as fifty righteous people are alive (*Pirke de Rabbi Eliezer* 25). □

Targum: English Translation
Exodus 28:36–38

36) *You shall make a blossom ornament of pure gold and engrave on it the seal inscription "Holy to Adonai."* 37) **It should hang on a cord of blue so that it should be part of the headdress. It should remain in front of the headdress.** 38) **It should be on Aaron's forehead so that Aaron can expiate the sins for the holy objects that the Israelites had consecrated, from out of their sacred gift offerings. It should be on his forehead at all times so that he might win acceptance for them in the presence of** *Adonai.* □

without end, living treasures with no limit, filled with all that exists, they only strengthen themselves to ascend from beneath their deep monotonous degradation to the heights of exaltation, the divine freedom, the source of joy and gladness. Each and every one of them urge all the deeds of the *tzaddik*, who continually performs the holy service. And his whole life is "Holy to *Adonai*." □

Perush: Explaining the Teaching

Our teacher is intrigued by the text's instruction to engrave the headdress with the inscription "Holy to *Adonai*." Does it reflect the diadem or the wearer? If it reflects the wearer, how is a priest holy to *Adonai*? He reasons that the priest is a holy vessel, a channel through which divine energy flows from heaven to earth. At the same time, the priest is the voice of the people. And so, the *tzaddik* is filled with holiness. □

Background The Baal Shem Tov (Besht) taught that there are certain individuals with superior spiritual qualities, much greater than other human beings.

This *tzaddik* is outstanding in his level of *devekut* (clinging to God), as well as the acknowledgment of the responsibility of one Jew to another. The Besht said, "Every Jew is a limb of the *Shechinah*." Through the principle of *devekut*

he teaches sinners to do *teshuvah*. He descends to the level of the sinner, associates with him, and then ascends—bringing the sinner to the level of goodness with him. Israel ben Eliezer Baal Shem Tov said, "When the *tzaddik* descends from his heights, it is an expression of the quality of mercy, in order that he may associate with the masses and elevate them." □

(61) Ki Tisa: *Shabbat*

The Teaching
from S. A. Taub of Modzhitz

"And they shall keep the *Shabbat*," "to do the *Shabbat*." Why is it stated twice? One possible answer is found in the Gemara (*Shabbat* 118b), which reads, "If only Israel were to keep two *Shabbatot* according to their laws, they would be redeemed in an instant."

Why, *specifically*, two *Shabbatot*? Perhaps because there are two dimensions to *Shabbat*. One mode is sitting still and not doing anything, keeping the word, the conduct, and the like. The other mode is getting →

Perush: Explaining
the Teaching

Drawing from the seemingly repetitive nature of the text where the observance of *Shabbat* is mentioned twice in succession, our teacher speaks of the two dimensions of *Shabbat*: being *and* doing. He wants to understand from this text the relationship between the two *Shabbatot* mentioned in *Shabbat* 118b. Thus, he derives "being" from the Hebrew →

Scriptural Context

This portion begins following the directions for the priestly garments and the ceremonies in which the priests exercised their authority. It contains another census, this time for the half-shekel Temple tax. The *Shabbat* is discussed (from which our text is taken) just prior to the actual giving of the stone tablets of the Decalogue, a prologue to the Golden Calf. □

Targum: English Translation
Exodus 31:12–17

12) **Adonai spoke thus to Moses:** 13) **You will speak to the Israelites and say [to them], "You [the Israelites] will indeed observe my *Shabbatot* since it [*Shabbat*] is a sign between Me and you throughout the generations in order for you to know that I am *Adonai* who sanctifies you. 14) And you will observe the *Shabbat* for it is holy to you. Anyone who profanes it will be put to death, for anyone who works on it will be cut off from among the midst of the people. 15) Let work be done for six days, but the seventh day will be a *Shabbat* of rest, holy to *Adonai*. Anyone who works on the *Shabbat* will be put to death. 16) *And the children of Israel shall keep the* Shabbat; *to do the* Shabbat *through their generations, an eternal covenant.* 17) It is an eternal sign between Me and the Israelites, for *Adonai* made the [world] heaven and earth in six days but on the seventh day, God ceased and rested. □**

From the
Tradition

Verses 16–17 from Exodus 31 are known as *Veshamru*. It has become part of the *Shabbat* liturgy. As such, it occurs in the Friday evening liturgy and also precedes the *Shabbat* morning *Kiddush*. In traditional synagogues, the congregation rises when these verses are recited. □

Background Taub was the name of the Modzhitz chasidic dynasty in Poland, whose founder was Israel of Modzhitz (d. 1921), son of Samuel Elijah of Zwole. One who emphasized music, he is often considered the creator of chasidic music as an art form. Much of his teachings praise music. His son Saul Jedidah Eleazer (d. 1947) was *av bet din* (head of the rabbinical court) in Rakov and Karzow before moving to Otwock, a city near Warsaw. While he led the Modzhitz *chasidim* following his father's death, he combined Torah with music, made the melodies of his comments in Modzhitz popular throughout the world, and published his father's sermons with his own. □

The Teaching *(continued)*
up and doing something, enjoying *Shabbat*, learning Torah and the like.

And this is why it is said, "If only Israel were to keep two *Shabbatot* . . .," which is to say, [if they were] to keep and to fulfill both dimensions of *Shabbat*, then "they would be redeemed in an instant."

For this reason we read in Exodus: "And they shall keep the *Shabbat*," which implies sitting still and not doing anything; and "to do the *Shabbat*," which implies getting up and doing something. Only then will the *Shabbat* they attain be "throughout their generations, an eternal covenant." For at last the children of Israel, having earned a time of unending *Shabbat*, will be "redeemed in an instant." □

Perush: Explaining the Teaching *(continued)*
ve-shamru (literally, "and they shall keep or guard, watch over"); he derives the doing from the Hebrew "*laasot*" (literally, "to do"). Our teacher recognizes that the only way to bring Messiah is through the being and doing of *Shabbat*, for in this being and doing we have a foretaste of the messianic. □

(62) Ki Tisa: *Shabbos* at Home

The Teaching from Ish Yehudah

Rabbi Yose, son of Rabbi Yehudah, said: Two divine messengers accompany a person on *erev Shabbat* from the synagogue to his home, one good and the other evil. When he arrives home and finds the candles burning, the table set, and the bed made, the good messenger says, "May another *Shabbat* be like this one," and the evil messenger, against his will, must respond, "Amen" (*Shabbat* 119b). →

Perush: Explaining the Teaching

Like so many other teachers, Ish Yehudah explains the use of the word *Shabbat* twice in one verse in his own particular way. Quoting from the sacred tradition, he argues that the *Shabbat* we experience at home ultimately is like the ultimate *Shabbat* of the future – the messianic time to come.

Building on this celebration of *Shabbat* in the home, which wards off the evil messenger that has accompanied the individual home, our →

Scriptural Context

Still very concerned with the Temple and its cultic system, this portion focuses on the investiture of the priests. The narrative continues with the requirement of the half-shekel contributory tax for Temple maintenance. Bezalel and Oholiab are chosen to complete the task of building, and the fiscal exchange (in this context) takes place between God and Moses – ending with Moses taking the two stone tablets that have been inscribed "by the finger of God." □

Targum: English Translation
Exodus 31:12–18

12) Then *Adonai* spoke to Moses, 13) "Speak to the Israelites. Tell them 'Keep my Sabbath, for it is a sign between Me and your children throughout the generations so that you should know that I am *Adonai*, who has [set you apart from the rest of the nations and thereby] consecrated you. 14) Keep the Sabbath for it is holy to you. The one who profanes the Sabbath shall surely die: whoever does work on it will be separated from among his kin. 15) On six days you [may] work but the seventh day is holy to *Adonai*. All who work on *Shabbat* will surely die. 16) *And the children of Israel shall keep the* Shabbat *to make* Shabbat *throughout their generations, an eternal covenant.* 17) It is a sign between Me and the Israelites for all time, for in six days did *Adonai* make the world but rested on the seventh day.' " 18) When [*Adonai*] finished speaking on Mount Sinai, [God] gave Moses two stone tablets of testimony that had seen the work of God [literally, written by the Finger of God]. □

From the Tradition

In *Shabbat* 118b we read: Rabbi Judah said in Rav's name: Had Israel kept the first *Shabbat*, no nation or tongue would have enjoyed dominion over them, for it is said, "And it came to pass on the seventh day, that there went out some of the people to gather [manna]" (Exodus 16:27), which is followed by "Then came Amalek" (Exodus 12: 8). Rabbi Yochanan said in the name of Rabbi Shimon bar Yochai: If Israel were to →

Background *Shabbat* is indeed a special time. In fact, we might even say it is metatime. Nearly all of Jewish life is measured in relationship to *Shabbat*. Yet, Rabbi Simchah Bunem used to say that when his *shtibl* was full of people on the Sabbath, he found it hard to teach Torah. Each person needs his own Torah and needs to be perfected in it. What I interpret for all, I withdraw from each. □

The Teaching (*continued*)

Le-dorotam, לדרתם, throughout their generations, in the Torah is written *chaseir,* defectively, that is, without both *vavs.* This gives us permission to misread it literally as *dalet hirek, resh kamatz, le-diratam,* which now means "for their dwelling places."

A person recognizes his dwelling on *Shabbat*: the candles burning, the table set, and the bed made, everything in order, the dwelling place of Israel wrapped in the holiness of *Shabbat,* divine messengers giving and receiving blessing, the presence of the Holy One. □

Perush: Explaining the Teaching (*continued*)

teacher tries to understand the unusual way the word *le-doratam* is written. It may also be found written with the two letter vavs included. Thus he asks why is it written in this way in this text. Like so many other teachers, he seeks the most profound meanings, especially in the context of *Shabbat.* He reasons that the word *le-doratam,* usually understood as "throughout the generations," might be understood as "in their dwelling places," for our homes take on a special character on *Shabbat.* □

From the Tradition (*continued*)

keep two Sabbaths according to the law, they would be redeemed instantly, for it is said, "Thus said *Adonai* of the eunuchs that keep my Sabbath, (Isaiah 56:2)" which is followed by "Even them will I bring to my holy mountain" (Isaiah 56:7). □

(63) Ki Tisa: Monday Morning Quarterback

The Teaching
from the Chatam Sofer, Moses Sofer

A period of time can only be understood once we are able to view the entire context of events and happenings. In the same way, we are only able to comprehend God's ways and recognize how God works in the world in retrospect. Only then is it possible to fathom even a little of what God does.

But at the time the event itself is happening, our understanding is unable to grasp God's doing. Instead we are simply astonished and mystified. As we read in Psalm 28:5, "For they do not comprehend Adonai's deeds, the work of God's hands."

And this is the real meaning of "You will see My back." [It is not referring to God's body but to our →

Perush: Explaining the Teaching

The Chatam Sofer reacts, as do most of our teachers, to the notion

Scriptural Context

Moses has descended the mountain, only to find that the Israelites had built "the Golden Calf." And so, Moses is told to lead the people away from Sinai. Moses pleads with God: how can he lead the people away in the aftermath of the broken covenant? Thus, the covenant is renewed. Moses ascends the mountain once again. And his face reflects the divine glory of God. ☐

From the Tradition

Jewish mystics called God by names that emphasized the unfathomable nature of God, like *temira de-temirin* (the hidden of hidden). However, rabbinic literature more often uses the term *Shechinah* to refer to a revelation of the holy in the midst of the profane. Certain philosophers consider the *Shechinah* to be the same kind of luminous material that emanates from God. ☐

Targum: English Translation
Exodus 33:17–23

17) And *Adonai* said to Moses, "Yes, I will do this thing that you have asked for you have gained my favor; I have singled you out by name [or provided you with a reputation]. 18) He [Moses] responded, "Show me your Glory." 19) And [Adonai] answered, "I will have My essence pass in front of you and I will spell out [for you] the reputation of *Adonai*: the grace I grant and the compassion I offer. 20) But you will not be able to see My face for no man [or woman] can see it and stand it [literally, 'live'.] 21) So *Adonai* said, "See that place near Me. Stand firm on the rock. 22) And as My glory passes by, I will place you in a cleft of the that rock and protect you with My hand until I have passed by [you]. 23) *Then, I will remove My hand and you will see My back, but My face cannot be seen.*" ☐

that we may see the back of God but not God's face. Yet he does not see the phrase as referring to God's body, so to speak, but rather to the perspective of time and ultimately to messianic time. We are only able to see the truth of God's ways in retrospect and at the End of Days, when "God's hand" will be removed entirely, we will have the full perspective of history behind us, and see the incredible design on the history of the world as designed by God. ☐

Background We spend a great deal of our spiritual energy trying to get a glimpse of the holy. Moses was given the opportunity to see God's glory after it had passed in front of him. Dov Baer of Mezerich offers us a more realistic path. He said that it is the duty of each individual to restore the holy sparks to their Source. As a result of this act, the individual may enter the palace of the Source of all Sources and thereby commune with God. ☐

The Teaching (*continued*)

perspective on time itself.] God says, in effect, "Only at the end of days will you see and understand Me." "But My face cannot be seen," not while the events themselves are happening, for "in the midst of things, you will not be able to see Me." □

(64) Va-Yakhel: One Congregation

The Teaching
from the Sefas Emes, Yehudah Aryeh Leib of Ger

There is a hint here that somehow through the experience of *Shabbat* the children of Israel were fused into one congregation, as suggested in the *Midrash*: Make for yourselves congregations to learn the laws of *Shabbat* and festivals, for the children of Israel are indeed a single unity, and only because of weekday turmoil is the congregation broken apart. But on *Shabbat*, when the disturbances →

Perush: Explaining the Teaching

The Sefas Emes reasons that since these verses follow one another, there must be a relationship between them. Thus, he ponders, what is the impact of *Shabbat*—and *Va-Yakhel*—the assembly into a congregation of the Israelites by Moses. (This action offers the name to this portion because it begins it.) Through *Shabbat*, Moses led the mixed multitudes of the Israelites to become a community. Only through *Shabbat* can the dispersed Jewish people become a community, and we, as *Shabbat* observers, feel part of such a community. Our teacher gains support for this lesson by recalling the final sequence of Torah readings. The Torah is a blessing [reward] for the *congregation* of Israel. This inheritance of Torah is a blessing because it enables Israel to become a congregation. And the secret irony of this community making is that all you have to do to achieve it is to learn how to be fully present. □

Scriptural Context

Here in this portion, after the details have been outlined for the Tabernacle, and the rules and regulations carefully articulated one at a time, the order to build the Tabernacle is finally given. The opening word of the *parashah*, *Va-Yakhel*—Moses assembled [made] a congregation—establishes a theme for the entire Torah portion. It ends a cycle that began in the assembling of the Israelites at the foot of Mount Sinai to build a golden calf. This assembly, however, is sanctified by God. As before, the Sabbath serves as a bridge between the building of the Tabernacle and a more profound purpose. □

Targum: English Translation
Exodus 35:1-2

1) *And Moses made a congregation of the whole Israelite community and said to them, "These are the things that* **Adonai** *has commanded you to do.* 2) *On six days you may work, but on the seventh day, you shall have a* **Shabbat** *of complete rest, holy to* **Adonai.** *"* □

From the Tradition

Mordechai Yosef Leiner of Izbica taught: In the building of the tabernacle, all Israel were joined in their hearts; no one felt superior to his fellow. At first, each skilled individual did his own part of the construction, and it seemed to each one that his own work was extraordinary. Afterward, they saw how their several contributions to the "service" of the tabernacle were integrated—all the boards, the sockets, the curtains, and the loops fit together as if one person had done it all. Then they realized how each one of them had depended on the other. Then they understood that what they had accomplished was not by virtue of their own skill alone but that the Holy One had guided the hands of everyone who had worked on the Tabernacle. They had merely →

Background It was the custom of Rabbi Shelomoh Kluger, the rabbi of Brod, to do the following at *Motza'ei Shabbat*. The minute three stars appeared in the sky, he would recite the evening service and make *Havdalah*. His disciples asked him, "Behold, since it is a commandment to take from the profane and add to the sacred, why not prolong the *Shabbat* a half hour?" Replied Rabbi Shelomoh Kluger to them, "There are many who profane the *Shabbat* in Brod, and there is nothing I can say. But it is in my power to add and bring those who profane *Shabbat* into a time when it is already the weekday." □

109

The Teaching (continued)
are gone, the unity returns.

Now Moses, our teacher, knew the whole Torah and through this was able to unify the children of Israel. Notice the sequence of "Torah" followed by "congregation" in *parashat Ve-Zot Ha-Berachah* (Deuteronomy 33:4): "Moses commanded us a Torah, an inheritance [for] the congregation of Jacob." This means that he bequeathed to the children of Israel the ability to become one congregation.

On *Shabbat* the spiritual power of Moses, our teacher, his memory is a blessing, and of the Torah, reveals itself. This is the reason why complete unity comes on *Shabbat*. As it is written in the *Ve-Shamru, Shabbat* "is a sign between Me and the children of Israel" (Exodus 31:17). This intimacy between God and Israel on *Shabbat* suggests that the other nations of the world want and have no part in *Shabbat*.

At the conclusion of the creation narrative in Genesis we read that on *Shabbat*, "God ceased from all the work of creation that God had done" (Genesis 2:3). During the six days of creation holiness is clothed in doing and in nature.

In the six days of doing [building, buying, selling, making, manipulating, wheeling, and dealing], resides great power for all the nations of the world, but the holiness is concealed. The children of Israel have an additional portion from on high, however, about [a strange kind of "not] doing": the sign of *Shabbat*. Therefore it is written in this week's *parashah*, "These are the things that *Adonai* has commanded you to do" (Exodus 35: 1), which is immediately followed by *Shabbat*: a time of doing nothing.

For this reason the only way to repair the workday doing is through receipt of the higher [spiritual] strength. The children of Israel alone, therefore, are able to repair the work of Creation for they alone possess *Shabbat*, the spiritual strength of knowing when to do nothing. □

From the Tradition (continued)
joined in completing its master building plans, so that "It came to pass that the Tabernacle was one" (Exodus 36:13). Moreover, the one who made the holy ark itself was unable to feel superior to the one who had made only the courtyard tent pegs.

Shabbat is the center and the axis of all the *mitzvot*, with the ultimate purpose of the sake of heaven. And this purpose is called *Shabbat*. The goal of the work of the tabernacle is the glory of Heaven, in order that the divine Presence might dwell among Israel. On this point all Israel were joined in their hearts, for the divine Presence would not dwell in the tabernacle if it were lacking so much as a tent peg. This is the meaning of "And Moses called together all the congregation of the children of Israel. . ." The section on *Shabbat*, therefore adjoins the one on the work of the tabernacle, because the root of the unification of Israel is in the commandments of *Shabbat*. □

(65) Va-Yakhel: The Rest of the Fire

The Teaching
from *Tiferet Yonatan*

In the first set of commandments, the reason given for the Sabbath was that it was a reminder of the Divine work of creation. "For in six days *Adonai* made the heaven and the earth and sea and all that is in them, and ceased on the seventh day; therefore *Adonai* blessed the Sabbath day and hallowed it" (Exodus 20:11).

But this technically does not refer to the work of making fire, for, as we learn in *Pesachim* 54a, fire was created at the conclusion of the Sabbath! ["Rabbi Yose said, 'It occurred to God to create two things on the eve of the Sabbath, but they were not actually created until the conclusion of the Sabbath, and at the conclusion of the Sabbath the Holy One gave the first Adam an idea, like the idea on high, →

Scriptural Context

The Israelites are in the desert, moving slowly from Egypt to Canaan. In the preceding *parashah*, they had made the Golden Calf. This portion opens with Moses instructing the people to build the Tabernacle, as a Divine gesture of forgiveness for the sin of the Golden Calf. The Sabbath and a cessation from work bridges the actual construction of the tabernacle and the more profound purpose for its construction. Here, the people are told to rest through the cessation of all labors – (understood by rabbinic tradition as those labors listed previously and associated with the building of the Tabernacle). Furthermore, the element of fire is introduced as another labor prohibited on the Sabbath (also not previously mentioned in regard to the building of the Tabernacle). □

Targum: English Translation
Exodus 35:1–3

1) Moses assembled all of the Israelites and said, "These are God's words that I speak. Therefore, you are obliged to do what I say. 2) Go ahead and work hard for six days, but rest on the seventh day. Separate that day and consecrate it to *Adonai*. If you work on that day, you will die. 3) *You shall not kindle a fire in any of your dwellings on the Sabbath day."* □

Perush: Explaining the Teaching

On *Shabbat*, we consider the world to be complete. Just before *Shabbat*, with one fell swoop, we clear our desks of their clutter, and enter the completed world of *Shabbat*. Fire, however, the only element not mentioned in the categories of prohibited work listed in the midst of building the Tabernacle, is puzzling for the commentator. Fire represents the primary factor in transforming one thing into another, such →

From the Tradition

There are thirty-nine kinds of work forbidden on the Sabbath. These are derived from the list of labors articulated in Exodus in the midst of the building of the Tabernacle. Right in the middle of the work is the *Ve-Shamru* text, in order to emphasize that even the building of the Tabernacle acts to conclude the story of creation (from which God rested) initiated in Genesis.

According to Rabbenu Bachya →

Background Yonatan (ben Nathan Nata) Eybeschuetz (1690/95–1764) was a talmudist and kabbalist who served as *dayyan* of Prague (1736–1740), and rabbi of Metz (1741–1749). He was elected rabbi of the Three Communities, Altona, Hamburg, and Wandsbek, in 1750 and was among the rabbis of Prague who excommunicated the Sabbatean sect – an action that plagued him throughout his life, since he was considered to lean toward Sabbateanism.

Eybeschuetz's son presented himself as a Sabbatean prophet – forcing the closure of his father's yeshivah, where he was a student. An excellent preacher as well as a talmudist, he published over thirty works in the field of *halachah*. His writings were considered masterpieces in pilpulistic literature. *Tiferet Yonatan* (1819), from which this selection is taken, was among his homiletic works. □

The Teaching *(continued)*
and so Adam found two stones and rubbed them against one another and made the lights of fire.' "] So, therefore, the making of fire should not be included among all those things from which God rested. One might think, consequently, that a person might get the idea that the work of making fire is permitted.

For this reason, an alternate explanation is offered in the second set of the commandments. In Deuteronomy the fourth commandment concludes, "Remember that you were a slave in the land of Egypt, and *Adonai* your God freed you from there with a mighty hand and an outstretched arm; therefore *Adonai* your God has commanded you to observe the Sabbath day" (Deuteronomy 5:15). Since here the creation of the world is not mentioned, and instead we are obligated to remember anew the going out from Egypt, we understand that making fire is forbidden on the Sabbath. □

Perush: Explaining the Teaching *(continued)*
as matter into energy. It symbolizes all human activity. Thus, we cannot use fire at all, in any of its forms. Our teacher suggests that the Deuteronomic version of the fourth commandment is set, not in the creation sequence as in the Book of Exodus, but in the context of Egyptian slavery and freedom. This context obviously has little to do with the creation sequence and thus permits the prohibition against fire on *Shabbat*. □

From the Tradition *(continued)*
every kind of work is included in the prohibition against kindling fire. For it is well-known that most of the work with which human beings occupy themselves is nothing more than one form or another of fire. Fire is the reason and the essence.

And it is for this reason that our sages ordained that we recite a blessing over the lights of fire during *Havdalah* at the departure of the Sabbath, since it is the commencement of the work of the six days of creation [which are about to begin again anew]. □

(66) Va-Yakhel: Daily Bride Price

The Teaching from Chafetz Chayyim

Observance of *Shabbat* is equivalent to all the other commandments in the Torah. According to *Exodus Rabbah* 25:11, the Holy One said to Israel, "If you merit to keep *Shabbat*, I will account it to you as if you had kept all the commandments in the Torah, and if you profane it, I will account it to you as if you had profaned all of the commandments." Furthermore, according to the *Midrash*, all those who keep →

Perush: Explaining the Teaching

For our teacher, *Shabbat* is the most important of all of the *mitzvot*—so important that he calls to our attention a midrashic text that credits the observer as if he had observed all of the *mitzvot*.

Calling on the well-known image of the loving relationship between Israel and God (personified in the Song of Songs), the Chafetz Chayyim explains *Shabbat* as a wedding gift from bride to groom. If one rejects the gift of one's lover or disregards it, this action pushes him or her away. Such is the case with Israel in the case of *Shabbat*. If we do not observe *Shabbat*, God's gift to us, we are in effect rejecting God as well. □

Scriptural Context

Finally, as a culmination of that which preceded, the building of the Tabernacle—with all of its details—is commanded. Moses convoked [*va-yakhel*] all of the Israelites and told them what God had said. Our text is taken from the beginning of the portion. □

Targum: English Translation
Exodus 35:1–4

1) **Moses convoked the whole Israelite community and said to them: These are the things that Adonai has instructed you to do:** 2) *On the seventh day shall be for you a Sabbath of complete rest for Ado-***nai. Whoever does work on it shall be put to death.** 3) **You shall kindle no fire throughout your settlements on the Sabbath day.** 4) **Moses further said to the community of Israelites: this is what Adonai has commanded.** □

From the Tradition

The power of community is often felt in the Torah text. While there are private moments in which God appears to individuals like Moses, it is in community where the Israelites are forged into a people. Like us, the ancient Israelites relate to the Divine on an individual basis but come together as a community to experience their destiny as a people. In community, we add our individual lives to that historical experience. *Shabbat* serves this purpose in a unique way. Not only is *Shabbat*, as we know it, special to the Jewish people, but it is also an ultimate symbol of the Jewish people. In our observance of *Shabbat*, a bond is forged through time and space. It represents the covenant between God and Israel. It offers us a taste of the messianic, and in doing so, if only for twenty-five hours, liberates us from this world. □

Background The Chafetz Chayyim, after the name of his first work (published in Vienna in 1873), was Israel Meir Ha-Koen (Kagan) Poupko (1838–1933). He came from humble origins and did not distinguish himself as a student, yet his writings have significantly influenced religious leaders and fascinated Jews through the decades. Hundreds of sayings of practical wisdom are attributed to him, although not all of them were truly his words. He operated a modest grocery store in Radun and never made the rabbinate the focus of his work. So many students came to learn from him, however, that his store became known as the *Chafetz Chayyim Yeshivah*. Later he actually opened a *yeshivah*, with Rabbi Naphtali Trup as its head. His most widely known and most-read work is called the *Mishnah Berurah*, but he also wrote a great work on the issues of gossip, slander, and talebearing. He traveled a great deal in order to encourage people to support Jewish institutions and was one of the founders of *Agudat Yisrael*. □

113

The Teaching *(continued)*

Shabbat are as if they had fulfilled the entire Torah.

And the reason is found in *Shabbat* 10, where we learn that "the Holy One says to Moses, 'I have a precious gift in My treasure house, called *Shabbat*, and I desire to give it to Israel.'"

If the bride returns to the groom the wedding gifts he gave her, it is a sure sign that she no longer desires him, and the marriage is off. It is the same with *Shabbat*. If the children of Israel do not keep the *Shabbat*, we are effectively returning the wedding present that God gave us and thereby demonstrate that we (God forbid!) no longer want the bond that is between Israel and the Holy One. □

(67) Pekudei: Gifts of Ecstasy

The Teaching
from Chiddushei Ha-Rim

Exodus Rabbah 51.2: "When Moses came to Bezalel and saw the amount of material left over after the Tabernacle had been constructed, he said to God, 'God of all the worlds, we have now made the Tabernacle and we have material left over; what shall we do with what is left over?' God replied, 'Go and make with them a tabernacle of the pact.'" [This seems to imply that a separate tabernacle was built within the holy of holies, where the tables of the covenant or "pact" were kept.]

But this is amazing. We find no mention anywhere in Scripture that a [separate] tabernacle and its utensils were constructed from what was left over.

This is because the *Midrash* is actually making another point. Moses asked God, "Already we have completed the work of the Tabernacle, but the people are still bringing free-will gifts." Replied the Holy One to Moses, "This religious enthusiasm is a sign of the people's freely giving spirit and the soul flame they feel. And they themselves are a living, faithful testimony that the Divine Presence will dwell in this tabernacle." □

Scriptural Context

This last section of Exodus begins with a summary of all of the materials used in the erection of the Tabernacle. After this summary, further instructions are given; this time there is a rehearsing of the necessary procedures to produce the priestly garments. Finally, when everything is finished, Moses comes and blesses the people. The anointing of the priests takes place and God's presence consecrates the Tabernacle. □

Targum: English Translation
Exodus 38:21–23

21) *These are the records of the Tabernacle, the Tabernacle of the Pact [Testimony], that were set forth at the word of Moses* – **the work of the Levites under the direction of Ithamar, son of Aaron the priest. 22) And Bezalel, son of Uri, son of Hur from the tribe of Judah, made all that God commanded Moses. 23) At his side was Oholiab, son of Ahisamach of the tribe of Dan, carver and designer, and embroiderer in blue, purple, and crimson yarns and in fine linen.** □

From the Tradition

The Tabernacle is called the Tabernacle of the Testimony because, according to rabbinic understanding, God had forgiven Israel for the building of the Golden Calf. Its presence (and God's acceptance of it) gave testimony to the whole world (cf. *Exodus Rabbah* 51:4). □

Perush: Explaining the Teaching

Our teacher tries to understand the seemingly repetitive use of the word *tabernacle*, which is further identified as the Tabernacle of the Pact. Is this the same? If so, then why the emphasis? Since we have no other indication that it was a separate tabernacle, nor were the extra materials left over from the first building used for the second, he assumes that Moses (through the *Midrash*) is attempting to say something else. The people are continuing to bring gifts. What shall I do with them? Since they are continuing to bring gifts, it is they who give testimony to the Tabernacle. □

Background It was the custom of chasidic leaders to place upon their Sabbath table twelve loaves of white bread in imitation of the Holy Temple. The Gerer *rebbe* once remarked that a *rebbe* who becomes a leader in order to gain fame or fortune will be dragged into Gehenna by his twelve loaves. □

(68) Pekudei: Holy Artisan

The Teaching
from Tiferet Shelomoh

Bezalel was not only an artist who executed all the work of the tabernacle and its utensils with skill. [As the text says, literally,] "he made *all* that God commanded Moses." This means that he fulfilled the entire Torah, all the commandments. This teaches us that the one who performs holy work must, himself or herself, also be holy. □

Perush: Explaining the Teaching

Our teacher is very interested in what he perceives as an emphatic use of the word *all* in regard to Bezalel. What does the text imply by including that word? He decides that the "all" refers not only to the commandments regarding the erection of the Tabernacle but to *all* of the commandments. This comes to teach us that one must be holy to do holy work and that holiness is achieved through the performance of *mitzvot*. □

Scriptural Context

Following the recapitulation of all of the materials used in the building of the Tabernacle, further instructions are given to the Israelites. Bezalel, the master craftsman, is the primary individual involved in the construction of the Tabernacle and in the section of text from which our teaching is drawn. □

Targum: English Translation
Exodus 38:21–23

21) These are the records of the Tabernacle, the Tabernacle of the Pact [Testimony], that were set forth at the word of Moses – the work of the Levites under the direction of Ithamar, son of Aaron the priest. 22) And Bezalel, son of Uri, son of Hur, from the tribe of Judah, made all that God commanded Moses. 23) At his side was Oholiab, son of Ahisamach, of the tribe of Dan, carver and designer, and embroiderer in blue, purple, and crimson yarns and in fine linen. □

From the Tradition

The folk etymology of Bezalel is "in the shadow or under the protection of God." Philo of Alexandria considered Bezalel as a symbol of pure knowledge. He inferred from the name that Bezalel knew God by seeing the Divine Shadow. In other words, he saw only God's works, not God's Divine Self as had Moses. □

Background Said Rabbi Isaac: A public appointment is not made without first consulting the public, in accordance with the text "See *Adonai* called by name."

Said the Holy Blessed One to Moses: Moses! Is Bezalel acceptable to you? He answered: *Ribbono Shel Olam!* If he is acceptable to You all the more so to me? God replied: Even so, go and tell the Israelites. He went and asked the Israelites: Is Bezalel acceptable to you? They answered him: *Mosheh Rabbenu!* If he is acceptable to the Almighty and to you, to us how much more so! (*Berachot 55a*). □

(69) Pekudei: Jewish Job

The Teaching
from *Divrei Yirmiyahu*

The Ramban (Nachmanides, Rabbi Moses ben Nachman) notes a difficulty with the verse: the words "all the work" seem to him to be redundant. Perhaps the explanation is that the intent of this text is to specify that the artisans did not employ foreign labor [of those who did not believe in the holiness of the task] in any work of the Tabernacle. Unlike the later case of the building of the Solomonic Temple, all the work [of the wilderness Tabernacle] was done exclusively by the children of Israel. □

Perush: Explaining the Teaching

Beginning with a question of redundancy that Ramban asks, our teacher wants to understand why "everything" and "all the work" are in the same verse. They seem to refer to the same thing. Acknowledging that nothing is redundant in Torah text, our teacher suggests that it is to emphasize the fact that the Israelites did indeed do all the work. No foreign labor was used for holy tasks that the Israelites were instructed to do. They did it all personally! □

Scriptural Context

This last section focuses on the actual erection of the Tabernacle. It begins with a statistical summary of the various materials used in its construction and continues with a description of the priestly garments. At the end of this section, Moses blesses the people. Our text is taken from the middle section of the portion, after the work of the Tabernacle had been completed. □

Targum: English Translation
Exodus 39:32–33, 42–43

32) **Thus was completed all the work of the tabernacle of the Tent of Meeting. The Israelites did so, just as** *Adonai* **instructed Moses, so they did. 33) Then they brought the Tabernacle to Moses, with the tent and all its furnishings: its clasps, planks, poles, posts and sockets. . . . 42)** *According to everything that God commanded Moses, so the children of Israel did all the work.* **43) And when Moses saw that they had performed all the tasks – as** *Adonai* **had instructed, so they had done – Moses blessed them.** □

From the Tradition

Seldom considered, commandments (*mitzvot*) imply a commander (*mitzaveh*). A story is told of a rabbi who met a gatekeeper of a city. He asked, "For whom do you work?" He replied, "I work for the master of this city; for whom do *you* work?" Not answering directly, the rabbi said, "I wish to hire you for my own employ." "And what will my task be?" asked the gatekeeper. The rabbi replied, "You will ask me every day, 'For whom do you work?' " □

Background The Ramban (or Moses ben Nachman, Nachmanides, 1194–1270) lived in Spain and was one of the leading talmudic scholars of the Middle Ages. His Spanish name was Banastrug da Porta. Some speculate that he was a physician. While it seems probable that he ran a *yeshivah*, there is no evidence available to support this claim. Trying to establish a compromise between the supporters and detractors of Moses Maimonides, he exerted great influence over Jewish public life in Catalonia. He was forced into public debate with an apostate Pablo Christiani, but King James I rewarded him for his conduct and elocution. Because of his work *Sefer Ha-Vikkuach*, he was accused of anti-Christian sentiment by the Dominicans. Nachmanides escaped to *Eretz Yisrael*, where he remained until his death. He published over fifty works. □

LEVITICUS

(70) Va-Yikra: Money, Food, and Sex

The Teaching
from Menachem Nachum of Chernobyl

"And he shall slaughter," alludes to controlling one's impulse to evil [which has three basic forms].

"On the . . . side" (literally, "the thigh") alludes to the urge for sex.

"The altar" alludes to the appetite for food, as we read in *Chagigah* 27a: "The table of a person resembles an altar."

And "north" alludes to the desire for wealth, as we read in *Bava Batra* 25b, "Rabbi Isaac said, he who desires to become rich should turn north," and also in Job 37:22 we read, "By the north golden rays emerge." →

Scriptural Context

This portion explains how the Israelites are to bring various sacrificial offerings to God and how the priests are to conduct the ritual so as to ensure its efficacy. □

Targum: English Translation
Leviticus 1:10–13

10) **If his [intended] sacrifice is from the flock, whether from the sheep or goats, for a burnt offering, the individual should select a male without blemish.** 11) *And he shall slaughter [the offering] before* **Adonai***; on the north side of the altar and Aaron's sons, the priests, shall dash its blood against all sides of the altar.* 12) **Next, he [the priest] should cut it into pieces and order the pieces with its head and suet on the wood that is on the fire that is on the altar.** 13) **But he [the priest] should wash the insides and the legs with water. The priest should offer it all and smoke it on the altar; [after all] it is a burnt offering made by fire issuing a sweet smell to** *Adonai.* □

From the Tradition

Euphemisms are used extensively in the Talmud and *Midrash* so that the rabbis might avoid vulgar expressions. A special euphemism is used to avoid expressions altogether, using the phrase *devar acher* (another thing), usually used to avoid reference to pork, but also referring to leprosy and sexual intercourse. The most common category of all are those euphemisms that are employed in order to avoid placing oneself in jeopardy – by opening oneself to misfortune, and, according to Jewish lore and legend, allowing the evil eye to cast its glance on one. □

Perush: Explaining the Teaching

Menachem Nachum of Chernobyl reads the text as an allegory. There are forces inside us that compel us to do things. Therefore, we must (metaphorically) slaughter them in order to free ourselves. In many ways, this "psychology" anticipates Sigmund Freud's construction of reality. Like Freud, Menachem Nahum suggests that our psyches are organized around sexual (genital), food (oral), and wealth (anal) themes. For him, the text is really speaking of our inner drives. "On the side" refers to our sexual drive. The altar refers to our oral drive to satiate our desire for food. And north speaks to our drive for personal wealth. These three drives may possibly estrange us from ourselves. If we are on the other hand able symbolically to "slaughter" them, that is, become aware of them and control them, we will be able to come closer to God. □

Background Menachem Nachum (1730–1787), a disciple of the Baal Shem Tov, settled in Chernobyl in the late eighteenth century and transformed it into a center for Chasidism. He wrote *Me-Or Einayim* (1798) and *Yismach Lev* (1798). He stressed the purification of the individual's moral attributes, and established the Twersky chasidic dynasty. He often includes the homiletic observations of Dov Baer (the *Maggid*) of Mezerich. □

The Teaching (*continued*)

Thus, if a person succeeds in uprooting these three lusts, then that person will be able to come "before *Adonai*." And just this is what our sages meant when they said in *Shabbat* 119b that "whoever responds 'Amen' with all his or her strength, the gates of paradise will be opened for him." And this is because when one answers, with all his strength, "Amen," since אמן (Amen) is really an acronym for אכילה (eating), ממון (money), and ניאוף (sexuality), he is responding with regard to the three categories he must control: eating, money, and sexuality. □

(71) Va-Yikra: Humility and Arrogance

The Teaching
from Simchah Bunem of Przysucha

The Aleph (א) of *Va-Yikra* (ויקרא), according to the Masoretic tradition, is smaller than the other letters.

Even though Moses attained the highest level, he never became impressed with himself because of it. He regarded himself with an exceedingly humble spirit. →

Scriptural Context

Now that the Tabernacle has been constructed (in the Book of Exodus), God calls out to Moses again. This time, God instructs Moses on the various aspects of sacrifices. ☐

Targum: English Translation
Leviticus 1:1–2a

1) *And* **Adonai** *called to Moses, speaking to him from the* **Ohel Mo'ed:** 2a) **"Speak to the Israelites and say to them. . . ."** ☐

From the Tradition

In a great act of intellectual self-confidence, the great philosopher Moses Maimonides included the laws of sacrifice in his great compilation of Jewish law, the *Mishneh Torah*. Even though the sacrificial cult had been stopped when the Temple was destroyed, Maimonides believed that the entire Temple cult would be reinstated once the Messiah arrived and rebuilt the Temple, and that the *Mishneh Torah* would still be studied! ☐

Perush: Explaining the Teaching

Hebrew, without upper-case and lower-case letters as we know them in English, nevertheless has been faithfully transmitted in Torah text through the masoretic scribal tradition. The orthographic peculiarity is the existence of several letters written either larger or smaller than the others. On first glance, appearing as they do, in the middle or at the end of words, their presence seems random. Thus, our teacher, Simchah Bunem of Przysucha, noting that the very first word of the Book of Leviticus concludes with a small *alef*, like centuries of teachers before him searches out its meaning. (The "scribal error" explanation is never admissible in sacred text.) We stay with the text until we have found an acceptable explanation for why the *alef* is small. One of the great exercises of Jewish intellect is to make apparent contradictions fit together.

Since God placed us in this world, we are bidden to pay attention to the world around us. Consider Moses. His sensation on top of the mountain was not of his own doing; rather, the sensation was caused by the mountain. But the reasoning presents us with a major cultural problem. Humility is not considered a virtue, especially if it leads to self-degradation. Thus, God creates a cycle between arrogance and humility. Martin Buber added that each person has a sacred unique reason for being. The humble and the arrogant play an indispensable role in the universe.

The explanation, therefore, of the small *alef* teaches a second lesson. Even in the call to Moses, the *alef* is humbled. God humbles all those who would be arrogant, almost forcing *teshuvah* on them. This is the cycle of God's world–God brings down all those who are arrogant and raises up those who are humble. As they became arrogant, God must lower them, as well. And so the cycle continues: humility to arrogance and back to humility again. ☐

Background Simchah Bunem of Przysucha, 1765–1827, was a *tzaddik* who was not a miracle worker. Since he taught that prayer should only take place after the individual has readied himself through meditation, he often delayed the time of prayer, a rather radical behavior in chasidic circles. His teachings were collected by his students in *Kol Simchah* (1859). Following his death, leadership of the Przysucha *chasidim* was taken over by the Kotzker *rebbe*. ☐

The Teaching (*continued*)

Like a person who stands on top of a high mountain, to whom it does not occur to magnify himself because of his high position (for it is not on account of himself but on account of the mountain), Moses knew that his exaltation was on account of God.

We read: "He brings the arrogant down to the earth (cf. Psalm 147:6) and raises up the humble on high" (cf. Job 5: 11). It appears to be an endless cycle.

If the Holy One humbles the arrogant, then the arrogant are made humble, but then [God only turns around and] raises up the humble so that once again the humble are arrogant. And so, it seems to go on forever.

[The explanation is that] the wicked, even when they stand at the entrance to Gehinnom itself, refuse to make *teshuvah*, so that even when God humbles them they stubbornly remain arrogant.

In opposition to this is the *tzaddik* who continues to be humble in his own eyes; even when God, may God's Name be blessed, raises him up, he remains humble and modest.

And this is the meaning of "God called to Moses." Even though God summoned him and brought him up to the heights, despite all this he remained modest and humble – a small *alef*. □

(72) Va-Yikra: Ultimate Sacrifice

The Teaching
from the Sefas Emes, Yehudah Aryeh Leib of Ger

This means that a person needs to offer to God his or her innermost strength and desire.

And this is the meaning of the teaching in *Pirke Avot* 2:4: "Make your will nothing in the presence of God's will."

[It is as if your own will] becomes the sacrifice. And somehow, through this sacrificial offering, you are able to bring all your deeds close to God.

[Now we understand the sense of] "from among you" as implying that this is all accomplished by means of submerging yourself into the larger totality of the Jewish people. □

Scriptural Context

Much of the book of Leviticus is devoted to rules regarding sacrifices. The beginning of the first Torah portion speaks of the offering called *olah* (literally, "what goes up"). This is generally what is referred to as the burnt offering, because the entire offering (except for the hide) is consumed by fire on the altar. □

Targum: English Translation
Leviticus 1:1-3

1) *Adonai* **called to Moses and spoke thus to him from the Tent of Meeting.** 2) **Speak to the Israelite people and say to them:** *A person among you who brings a sacrifice to God* **shall choose the offering from the herd or from the flock.** 3) **If his offering is a burnt offering, he shall make his offering a male without blemish. He shall bring it to the entrance of the Tent of Meeting for acceptance in his behalf before** *Adonai.* □

From the Tradition

Devekut is communion with God. The word occurs in the Bible, most frequently in the Book of Deuteronomy, in reference to one cleaving to God. Sometimes it is simply being near to or close to God, but for the *chasidim*, it is a much more intense state. It is to be achieved during meditation or prayer, done with the proper *kavanah* (intention). It is the highest level on the spiritual ladder and is reached after the individual has mastered fear and love of God. *Devekut* is momentary. The goal is to string these moments of communion together so that one's life—even and especially the ordinary moments—is one long string of presence "in" God. Some mystics believe that *devekut* itself is a ladder on which one climbs the various *Sefirot*, or divine emanations. □

Perush: Explaining the Teaching

Like so much chasidic spirituality, the Sefas Emes is interested in how the Torah provides us with the opportunity to learn more about ourselves. He is intrigued by the phrase "from among you." When we bring sacrifices, we are also presenting ourselves before God—that is why we do not send them with anyone else. That is the ultimate sacrifice. It is not that God cannot pierce our inner selves. Rather, the burden of the Sefas Emes's teaching is that through this process God is providing us with a way to pierce ourselves and reveal our inner truths for us to see, as well. But we can only accomplish this, says our teacher, if we submerge ourselves into the totality of the people of Israel. That is the secondary meaning of "from among you"—the collective you, the people of Israel. □

Background The Sefas Emes has a special fascination with our individual "innermost essence." He searches the text to get a glimpse at the "essential" you—what really is at the innermost core of the individual, and the touchstone for all spirituality. □

(73) Tzav: Sacrifice Study

The Teaching
from Simchah Bunem of Przysucha

Behold it is said in 1 Samuel 15:22, "Does *Adonai* delight in burnt offerings and sacrifices as much as in obedience to *Adonai*'s command? Surely, obedience is better than sacrifice, compliance than the fat of rams."

It says in the *Gemara* (*Menachot* 110): "All who occupy themselves in Torah have no need for the burnt offering, the meal offering, the sin offering, nor for the guilt offering."

And this is Scripture's intention here: "Command Aaron and his sons, saying" that they shall say to the children of Israel—"This is the Torah of the burnt offering," that is, the principle is in the Torah of the burnt offering. Better that they should learn the Torah of the burnt offering than that they bring a sacrificial offering. □

Scriptural Context

After the Torah has introduced the sacrificial offerings in the first five chapters of Leviticus (in *Parashat Va-Yikra*), this portion begins by reiterating these sacrifices and providing new information. □

Targum: English Translation
Leviticus 6:1–2

1) **Thus *Adonai* spoke to Moses:** 2) **"*Command Aaron and his sons saying, 'This is the Torah of the burnt offering.' The burnt offering itself* should remain where it is burnt on the altar all night until morning as the altar fire keeps it aflame."** □

From the Tradition

Salt, an indispensable ingredient of sacrifice, was symbolic of the moral effect of suffering, which purifies the individual and causes sins to be forgiven (*Berachot* 5a). Since the table on which we eat has been transformed into an altar (reflective of the ancient Temple altar), we salt *challah* before we eat it on *Shabbat*. □

Perush: Explaining the Teaching

Our teacher in this text brings together (in order to resolve) the apparent conflict between Leviticus 6:2, which seems to be in favor of sacrifice, and 1 Samuel 15:22, which seems to imply that the performance of *mitzvot* is preferred over the bringing of offerings for intended sacrifice. Furthermore, what is meant by the peculiar construction "Torah of the burnt offering?" Rabbi Simchah Bunem suggests that since Torah encompasses all *mitzvot*, including sacrifices, then its study, including the study of burnt offerings, is tantamount to the actual sacrifice of burnt offerings. □

Background According to the *Kabbalah*, the mystical conception of the nature and purpose of the sacrifice explains the act as a process that brings about the dynamic union of the Divine powers, the *Sefirot*. Sacrifice also restores the soul of humankind and other created elements to their place of origin, namely, to the *Sefirah* of which they had originally been part. □

The Teaching
from the Sefas Emes, Yehudah Aryeh Leib of Ger

According to the burning of the refuse, so is the measure of the holiness of a person.

We know that there are forty-nine ways something can be ritually pure and forty-nine ways it can be ritually defiled, one corresponding to the other.

There is also in the heart of every Jew forty-nine gates.

It says in the Zohar, concerning our verse, "This is the Torah [often translated as ritual] of →

Perush: Explaining the Teaching

Our teacher is fascinated with the relationship between the priest who takes up the ashes and the sacrifice itself – both ascending to the altar. We long for God just as the flame travels heavenward. The sacrifice represents our own evil thoughts and deeds, which are consumed on the altar by holy flame, and we, in turn, are made holy. For the Sefas Emes, this is hinted at in the ritual introduced in Leviticus 6:2 as the "Torah of the burnt offering" but elucidated in the specific action of →

Scriptural Context

The ritual for the various offerings are further detailed. While our text is taken from the ritual of the burnt offering, the meal offering and sin offering are also explained. The portion continues with even more laws of sacrifice: the *shelamim*, the thanksgiving (*todah*) offering, and the *nedavah* (freewill) offering. □

Targum: English Translation
Leviticus 6:3–6

3) *And the priest shall dress in a linen robe and linen pants next to his body, and he shall take up the ashes in which the fire has consumed the burnt offering on the altar and set them beside the altar.* 4) **He should remove his priestly garb and put on new garments and take the ashes outside the camp to a [ritually] pure place. 5) The fire on the altar should be permanent, never to go out [for lack of fuel], and the priest should every morning feed it with wood and transform the fit parts of the** *shelamim* **[wellbeing] offering into smoke. 6) A continuous flame should be kept burning on the altar, never to go out.** □

From the Tradition

Simchah Bunem of Przysucha taught: "And he shall take up the ashes. . . ." Just this is the first gesture of service, even for the high priest himself when he enters the innermost chamber of the tabernacle. In this way the priest, the elect of the people, will not forget even when he comes into such a holy and awesome place, the simple material tasks of the people.

And this is the reason for the commandment in the Torah "And he shall strip off his clothing and put on other clothing. . . ." (Leviticus 6:4). He shall put on common clothes and busy himself in common work in order that he should remember to pray for the ordinary and simple needs of the common people. □

Background from Shem Mi-Shmuel, Shneur Zalman of Liadi *Zevachim* 48a-b: Where is the burnt offering slaughtered? – in the north. Why does Scripture attach the slaughtering place of the sin offering in the north with the burnt offering? It is as if the main idea of the sacrificing in the north depends on the burnt offering, and the sin offering is dragged along after it.

My revered father, his memory is a blessing, Rabbi Abraham of Suchtchov, offered the following explanation. The reason the location of the slaughtering of the burnt offering is in the north (צפון, tzafon) is because the burnt offering is the result of the meditations of a person's heart, which themselves are hidden (צפון, tzafun) within a person. And for this reason, its location is also hidden.

But why then is the location of the sin offering also burdened with being hidden? Behold, the sin offering is the result of a →

The Teaching (continued)

the burnt offering, it goes up." That is to say, the burnt offering springs up in much the same way as an evil thought in one's mind.

In other words, no sooner is there a Torah of burnt offerings (that is, things that "spring up") than there are also evil thoughts, one corresponding to the other.

But here too we also have the possibility of an ascent for strange thoughts when, like the sacrifice, they are burned. This is because on the coals on top of the altar, in the flames of the fire, there is a longing for God.

And just this is the hinted-at meaning in the gesture of the raising up of the ashes, elevating the ashes, after the flaming, for we read, "And he shall set them beside the altar" (Leviticus 6:3). In other words, after he has turned them into ashes, and transformed them, there shall be reserved for him a place in holiness. □

Perush: Explaining the Teaching (continued)

bringing the ashes and placing them beside the altar. We have the opportunity to be made holy on the altar of God if we are only willing to place ourselves and our misdeeds on God's altar and be made holy (whole) once again.

The focus on forty-nine is taken from the Talmud, where Rabbi Meir suggests that a person may sit in the *Sanhedrin* only if he knows the forty-nine ways that someone can become ritually pure. This leads the Sefas Emes to the mystical notion of forty-nine gates in the person's heart, probably corresponding to the forty-nine days of *Sefirah* – an anticipation of the revelation of Torah – and a pun on an abbreviation for forty-nine days of impurity.

Our teacher also makes mention of *machshavot zarot*, evil or alien thoughts. This was an early concept of the *chasidim* which, in general, was later abandoned. The *chasid* was taught to avoid thoughts of self during prayer. Ideally, one should lose oneself in the Divine. Yet thoughts of self inevitably intrude. These (alien) thoughts were categorized as: (1) strange love (sexual fantasies of sin); (2) pride (false piety or false wisdom); and (3) idolatry (irreligious thoughts including an attraction of Christianity and a denial of Judaism). The dialectic was either to push them out of one's mind or hold on to them and elevate them to the source of all thoughts, namely God. □

Background (continued)

revealed transgression, on account of an open act, the very opposite of a burnt offering (resulting from private meditations of a person's heart).

The concern, however, is regarding the one who commits a mistake – if it should happen that a person should commit a sin accidentally. It is certainly that he yearned long ago for that thing [his sin]. Therefore he must strive to do it. As a result, something will happen that he commits a transgression on account of it [the striving] by accident.

And the atonement is for the first [unconscious] desire. And for this reason, the atonement of the sin offering is for the root of the thought. Therefore [like the original, unconscious thought that spawned it] it must be hidden [in the north]. Scripture connects the sin offering with the burnt offering to teach that even the atonement of the sin offering involves the original hidden meditation. □

(75) Tzav: Unleavened Behavior

The Teaching
from *Kelei Yakar*

The sin offering and the guilt offering are brought for atonement of sin, which is called "holy of holies." This is because a perfect *tzaddik*, who has never sinned at all, is "holy," whereas one who sinned and turned in *teshuvah* (repentance) is the "holy of holies."

This is because, as we read in *Sanhedrin* 99a, "A perfect *tzaddik* is unable to stand in the same place as one who has turned in *teshuvah*."

And, as our sages teach in *Yoma* 86a, "The wicked acts of one who turns in *teshuvah* from love are transformed for him into merits!"

And this is the great level to which only a perfect *tzaddik* cannot attain.

And for this reason, the *matzah* needs to be in a holy place, for also it represents a dimension of the holy of holies, since it represents the removal of "the yeast in the dough" (*Se'or she-be-isah*), which profanes the holiness of a person. □

Scriptural Context

For the second time in the Book of Leviticus, the various sacrificial offerings are discussed. New material has been added to the discussion, essential to the sacrificial cult. Our text is taken from the discussion concerning the meal offering. □

From the Tradition

According to the *Zohar*, sacrifices are significant in the cosmic fight between good and evil in the Divine world. It even goes as far as to state that the flesh of the sacrifice is intended to placate the *sitra achra*, the evil power, but God received the *kavvanah* of the one offering the sacrifice. □

Targum: English Translation
Leviticus 6:7–11

7) This is the ritual [Torah] of the meal offering. The Aaronides should present it before *Adonai* in front of the altar. 8) A handful of the choice flour and oil of the meal offering should be taken from it. 9) *What is left of it shall be eaten by Aaron and his sons; it shall be eaten as unleavened bread [matza] in the holy place.* They should eat it in the enclosure in the Tent of Meeting. 10) *It shall not be baked with leaven [chametz]; I have given it as their portion from My offering by fire; it is the most holy, like the sin offering and the guilt offering.* 11) Only the males among Aaron's descendants may eat from it, as their entitlement throughout the generations from *Adonai*'s fiery offerings. Anything that touches it is consecrated [made holy]. □

Perush: Explaining the Teaching

Our teacher is puzzled at why the priest's portion of this offering alone is not to be prepared with leaven (a recapitulation of Leviticus 2:11). For the rabbis, leaven is also a symbol for moral corruption. Searching for the connection, our teacher calls to mind texts from *Sanhedrin* 99a and *Yoma* 86b where the behaviors of *tzaddikim* and *baalei teshuvah* are discussed. This action therefore is of a transformative nature; it is more than a simple cultic observance. The *matzah* (without leaven) represents the person who has made *teshuvah* where leaven (moral corruption) has been transformed into acts of holiness, and the one who has turned in repentance has actually become holier than the priest. □

Background Because the evil powers of humans are embedded in one's flesh and blood, say the mystics, flesh and blood have to be sacrificed. □

The Teaching from R. Meir (of Lublin [or Rottenberg])

Rashi: [We know that] the eighth day [here refers to] the consecration [of the priests into the priesthood that was just completed in the preceding chapter and took seven days]. And [according to *Midrash Sifra*] it was the first day of the month of *Nisan* on which the wilderness Tabernacle was also erected. And [for this reason, the day] received ten crowns [or, distinctions].

In *Shabbat* 87b, we read, "And it came to pass in →

Perush: Explaining the Teaching

In this lesson, our teacher focuses on the fact that Moses summoned Aaron and his sons, as well as the elders. Later, we read that God only appeared after the sacrifices took place on the eighth day, but not before. Why the eighth day? Here he relates the construction of the Tabernacle (and the consecration of the priests who will serve it) to the creation of the world, borrowing from *Megillah* 10b. While it is the eighth day of consecration, it is the first day of the second year, the first day of the month. Thus this first day (even within →

Scriptural Context

In this section of Leviticus, the specific articulation of laws is interrupted so that the priests might be consecrated and the tabernacle dedicated. (These rites had already been specified in Exodus 29:1–37.) The service will climax in the next portion by an appearance of the Divine Presence in the midst of the ceremony. □

Targum: English Translation Leviticus 9:1–6

1) *And it came to pass on the eighth day that Moses summoned Aaron, his sons, and the elders of Israel.* 2) He [Moses] said to Aaron, "Take a calf from the herd as a sin offering and a blemish-free ram for a burnt offering and bring them before *Adonai*. 3) Then speak to the Israelites thus, 'Take a he-goat for a sin offering, a calf and a lamb, blemish-free yearlings, [all] for a burnt offering, 4) and an ox and a ram for a well-being offering as a sacrifice before *Adonai*, [as well as] a meal offering mixed with oil. Because *Adonai* will appear to you today.' " 5) They brought the things that Moses had instructed [them] to the front of the Tent of Meeting. So the whole community came before and stood before *Adonai*. 6) Moses said, "This is what *Adonai* has commanded you to do, that *Adonai*'s presence may appear to you." □

From the Tradition

We read in *Yafet To'ar* that Rashi taught: [A calf was selected] to make known to Aaron that the Holy One had granted him atonement for the the Golden Calf that he had made.

Our sages, in Rosh Ha-Shanah 26a, note a difficulty here: "Rabbi Hisda said, 'Why does not the high priest enter the inner precincts [on Yom Kippur] in garments of gold to perform the service there? [Instead he wore only garments of linen (Leviticus 16:4, 23).] [It is] because the accuser [who originally caused the problem] cannot act as a defender [and repair the damage].' " And the "calf" was made of gold.

According to the same reasoning [also in *Rosh Ha-Shanah* 26a, we read in the →

Background Meir ben Jacob Ha-Kohen Schiff, known as the Maharam (1605–1641), was born in Frankfurt-am-Main and, by the time he was seventeen, was rabbi of Fulda and head of its *yeshivah* there. Most of his extensive writings were destroyed by a fire in 1711. Because he does not intend to give the reader halachic decisions, his work always includes a bibliography to direct the reader further. □

The Teaching (continued)

the first month of the second year, the first day of the month, that the wilderness Tabernacle was set up" (Exodus 40:17). A mishnaic teacher taught that for this reason, that day received ten crowns. It was the first day of creation (that is, Sunday). Rashi's interpretation is that it was the first day of the week. But this is perplexing. What is so special about the first day of the week? Every Sunday is the first day of creation.

The main idea here is this: the creation of the world was ordained according to the construction of the wilderness tabernacle. As we read in *Megillah* 10b, " 'And it came to pass on the eighth day,' and it has been taught, on that day there was joy before the Holy One, as on the day when heaven and earth were created." And ten crowns correspond to the passage in *Pirke Avot* 5:1, "With ten sayings was the world created."

This is according to a teaching of the sages in *Genesis Rabbah* 3:8, "According to normal syntax, the passage should be written: 'And there was evening and there was morning, a first day,' to conform with the way all the other days are written, 'second,' 'third,' 'fourth,' and the like. Why then is it written here instead 'one day,' "? Because, as the *Midrash* continues, "Rabbi Judah said, it was the day on which the Holy One, was one in the universe."

And so when was it said, "a first day"? In Numbers 7:12, "And it came to pass that the one who presented his offering on the first day [of the consecration of the newly completed wilderness tabernacle] was Nachshon, son of Amminadav. . . ." Just this is the first of the work of creation. ☐

Perush: Explaining the Teaching (continued)

the eight-day counting) reflects the first day of creation when heaven and earth were created. It was written in this peculiar way, says R. Meir, in order to make it conform to the way we refer to days, in general, in Hebrew [*Yom Rishon, Yom Sheni,* and so on]. The important part of the lesson is that through the "creation" of the Tabernacle, the dwelling of God's presence was encouraged. Just as in the last day of creation, according to *Genesis Rabbah* 3:8, God's presence was at one with the universe. Our goal in building the *Mishkan,* whether as the desert tabernacle or as modern structures for worship, is to provide a context to bring God closer to us, so to speak. ☐

From the Tradition (continued)

Mishnah that] all kinds of *shofars* are ritually acceptable except [ones made from the horn of] a cow. [And the horn of cow in Hebrew is a *keren* and not a *shofar.*]

But [if the accuser may not act as defender] why did God command Aaron here to take a calf?

The explanation is that the teaching that the accuser cannot act as defender is used if the matter involves a completely different category and thus provokes stern judgment. But if the matter comes to make atonement for a sin which one committed, then precisely the very instrument with which he disgraced himself becomes the instrument of his repair.

And just this is suggested in the *Midrash*. The pascal offering was a lamb in order to make atonement for the idolatrous worship of the constellation of Aries [*taleh*, "lamb or ram"]. And thus it is said, "Let the gold of the Tabernacle come and make atonement for the gold of the calf." And therefore here also, let the sacrifice of the calf make atonement for the sin of the calf. ☐

(77) Shemini: Happy without Wine

The Teaching
from Simchah Bunem of Przysucha

[*Leviticus Rabbah* 12.3], commenting on this verse cites Psalm 19, "The precepts of *Adonai* are right, rejoicing the heart. . . ."

One possible way to explain the *Midrash* is that God cannot dwell amidst sadness. And the priest is required, therefore, to offer sacrifices to God in a spirit of exaltation and joy. But why then would he be forbidden to →

Perush: Explaining the Teaching

Our teacher is puzzled by the prohibition against wine, when he knows that wine not only is often used for the specified purpose of sanctification but also because there is the well-known text "Wine rejoices the heart." Why then would the Torah proscribe such joy in the midst of serving God? The opposite should be true. Simchah Bunem offers an explanation that not only teaches us about the ancient priesthood but – since "Israel is a kingdom of priests, a holy nation" – also about ourselves. Our relationship with God should be pure. And our joy must come purely from the service of God and not through any secondary "chemical" means. This allows for exaltation that soars heavenward unencumbered by any mundane, earthy assistance such as wine or strong drink. Only from living according to Torah can we gain ultimate joy. □

Scriptural Context

Now consecrated, Aaron and his sons have taken on the cultic functions of the Tabernacle. The *parashah* begins with the prohibition of intoxicants of any sort, for the priests are responsible for the welfare of the community. □

Targum: English Translation
Leviticus 10:8–11

8) **The Adonai spoke to Aaron thus,** 9) *"Drink no wine nor strong drink, neither you nor your sons with you when you enter the Tent of Meeting, so that you shall not die; it is an everlasting law throughout your generations.* **10) For you must make a distinction between [what is] sacred and [what is] routine [alternately, profane], between the [ritually] unclean and clean. 11) And you must teach the Israelites all of the laws that *Adonai* imparted to them through [the agency of] Moses.** □

From the Tradition

The prohibition against wine or strong drink (probably a beerlike drink since distilled liquors were unknown in the ancient world) for the priests alone was only relevant during their official duties. At other times, they were free to drink just as were the Israelites. Among the many speculations about this, was that Nadab and Abihu may have been intoxicated when they attempted to make an unofficial offering. Hence, they were killed. The Bible does speak, however, of Nazirites who took a vow to abstain from wine and never to cut their hair – as an additional sign of dedication to God (cf. Judges 13; 1 Samuel 1:1; Amos 2:11ff). While some of these biblical personalities were dedicated to such a life by their parents, there is a provision for individuals to make such a vow to become a Nazirite (man or woman) for a specified length of time. This vow allows the layperson to be given a status similar to a priest. The Nazirite may cut his or her hair at the end of this period to signify the →

Background Raba said: It is the duty of a man to get so drunk on Purim that he cannot tell the difference between "cursed be Haman (the villain)" and "blessed be Mordecai (the hero)."

Raba and Rabbi Zeira joined together in a Purim feast. They got drunk, and Raba arose and cut Rabbi Zeira's throat. On the next day he prayed on his behalf and revived him. Next year he said, "Will your honor come and we will have the Purim feast together?" He replied, "A miracle does not take place on every occasion!" (*Megillah* 7b). □

The Teaching (*continued*)
drink wine? Surely wine causes joy; "Wine rejoices a person's heart" (Psalm 104:15).

The explanation is that when the priest enters the Tent of Meeting to perform the holy service, into the Holy of Holies, he must attain a feeling of exaltation and happiness from the sheer joy of doing what God wants. The Torah, the way of God, needs to be the source of his inspiration and the wellspring of his joy.

And only this constitutes the fulfillment of what God wants of us. [For this reason, the priest is told,] drink no wine, nor strong drink, he needs to fill his heart with joy [from what he does]. According to the psalm, "The precepts of *Adonai*—make the heart rejoice." □

From the Tradition (*continued*)
end of the period. This hair was to be burned together with the offering the individual was required to bring at the end of his Nazirite status. Since this vow was closely connected to the Temple cult (through this final offering), it was discontinued following destruction of the Second Temple. These vows were discouraged by the rabbis who believed that asceticism was inconsistent with the spirit of Judaism. □

(78) Shemini: Lower than Angels

The Teaching
from Chatam Sofer, Moses Sofer

"Rabbi Simlai observed that just as the creation of human beings [is recounted] after all the cattle, beasts, and birds in the creation story, so the Torah [of human beings] is explained after the Torah of cattle, beasts, and birds (Rashi; also *Leviticus Rabbah* 14:1).

Indeed, even though human beings are the chosen of creation, the select ones of the universe, in the words of Psalm 8:6, "little lower than the angels," let people not consequently think in their hearts that they therefore rule the world and are permitted to break through all boundaries, priding themselves and becoming arrogant, calling themselves *Übermenschen*. →

Scriptural Context

Following the description of dietary laws, this portion ends with the designation of defilement (or ritual impurity) through contact with animal carcasses. The next portion begins with a discussion of similar ritual impurities associated with childbirth. Our text is taken from the vantage point of this transition from one Torah portion to the next. □

Targum: English Translation
Leviticus 11: 46–47; 12:1–2

46) These are the instructions concerning animals, birds, all living creatures that move in water, and all creatures that swarm on earth, 47) for distinguishing between the unclean and the clean, between the living things that may be eaten and the living things that may not be eaten. 12:1) Adonai spoke to Moses saying: 2) Speak to the Israelites saying, "When a woman conceives and bears a son, she shall be ritually impure for seven days, she shall be impure as during the days of menstruation." □

From the Tradition

Ritual purity or impurity is a state preventing an individual (or object) from having contact with the Temple or its cult. This state can be transferred through contact from person or thing to another and can only be corrected through prescribed rituals. It was central to all classical religions and usually resulted from "contamination" through contact with death. For this reason we today still ritually wash our hands when leaving the cemetery. This may also explain the surprising "defilement" at childbirth: the thin veil between life and death has been opened for a moment and elaborate ritual procedures for protection are required. □

Perush: Explaining the Teaching

The Chatam Sofer teaches us that ritual impurity is a metaphor for ethical contamination. Learning this from the sequence of instructions from animal to human beings, he reasons that the Torah teaches us to remember that although we are at the center of creation, and at times, only a little lower than angels, on account of our sins, we can just as easily be even lower than cattle and carrion. Animals are ritually impure at death, not in life. Only human beings, through righteous acts, can control their ritual purity. Thus, our teacher also makes a claim for the moral exercise of free choice.

Our Torah is always challenging us on the one hand to increase our self-esteem as a Jew while simultaneously maintaining our humility as an individual on the other. Only a religious life keeps this "up and down" motion in check and prevents us from getting "motion sickness." All this, Simchah Bunem learns from the juxtaposition of the end of one Torah portion with the beginning of the next. □

Background According to *Song of Songs Rabbah* (1:2 par. 3), "Just as water purifies from ritual impurity, so does the Torah purify the impure from one's heart." □

The Teaching (*continued*)

For this very reason, the Torah sets the laws of cattle before the laws of people, in order to teach us: While the *tzaddikim* and the righteous ascend even higher than angels, and people of high qualities are able to attain the highest levels, nevertheless remember that in contrast to this, those afflicted with leprosy [the paradigm for spiritual defilement] and ritual impurity – defiled and contaminated on account of sins – behold, they are at a low level, inferior to cattle, worse than beasts and carrion.

Thus their ritual impurity is all the worse. Cattle after all cannot be ritually impure while they are alive, only people can. And the corpse of a beast only defiles someone who touches or carries it, while a person can defile someone else who is merely in the same tent.

Similarly, a person who has attained a high level of religious development through exercising freedom of choice, that same person can easily abuse that same power and sink into the depths of Sheol below. □

(79) Tazria: Torah, *Chuppah,* and Good Deeds

The Teaching
from *Beit Kotzk,* the school of
Menachem Mendl of Kotzk

Once, at a gathering of the *Chasidim* of Kotzk, Rabbi Neta Noach of Wyshograd explained that this means that just as the infant has entered the covenant without arrogance, ulterior motive, or perverse intention, so may he enter the study of Torah and marriage.

Rabbi Hirsch of Grobovitz spoke after him: I have always had a different interpretation. Just as he has entered the covenant in order to change from being an uncircumcised non-Jew into a Jew, may he enter the study of Torah and marriage with this very same purpose. [So may the study of Torah and marriage likewise transform him into a complete Jew.] □

Perush: Explaining the Teaching

Our teachers are fascinated by the nuances of text of the *brit milah* liturgy, and especially the relationship between "Torah, *chuppah,* and good deeds." From the school of Kotzk, we learn that as one enters the covenant with no malice or manipulation, one should fulfill *all* of the rituals of Jewish life with the same purity. In particular, one should study Torah and marry with the same innocence, for if one can remain modest in the study hall and at home so will one live in all of his or her dealings. One of the rabbis in Kotzk added to this teaching. Hirsch of Grobovitz believed that *brit milah* contained the potential to actually transform the individual. Just as *brit milah* transformed the individual into a complete Jew, Torah study and marriage are also necessary to fulfill the individual. □

Scriptural Context

This portion focuses primarily on the ways one can become ritually defiled, for example, through childbirth or leprosy. Since our text is taken from the liturgy for *brit milah* (circumcision), which also involves blood, its lesson is related to this Torah portion. □

Targum: English Translation
from the liturgy for *brit milah*

Just as he has entered into the covenant (of circumcision), so may he enter (the study of) Torah, the **Chuppah** *(marriage canopy), and doing of good deeds.* □

From the
Tradition

Since the promise that Abraham's seed should inherit the Land of Israel is tied to the rite of circumcision, it is considered a very important commandment. The philosopher Baruch Spinoza once said that this rite alone was sufficient to insure the survival of the Jewish people (*Tractus Theologica-Politicus* 3:53). In *Shabbat* 137b the rabbis declare that were it not for the blood of the covenant, heaven and earth would not exist. According to *Pirke de Rabbi Eliezer* 29, Abraham circumcised himself on the tenth of *Tishri,* the date later observed as Yom Kippur, the Day of Atonement. □

Background Jewish liturgy is sacred text. In a unique form of dialogue, it is the expression of the Jewish people's yearning to respond to God's revelation and instruction through *mitzvot.* □

(80) Tazria: The Fourth Path

The Teaching
from Gevurot Shelomoh, Rabbi Shelomoh Kluger

"A person" is mentioned four times in this biblical context. Here, "When a person has on the skin of his body a swelling . . ." (Leviticus 13:2); "A person from among you who will make an offering . . ." (Leviticus 1:2); "When a person dies in a tent . . ." (Numbers 19:14); and "People and animals you deliver, O *Adonai*" (Psalm 36:7).

These four verses allude to the four paths to *teshuvah*, returning to God, which are cited by our sages [in →

Perush: Explaining the Teaching

While many moderns avoid this portion, some teachers remain undaunted and try to unravel the mystery of these texts with the same enthusiasm as the passages. Torah is Torah and we are obligated to try to understand it, for in doing so we come closer to God. In this case, Rabbi Shelomoh Kluger is attempting to understand why the Torah focuses on the individual rather than the people as a whole. He notes four places where the Bible uses a similar construction and deduces that these four examples represent the four paths of *teshuvah*, of return to God, as cited elsewhere by the sages. Through *teshuvah*, one can be healed in a myriad of ways. □

Targum: English Translation
Leviticus 13:1-3

1) **Adonai spoke thus to Moses and Aaron: 2)** *When a person has on the skin of his body a swelling, a rash, or a discoloration, and it develops into a scaly affection on the skin of his body,* **it shall be reported to Aaron the priest or to one of his sons, the priests. 3) The priest shall examine the affection on the skin of his body: if hair on the affected patch has turned white and the affection appears to be deeper than the skin of his body, it is a leprous affection; when the priest sees it, he shall pronounce him unclean. □**

Scriptural Context

Tzaraat, customarily translated as "leprosy," is the salient theme of this very strange portion. While Hansen's disease (leprosy) is specific, *tzaraat* seems more likely any scaly skin condition as well as metaphor for any terrible disease such as cancer or AIDS, that is to say, the scourge of any particular generation. In our Bible text, *tzaraat* can also afflict garments, and even the walls of homes. □

From the Tradition

As it is described in the Bible, leprosy encompassed a variety of skin ailments, some transient and others chronic, often leading to death. Thus, what we know about Hansen's disease only gives us some insight into what is described in the Bible. In order to separate the ritual as described in the Bible from what might have been considered magic in the ancient Near East, the priest performed the ritual only after the leprous condition had been resolved.

When the Temple was destroyed, the laws of leprosy became obsolete, so the rabbis revived them by offering moral lessons, primarily by punning *metzora* as *motzi shem ra* (spreading a bad name, that is, libel or slander). Thus they reasoned that leprosy was the punishment for this kind of evil and cited Miriam's slander of Moses in Numbers 12:1–15 as an example. □

Background Shelomoh ben Yehudah Aaron Kluger (1785–1869) was known as the *Maggid* of Brody, where he spent fifty years of his life. Also known as Maharshak, he was a prolific writer who wrote hundreds of responsa. He is said to have written 375, the *gematria* equivalent to his name (Shelomoh/Solomon)–the known list of his books reaches nearly 175. He was extreme in his Orthodoxy and fought against the Enlightenment. □

The Teaching (*continued*)
Midrash Yalkut Shimoni on Psalm 25].

They asked Wisdom, what is the punishment for a sinner? Replied Wisdom, "Trouble pursues sinners," meaning, they will be afflicted with divine punishments. This is an allusion to "When a person has on the skin of his body a swelling . . ." (Leviticus 13: 2).

They asked Prophecy [the same question] and it replied, "A person who sins shall die." This is an allusion to "When a person dies in a tent . . ." (Numbers 19:14).

They asked Torah and it replied, "Let the guilty bring forward [an offering] and make atonement for himself." This is an allusion to "A person from among you who will make an offering . . ." (Leviticus 1:2).

They asked the Holy One of Being, and God replied, "Let the person make *teshuvah* and atonement for himself." This is an allusion to "People and animals you deliver, O *Adonai*" (Psalm 36:7).

In other words, by means if the act of *teshuvah*, returning to God, a person is saved from death punishments, offering sacrifices, and animals from slaughter. [As in the conclusion to Jonah, "and much cattle," animals pay for *our* sins.] □

(81) Tazria: Showing the Priest

The Teaching
from *Sippurei Chasidim*

Rabbi Asher of Stulin would complain about the *chasidim*. When they came to the *rebbe*, they would accentuate their good points and conceal the bad.

When I – said the *tzaddik*, Rabbi Asher of Stulin – would study *midrash* in the presence of my teacher and rabbi [Shelomoh of Karlin] – and he would kiss the tips of his fingers at the mention of his rabbi – I would conceal from him the good. This is because there is no one except God who gives "reward and punishment," [certainly not my teachers!]. Nevertheless, I would show him the evil in me [for the teacher is like a priest who heals]. And for this reason, the priest needs to see the affection. □

Perush: Explaining the Teaching

In this text the priest is given the authority to determine whether or not an individual has *tzaraat*. Our teacher suggests that the condition of *tzaraat* is like an individual who tries to conceal his or her evil from a teacher. But this is impossible, for the *tzaddik* is able to see "through" the pretense, just as the priest can "see through" the white patch in order to determine whether the individual is really pure or only seems to be so. □

Scriptural Context

One of the better known and least understood portions of the Torah, this portion is concerned with ritual impurities, which the Torah expresses in graphic terms and which encompass a variety of afflictions of the skin. In our text, the priest is called to determine the status of the infection since such infections often reflect moral impurity as well. □

Targum: English Translation
Leviticus 13:9–13

9) *When a person has a scaly infection, he shall be brought to the priest.* 10) **If the priest finds on the skin a white swelling that has turned some hair white, with a patch of discolored flesh in the swelling 11) it is chronic leprosy on the skin of his body, and the priest shall pronounce him unclean. He does not have to isolate him, since he is unclean. 12) But if the eruption has spread over his skin so that it covers the skin of the affected person from head to toe, wherever the priest can see, 13) if the priest sees that it covers the [afflicted] person's entire body, he shall pronounce the afflicted person clean. He is clean because he turns all white.** □

From the Tradition

In *Bava Metzia* 86a, concerning the "diagnosis" of *tzaraat*, (leprosy) by the priest, there is a dispute over whether the person whose diagnosis is in doubt is ritually clean or not. The debate is taken to the heavenly court, which rules in favor of God's judgment. However, Rabbah bar Nachmani turns over God's judgment and God lets it stand. This teaches us that, in fact, human beings, teachers of Torah, are involved in the deliberation of God's decrees even when they appear to contradict divine authority. □

Background In the *Sanhedrin* 52a, the rabbis are perplexed over the instructions to the priest in Leviticus 13:9–13. There they draw a different lesson, suggesting that the afflicted ones are like Korach, who rebelled against the authority of Moses. □

(82) Metzora: Sacred Speech

The Teaching
from *Akeidah*

Arachin 15b: "Resh Lakish said: 'What is the meaning of "This shall be the ritual for a leper (*metzora*, מצרע)...'? [It means] 'This shall be the law for one who brings out a bad name (*motzi shem ra*, מוציא שם רע).'"

The power of speech is the most sublime thing a person has; it elevates one from the category of animals to the level of being "a speaker." We read in Genesis 2:7, "God blew into Adam's nostrils the breath of life and Adam became a living being." But the text is translated into Aramaic [not as, "the breath of life", but] as "the spirit of speaking." And this quality is what makes a human being.

Scriptural Context

This portion focuses on leprosy and the purification of a leper by the priest. The biblical author believed that such bodily decay reflected some sort of inner moral or spiritual decay as well. Once the priest determined that the leper was unclean, the two stages of purification could begin. □

Targum: English Translation
Leviticus 14:1-7

1) *Adonai* spoke thus to Moses: 2) *This shall be the ritual for a leper at the time that he is to be cleansed:* When it has been reported to a priest, 3) the priest should go outside the camp. If the priest sees that he has been healed of his scaly affection, 4) the priest should instruct that two live, clean birds, cedar wood, crimson thread, and hyssop be brought for him who is to be cleansed. 5) The priest should order that one of the birds be killed over fresh water in an earthen vessel. 6) He should take the live bird, with the cedar wood, the crimson thread, and the hyssop, and dip them together with the live bird in the blood of the bird slaughtered over the fresh water. 7) He should sprinkle it several times on him who is to be cleansed of the eruption and cleanse him; he shall set the live bird free in the open spaces. □

From the Tradition

The sages prohibited slander, slurs, and defaming others–even when the derogatory remarks were true. They recognized the power of a spoken word to build or ruin relationships between people, and even called the tongue an elixir of life (*Leviticus Rabbah* 16:2). □

This also is the intention of the passage in Isaiah 40:6-7, "All flesh is like grass.... The grass withers, the flower fades, but the word of our God endures forever." This teaches that the body of a person, which is flesh, is like grass that withers and fades but the power of speech within a person–the word of our God–endures forever.

But if a person misuses this gift for evil, for wickedness and perversity, in the service →

Perush: Explaining the Teaching

In this difficult section of the Torah, our teacher reads the disease of leprosy metaphorically–not as a physical disease but as symptomatic of a character defect. *Metzora* becomes an acronym for the "one who brings out an evil name." To bolster his position, he cites the Aramaic translation of Genesis 2:7 and Isaiah 40:6-7. Thus, for the rabbis, the cleansing of the leper was not for hygienic purposes, it was also to purify the soul of the leper–as the one who had spoken evil. □

Background Mar, the son of Ravina, ended his daily prayer with these words, "My God, keep my tongue from evil and my lips from speaking guile" (*Berachot* 17a). This meditation has since been added to the end of the *Amidah*. □

The Teaching (*continued*)

of his or her own baser, materialistic gratification, then such a person perverts and defiles the ultimate goal of creation. Such a person is like one to whom the king gave royal robes and who proceeded to put them on his donkey!

The Torah says, "This shall be the ritual for a leper," one who brings out an evil name. Behold this is a perversion; this is not the way of a lofty human being, but the way of a leper. □

(83) Metzora: The Red Thread

The Teaching
from Abraham Joshua Heschel of Apta

Rashi: [Punning on the Hebrew for crimson thread, *tolaat shani*, asks] how should one repair oneself in order that he or she may be healed? You must abandon pride and regard yourself lowly as a worm (*tolaat*) and hyssop.

Hyssop alludes to a person's needing to make him- or herself lowly like a hyssop bush, "of this earth." Likewise one also needs the wood of a cedar tree, which alludes to needing to make oneself feel grand, that is to say, "heavenly." As we →

Perush: Explaining the Teaching

Punning on the Hebrew for crimson thread, which sounds like the word for worm, and then on the stately cedar tree, Abraham Joshua Heschel of Apt draws a lesson for the Jewish people, who are themselves a kingdom of priests. True healing demands a balancing of pride and humility. Cleansing the self of moral decay is arduous, and only possible once we can balance pride and humility.

There is a well-known chasidic teaching attributed to Simchah Bunem of Przysucha: An individual should keep a scrap in each pocket. On one should be written, "You are nothing but dust and ashes"; on the other should be written, "The whole world was created for me." When down, you read one; when you are feeling arrogant, you read the other. Heschel's insight reminds us that the key is to remain in the balance. □

Scriptural Context

The theme of this portion follows directly on the previous one. While *Parashat Tazria* focused on impurity and defilement, specifically from *tzaraat*, this portion provides a ritual mechanism for purification. Our text is taken from a section in which the priest is instructed regarding the preparation of a mixture necessary for the individual to regain a state of purity. □

Targum: English Translation
Leviticus 14:1–4

1) *Adonai* **spoke thus to Moses:** 2) **This is to be the ritual for the leper at the time he is to be cleansed. Once it has been told to the priest,** 3) **the priest shall go outside the camp. If the priest has seen that the leper has been healed from the scaly infection,** 4) *then shall the priest command to take for the one who is to be cleansed two live, clean birds, cedar wood, crimson thread, and hyssop* **to be brought for him who is to be cleansed.** □

From the Tradition

The hyssop is a small plant that grows in the rocks and in stone walls. While it was used with the cedar in rites of purification, it was usually described in distinction to the lofty cedar trees. While it may be that hyssop was plentiful and that that was the reason it was often chosen for the purposes of purification, the sages contend that it was chosen because, unlike the cedar, which symbolizes pride, it symbolizes humility. □

Background Abraham Joshua Heschel of Apta (Opatow) (d. 1825) was a disciple of Elimelech of Lyzhansk and probably Jehiel Michael of Zloczow. He served as rabbi in several communities (including Kolbuszowa Apta from 1809 to 1813) before settling in Medzibozh, where he remained until his death. He led a public fast as protest against the discriminatory legislation passed by Czar Alexander I. Acknowledged by many as the preeminent authority in his old age, he was called on to ex-

communicate other *rebbes* during a controversy between the Bratzlaver and Przysucha *chasidim*, but worked hard to maintain harmony between the groups.

His epitaph, for which he was known, was simple: *Ohev Yisrael* (lover of Israel). He was a religious ecstatic who was fascinated by Jewish leadership. He focused on practical "tzaddik-ism" and maintained that through wisdom a *tzaddik* is able to bind Israel to heaven and bring prosperity to the Jewish people. □

The Teaching (*continued*)

read in 2 Chronicles 17:6, "His mind was elevated in the ways of *Adonai*."

For this reason a person also requires some kind of balancing line to know where to stand in order to balance the scales: whether one should feel grand in the service of God or whether one should feel lowly and earthbound.

The whole notion of scales implies that one should maintain balance in the middle in order not to tip to one side or the other, but to remain centered on a line as thin as a strand of hair.

And just this is the allusion to "the crimson thread," which must be brought along with the cedar and hyssop. □

(84) Metzora: Sorrow Not Impurity

The Teaching
from *Yalkut Penimim*

Mo'ed Katan 8a: It was seen by me and not by the aid of some artificial light, teaching that we do not look for plagues at night.

And thus our sages taught in *Mishnah Nega'im* 2:3: A priest blind in one eye or whose sight is dim may not inspect symptoms, as it is said in Leviticus 13:12, "as far as appears in the eyes of the priest." Windows in a house that is dark may not be opened up in order to inspect its leprosy symptoms.

We have here a moral lesson and a suggestion to the priests of the people

Scriptural Context

This section of our Torah portion focuses on the *tzaraat* of houses. The priest examines the house and then follows the prescribed method to cleanse it. Unlike the cure for a person, the law here is more severe. If a house is not able to be purified, it is to be destroyed totally – so that the plague does not spread. □

From the Tradition

The Gerer *rebbe* taught that a candle, wick, and oil give forth light by diminishing themselves. It is likewise with us. As our material wants are diminished we give out spiritual light. □

Targum: English Translation
Leviticus 14:34–36

34) **When you enter the land of Canaan, which I give to you as a possession, and I inflict an eruptive plague upon a house in the land you possess, 35)** *the owner of the house shall come and tell the priest, saying, "Something like a plague was seen by me in the house."* **36) The priest shall order the house cleared before the priest enters to examine the plague, so that nothing in the house may become unclean; after that the priest shall enter to examine the house.** □

and their leaders that they not search for defects in the people as long as there is darkness around them. If the situation of the people is bad, showing symptoms of plague, such symptoms are not necessarily signs of ritual impurity. There is some reason to believe that the plague has not contaminated the inner essence of the people but rather only a superficial manifestation, a passing phenomenon, and it has only been distress that has brought the people into the power of such degraded spirit and deep depression. □

Perush: Explaining the Teaching

Like many teachers who read *tzaraat* as a metaphor for moral behavior, here our teacher draws a lesson from the instruction about the homeowner seeing the leprosy in his house. How is it, he inquires, that one *sees* a plague on one's house? We know elsewhere that the tradition states that a priest with impaired vision may not use artificial light in order to see whether in fact the house is infected. Thus, we do not look for defects in others when darkness surrounds us. This " darkness" may be the situation of the Jewish people or the bad straits in which an individual finds himself or herself, and that is what causes the "appearance of the plague." Thus, there is reason to hope that the plague has not infected the essence of the person or the people but rather is only superficial and able to be remedied. □

Background The Baal Shem Tov sent his disciples out to help people improve themselves. One disciple, Mendel of Bar, returned to Medzibozh from a journey. The Besht said to him: A broom can sweep clean a courtyard but in doing so it becomes soiled. Go now and cleanse yourself of any offenses of which you may be guilty. □

(85) Acharei Mot: Dying to Serve

The Teaching from Likkutei Ha-Besht

The phrases "after the death of . . ." and "they died" seem to be redundant. The apparent repetition can be reconciled when we consider the words of the sages in *Midrash Genesis Rabbah*, 44:5 (and in Rashi to *Sotah* 33, and in *Parashat Re'eh*): Every place where the word אחר (*ahar*, after) is used, it means "next to" or "dependent upon," and wherever אחרי (*acharei*, after) is used, it means "divided" or "distant."

And this is the explanation of [the first reaction of death] "after (אחרי, *aharei*) the death of the two sons of Aaron. . . ." The fear of death was distant from them, for every moment they stood face-to-face with death. On the other hand, when the text says, "when they drew near before *Adonai* and they died," it means that every moment that they approached *Adonai* they died (literally, "their souls blossomed"), for they continually gave their souls over to the service of God. □

Scriptural Context

While this portion does not deal with the deaths of Nadab and Abihu (since they really died in the previous portion), the name of this portion – taken from its first verse – calls our attention to their deaths. As a result, a great deal of attention is given to the deaths of Nadab and Abihu within the context of this portion. The portion actually deals with Yom Kippur, the laws of holiness, and sexual offenses. □

Targum: English Translation
Leviticus 16: 1-3

1) *And* Adonai *spoke to Moses after the death of the two sons of Aaron when they drew near* Adonai *and died.* 2) *Adonai* said to Moses, "Tell your brother Aaron that he is not to come whenever he wants into the inner sanctum behind the curtain, in front of the cover that is upon the ark so that he should not die, since I appear over the cover. 3) Thus, only Aaron will [be permitted] to enter the inner sanctum – with a bull of the herd as a sin offering and a ram for the burnt offering. □

From the Tradition

According to the Talmud, the deaths of Nadab and Abihu were caused by "two streams of fire . . . branched off into four, and two entered each of the nostrils of Nadab and Abihu." Their souls were burned but no external injury was visible (*Sanhedrin* 52a). □

Perush: Explaining the Teaching

Like many who read this text and about the deaths of Nadab and Abihu preceding it, the Baal Shem Tov struggles to understand how God could let the altar flame consume Aaron's sons so soon after they had been consecrated to God's service. He finds an explanation in an apparent redundancy. In Leviticus 16:1, the death of the young men is mentioned twice. Why? He suggests that there is an important distinction in the Hebrew between *achar* (after) and *acharei* (after).

Perhaps one death, so to speak, refers to physical death, while the other death is really a loss of self to the Ultimate Self, namely God. Each time one serves God – as did the priests – their selves died, for they had given themselves over to (the service of) God. □

Background Israel ben Eliezer Baal Shem Tov, who was known by the initials of the Baal Shem Tov (Besht), lived from about 1700 to 1760. He was a charismatic leader who founded Chasidism. Tales abound about him, as he traveled to effect cures and teach his newfound disciples. According to legend, he reached the highest levels of mystical ecstasy and closeness to God. At the core of his teaching is *devekut*, literally, "a bonding to God," which he believed was the foundation for all the routines of daily life. He taught that "if the individual is occupied with the material needs, and his thought cleaves to God, he will be blessed." □

(86) Acharei Mot: Jewish Clothes

The Teaching
from Menachem Mendl of Kotzk

During the reign of Czar Nicholas I of Russia, a decree was issued by the government that Jews were required to wear hats with visors [or brims] just like Gentiles. This created a storm among the Jews: "A Gentile law"–"Let him be killed rather than transgress." [During times of persecution people can die even over something as trifling as a shoelace.]

Chasidim sat in the study house of Rabbi Menachem Mendl of Kotzk in heated and furious debate. Some were religiously strict, others lenient. Suddenly, the *rebbe* opened the door and asked, "Why the commotion? What has happened?"

They replied to him that the government had issued a decree that Jews must change the way they dress, and clothe themselves like Gentiles. "The clothing of Jews is only *tallis* (alternately, *tallit*) and *tefillin*," snapped the *rebbe*. And he closed the door as he left. □

Scriptural Context

This section of the Torah portion focuses on sexual behavior and offenses. The text under discussion introduces this section and provides a context for that which follows. □

Targum: English Translation
Leviticus 18: 1-4

1) *Adonai* spoke thus to Moses: 2) "Speak to the Israelites and say to them, 'I am *Adonai* your God.' 3) You shall not mimic the practices of the land of Egypt where you lived or of the land of Canaan where I am taking you. *And in their ways, you shall not walk.* 4) You should follow [only] My rules so that you may be guided by them. I am *Adonai* your God." □

From the Tradition

After the exile from *Eretz Yisrael* and the first Diaspora, the Jewish people began to adopt the fashions of their non-Jewish neighbors more readily. The *tallit* was therefore discarded as a daily garment and generally restricted to prayer.

Later the *tallit katan*, a small *tallit* generally worn under the shirt, was reintroduced. It is still worn today by observant Orthodox Jews. □

Perush: Explaining the Teaching

Like so many of the Kotzker's teachings, there is a simple but profound truth implicit in what appears to be an abrupt statement that leaves little room for dialogue. One might say that Menachem Mendl dismissed the discussion as trivial by refusing to deal with it. Yet, if we explore the text more deeply, the Kotzker is suggesting, as befits his retreat from the world, not to worry about silly little hats with visors. Instead, focus your attention on the essence of Judaism, that is, *tallit* and *tefillin*. If you do this, implies the Kotzker, the way of the Gentiles (and the clothing they wear) will be irrelevant. □

Background The kabbalistic meditation prior to wearing *tefillin*: You have instructed us to lay the *tefillin* on the head as a memorial of Your outstretched arm; opposite the heart to indicate the duty of subjecting the longings and designs of our heart to Your service; and upon the head, over against the brain, thereby teaching that the mind, whose seat is in the brain together with all senses and faculties, is to be subject to Your service. □

(87) Acharei Mot: By What Do You Live?

The Teaching
from *Degel Machaneh Ehpraim*

אשר יעשה אתם (*asher yaaseh otam*)—אתם (*otam*) is written defective, *chaseir* א, *alef*; ח, *tav*; ם, *mem*), the letters of אמת (*emet*, truth). One who acknowledges the truth, tells himself the truth, walks in the way of truth, and thus makes truth the foundation of his life, is one "who lives by them." And this is the mystery of prolonging and fulfilling one's life. □

Scriptural Context

This text is an introduction to the laws regulating sexual practices and offenses. Not only should you not copy the practices of others, teaches the Torah, but you must also follow the way that Gods shows you. □

Targum: English Translation
Leviticus 18:4-5

4) You should follow [only] my rules, so that you may be guided by them. I am *Adonai* your God. 5) *And you shall keep my laws and my decrees; a person shall observe them and live by them; I am* **Adonai.** □

From the Tradition

It is permitted to deviate from the truth only to establish peace (*Yevamot* 65b). □

Perush: Explaining the Teaching

Defective or *chaseir* writing refers to Hebrew written without the help of two "consonantal" vowels (either *vav* for *holem* or *yod* for *chirik*) when Hebrew is written without any vowels at all. Our teacher deduces his lesson by an irregularity of this Hebrew spelling and the juxtaposing two letters in the word for "truth," or *emet*. From this one learns that to live a life of Torah, one must live a life of holiness, searching for it always, wherever one is, whatever one does, to always be truthful with oneself and with others as well. □

Background There was once a peddler who arrived in Vilna one cold winter's night with his wagon loaded with merchandise. The people of the town were all fast asleep. The streets were desolate, cold and dark. Light shown from only one window. Nearly frozen from the cold, he entered this house and found the rabbi sitting busy in the words of Torah. The Gaon brought him food to eat and something warm to drink, and prepared a place for him to spend the night.

Then suddenly, with a burst of emotion, the peddler asked, "Rabbi, will I at least merit the world to come (will I at least find some ultimate meaning)?"

"You already have life in this world," asked the sage, "that you are asking about the world to come (Ultimate Meaning)!?"

"What is this world?" sighed the traveler, from the depths of his heart. "All week long I wander from one place to another. I have neither rest nor peace of mind. I don't even have enough free time to pray properly. I have only pressure, worry, exhaustion. For me, that is life in this world."

"If so," replied the rabbi, "if just staying alive in this world, for which you work so hard, looks that miserable, why do you look for ultimate meaning and fulfillment in the world to come—for which you do nothing!" □

(88) Kedoshim: Begin with Parents, End with *Shabbat*

The Teaching
from Chatam Sofer, Moses Sofer

What is the relationship here between revering parents and keeping *Shabbat*? An explanation may be found in *Leviticus Rabbah* 14:5, which reads: "King David said before the Holy One, 'Lord of the Universe, did my father, Jesse, have the intention of bringing me into being?' Wasn't his intention really just his own pleasure? And you know that this is so because after they had satisfied their desire, he turned his face in one direction and she turned her face in the other! . . . And this is what David meant when he said in Psalm 27:10, "Though my father and mother abandon me, the Lord will take me in." [Freud said that when it comes to our birth, chance rules our lives. We want to think that our parents said, "Now, let us cohabit and create the perfect human being!"]

"Though my father and mother abandon me" seems to imply here that their only function was the beginning of life; and "the Lord will take me in" implies that afterward one grows up and understands about God's plan.

Now *Shabbat* is the culmination of the work of creation. And if we were supposed to preoccupy ourselves only with the beginning, we would logically sanctify Sunday, since it is the first day of creation. But if this is so, it seems that commandments about *Shabbat* and honoring parents contradict one another. →

Scriptural Context

This portion contains what many regard as the loftiest chapter in the Book of Leviticus. The "holiness code" (*Kedoshim*) summons the Israelites to a life of holiness according to the specific set of articulated behaviors. □

Targum: English Translation
Leviticus 19:1-3

1) *Adonai* spoke to Moses thus 2) Speak to the entire Israelite community and tell them, "You will be holy [wholly different] because I, *Adonai*, your God, am holy. 3) *A person shall revere his mother and his father; My Sabbaths you shall keep.*" □

From the Tradition

The Ketev Sofer taught: Not only while you are supported by your parents, while they feed you from their table, clothe you, and satisfy all your needs are you obligated to honor them but even when you become "a person," no longer reliant on their nurture, an independent person on your own, even then, "a person shall revere his mother and his father." □

Perush: Explaining the Teaching

The theme of the Chatam Sofer's explanation is that the holiness of the goal (*Shabbat*) takes precedence over the holiness of the origins (honoring parents). The problem, therefore, is how to reconcile these somewhat conflicting biblical sequences, which according to our teachers are intentionally placed one after another to teach a lesson. Thus, we must both honor our parents and observe *Shabbat* in order to fulfill our obligations regarding the "importance of origins" and "the goal of creation."

Background Moses Sofer (1762–1839), also known as Chatam Sofer, was the leader of Orthodox Jewry. He founded a *yeshivah* in Pressburg, Hungary, where he served as rabbi from 1806 and remained the rest of his life. An ardent opponent of Reform Judaism and innovation of any sort, he exercised the talmudic instruction *"Chadash asur min Ha-Torah"* – any innovation is strictly forbidden. He was convinced of the perfection of the Jewish way of life in Germany and Poland toward the end of the eighteenth century. His ruling that the *Shulchan Aruch* (*Code of Jewish Law*) remain as the authoritative code won him great support throughout Europe. □

The Teaching (*continued*)

The explanation is that with the honoring of parents, we are commanded regarding revering the importance of origins, while with the keeping of *Shabbat*, we are commanded regarding the goal of creation. And for this reason we are commanded to both honor parents and keep *Shabbat*. □

(89) Kedoshim: Communal Holiness

The Teaching from Chatam Sofer

Rashi, citing *Midrash Sifra (Torat Kohanim)* and *Leviticus Rabbah* 24:5, observes that the apparently redundant phrase of "the whole congregation of" in our verse, teaches us that this *parashah* was uttered in the presence of the whole congregation.

This does not mean the hermit's holiness of isolation and seclusion as a means of seeking the holy way. On the contrary, what is spoken of is the holiness of the community, a holiness that springs precisely from being within a community, a congregation, mingling with other human beings. □

Perush: Explaining the Teaching

In this particular context, the Torah emphasizes the fact that Moses is to speak to the *entire* people of Israel. Like other teachers who have commented on this text, the Chatam Sofer wonders why there is an emphasis on the public nature of this particular instruction. Rashi argues that this entire Torah portion was uttered in the presence of the entire Israelite nation – perhaps because it formed the essence of *menschlichkeit* for the Jewish community. All needed to hear it because it focuses on the relationship one has with his or her neighbor.

But the Chatam Sofer sees more in the text. It is a warning against isolationism as a means of seeking the holy. There is holiness in the human family. The Jew, he would argue, seeks God in community, not in isolation. □

Scriptural Context

In this Torah portion, we reach perhaps the climax of the entire Book of Leviticus. It is also a section oft quoted in contemporary Jewish life, for it sets forth the pattern of behavior to be emulated for one to lead a holy life. Our text is taken from the central material, said to be spoken publicly because it contains so many laws basic to the "holiness" of the Jewish people. □

Targum: English Translation
Leviticus 19:1–2

1) *Adonai* **spoke thus to Moses: 2)** *Speak to the whole congregation of the Israelites and you shall say to them, "You shall be holy for I,* **Adonai***, am holy."* □

From the Tradition

Midrash Sifra, also known as *Sifra De-Vei Rav* or *Torat Kohanim*, is a halachic *midrash* to the Book of Leviticus. The term was used by the *amora'im* (rabbis of the Talmud) to refer to laws derived from the Book of Leviticus using exegesis of the text. The *Sifra* is a collection of various interpretations assembled by the editor. It follows the format of the biblical text, expounding the book of Leviticus chapter by chapter, verse by verse, even word by word.

Background The Baal Shem Tov taught that self-denial should only be practiced at the beginning of one's self-discipline, until the point when the *yetzer ha-ra* is subdued. Later one should live and work in community; otherwise one will become haughty and arrogant. □

(90) Kedoshim: Misusing Your Heart

The Teaching
from Otzar Ha-Machshavah

Rabbi Yechiel Meir of Gostynin once scolded two of his followers. They were trying to collect an appropriate sum of money for a charitable cause from some wealthy *chasidim* who had visited with him in Gostynin for a short time.

It seems there was among them, however, a wealthy Jew from Warsaw who only wanted to give a trifling sum. The matter so angered the two of them that they continued to argue over it, and so they recounted the whole matter to the rabbi.

Said Rabbi Yechiel Meir to them, "It is written, 'You shall not hate your brother in your heart. . . .

"If *Adonai* has graced you with a good heart, behold this is a gift God has given you. So, God forbid you should hate your brother on account of it [thinking to yourselves that you are better or more generous than him and that he] does not have a good heart like you. 'You shall not hate your brother *with* you heart.' " □

Scriptural Context

This Torah portion focuses on the holy separateness of the people of Israel. It delineates those laws that raise the daily behavior of the individual to holy proportion while maintaining a profoundly human quality. Our text is taken from a section that emphasizes the importance in maintaining a just relationship between individuals. □

Targum: English Translation
Leviticus 19:17–18

17) *You shall not hate your brother in your heart.* **Reprove your neighbor but do not incur any guilt because of him.** 18) **Do not take vengeance or bear a grudge against your neighbor. Love your neighbor as yourself. I am Adonai.** □

From the
Tradition

Yechiel Meir, a pupil of Menachem Mendl of Kotzk, had a reputation for holiness and was referred to, even in his youth, as one of the thirty-six *tzaddikim* (considered by tradition to sustain the world). He led a modest life, which gained him popularity among the common folk. Also known as *Der Tillim Yid* (the Psalm Jew), Yechiel Meir advised his people on the use and repetition of psalms as the most potent form of prayer. □

Perush: Explaining the Teaching

One of the many phrases from this section of Torah that has been absorbed into the language of Western culture, our teacher seeks an ethical lesson with subtle but deliberate misreading of the text that goes beyond the obvious. A story of Yechiel Meir is told regarding what might easily be an exchange today among synagogue or community fund-raisers. If God has given you a good heart, Yechiel Meir suggests, which prompts you to give generously to *tzedakah*, then don't use that same heart – the one God gave you – to hate your brother because you feel his charitable contribution does not measure up to yours. The text translates the pronoun *"in* your heart" to *"with* your heart." Perhaps, don't hate someone with a gift God has given you, that is, don't hate your brother with your gift. □

Background Gostynin is a town in central Poland whose Jewish population reached nearly 2,300 on the eve of World War II. Between the years 1823 and 1862 there were special residential quarters already established in the town for its Jewish residents. The old Jewish synagogue, once destroyed by fire, was rebuilt in 1899. It was built near the "valley of the dead," recalling the old Jewish cemetery nearby. The chasidic leader Yechiel Meir Lipscheutz lived in Gostynin in the late nineteenth century. □

(91) Emor: The Leader Is Blind

The Teaching
from Simchah Bunem of Przysucha

Leviticus Rabbah 26:7, end: Rabbi Joshua of Siknin said in the name of Rabbi Levi, the text teaches us that the Holy One showed Moses every generation and its judges, every generation and its kings, every generation and its sages, every generation and its leaders, every generation and its lieutenants, every generation and its officers, every generation and its philanthropists, every generation and its robbers, every generation and its prophets.

Why was it necessary to show Moses every generation together with its leaders? Or a generation together with its philanthropists? Wasn't it enough just to see the leaders and the philanthropists?

But had Moses seen that Simchah Bunem of Przysucha, who, in his later years was blind, was a leader of Israel, Moses would have been surprised and shocked. He would have cried out, "Is it possible [that a blind old man could lead Israel]!"

But when Moses saw the generation, he understood that for *Chasidim* like these even Simchah Bunem was able to be a rabbi and a leader. □

Scriptural Context

This section of the Torah details the Temple cult in its entirety. Here we find the focus on the priesthood, its role and rule. To ensure the efficacy of the sacrifice, rituals for the officiant had to be performed with the utmost care and precision. □

Targum: English Translation
Leviticus 21:1–4

1) *And* **Adonai** *told Moses, say to the priests, the sons of Aaron, and say to them:* **None [among you] shall defile himself by any [dead] person who is your kin.** 2) **Except for those relatives that are closest to him: mother, father, son, daughter, and brother,** 3) **also for an unbetrothed sister, alone to him because she is not married, for her, he may defile himself.** 4) **But he should not defile himself as a relative by marriage to defile himself.** □

From the Tradition

There is a sense that a leader can only lead where people are willing to follow. Said Rabbi Isaac: A public appointment is not made without first consulting the public, in accordance with the text, "See, *Adonai* has called by name" (*Berachot* 55a). □

Perush: Explaining the Teaching

Sensitive to the frailties of the human being, knowing that the priests should be as "perfect" as the sacrificial offerings, Simchah Bunem cites a story from the *Midrash* in which Moses was shown future generations with their leaders. Simchah Bunem was himself blind in his later years – even as he remained a leader of his *Chasidim*.

Leaders are really only functions of and relative to those who follow. Where there are no followers, there can be no leader. With such holy followers as were those of Simchah Bunem, even a blind *rebbe* could be a leader. And so it is that the blind may be flooded by light and still lead Israel. This passage is indeed intriguing because it reflects the teacher's own predicament so that a lesson might be drawn from his own life. In that way, as in so many other instances, our teachers and their lives become sacred texts in themselves. □

Background Leadership is important to the people of Israel. Leaders have the capacity to lead the Jewish people toward God or away from God. Thus, tradition (*Chagigah* 5a) teaches that over these does God weep daily: over the one who is able to study the Torah and does not; over the one who is unable to devote the time to Torah and study it; and over the public leader who is arrogant in his leadership. □

(92) Emor: Material Relations

The Teaching
from She'arit Menachem

We have a tradition in the name of Rabbi Menachem Mendl of Kotzk that he taught that the main idea was that the high priest should be separated and set apart from all material relations so that he may not feel any connection coming from the side of the his body. Indeed these matters are discussed in *Sefer Ha-Hinuch* (commandment 270).

"And the high priest is set apart" so that he can be a holy of holies. Despite his being [just an ordinary] physical person, nevertheless his soul should continually dwell with the angels on high, therefore they never permit him to become ritually defiled. He must remove himself completely from human nature and be one who erases from his heart all the cares of this decaying world.

From his great cleaving to God, the joining of his soul with heaven, therefore, the death of [even] a relative will not disturb his soul because already he has departed from them while he was still alive. □

Scriptural Context

This Torah portion celebrates the life of the priesthood, identifying laws that distinguish the role and lifestyle of the priest from those in the community. □

Targum: English Translation
Leviticus 21:10–12

10) *The priest who is exalted above his fellows, on whose head the anointing oil has been poured, and who has been ordained to wear the vestments, shall not bare his head or rend his vestments.* 11) *He shall not go in where there is any dead body; he shall not defile himself even for his father or mother.* 12) **He shall not go outside the sanctuary and profane the sanctuary of his God, for upon him is the anointing oil of his God, Mine,** *Adonai's.* □

From the Tradition

Sefer Ha-Hiunuch, a book of *mitzvah* education, uses the lens of the weekly Torah portion and the *mitzvot* explicit in each portion to teach the (intended) young student the system of *mitzvot*. Often, this text is studied by families on *Shabbat* afternoon. It was the product of a thirteenth-century Spanish Jewish environment. Spain was a major center for Jewish education in the Middle Ages. Maimonides' own *Sefer Ha-Mitzvot* dates back to this community only one century earlier. The most revealing text in all of *Sefer Ha-Hinuch* is "Talmud Torah is the mother of all *mitzvot*." □

Perush: Explaining the Teaching

Our teacher is fascinated by the separateness of the priest. Since even the relationship of one verse to another comes to teach us something, what is the relationship to the text of Leviticus 21:10 of the following verse? He suggests, relating a teaching from *Sefer Ha-Hinuch*, that the Kotzker contended the separation of the high priest was from all material matters, even those of the body, such as death. He further suggests that since the priest is a holy vessel, he must not be ritually defiled. This means that it, in fact, is impossible to ritually defile him since he is already separate from the material world – he is with the angels. Nothing can disturb the ritual purity of his soul, even the death of his relatives, since he has already left them (separate in his holiness) when they were still alive. □

Background To this day, it is customary to bury *kohanim* at the end of a row and to place a path several feet away from the grave so that priestly relatives may visit the grave without coming in close contact with the body. You will also find double doors in some hospital morgues so that descendants of priests may visit relatives and not come in contact with the dead and become thereby ritually defiled. □

(93) Emor: The Sixth Day of Creation was Sukkot

**The Teaching
from Kol Kol Yaakov, Yaakov
Hamburger**

"To make atonement for the first sin" (*Genesis Rabbah*) 2: 3)

"Which first sin is being spoken of here? In *Midrash Rabbah*, *Parashat Bereishit*, in the verse "And there was evening and there was morning, one day," meaning one that says "*echad*."

This is *Yom Ha-Kippurim*. Which is to say that the first day of the six days of Creation was Yom Kippur. This means, consequently, that the sixth day was the day on which *Adam Ha-Rishon*, the first human being, was created, and [therefore, also] the first day of Sukkot, and on that very day, according to the reasoning of the sages, Adam ate from the tree of knowledge. So therefore, "And on the first day you shall take the product of *hadar* trees (*etrogim*) . . . to make atonement for the first sin." □

Scriptural Context

This portion fixes times and seasons for Israelite celebrations. They establish for generations to come an opportunity to re-tell the events of the past so that they might be remembered into the future. □

Targum: English Translation
Leviticus 23:39–43

39) **On the fifteenth day of the seventh month, when you have gathered in the harvest of the earth, you shall observe a festival of *Adonai* for seven days. The first day will be a complete rest as will the last day.** 40) *And on the first day you shall take the product of hadar trees (etrogim)*, **branches of palm trees, boughs of leafy trees, and willows of the brook. You shall rejoice before *Adonai* your God for seven days.** 41) **You shall observe it for seven days each year as a festival of *Adonai* in the seventh month. It shall be a law for all time throughout the generations.** 42) **You shall live in *sukkot* for seven days; all Israelites shall live in booths,** 43) **so that future generations will know that I made the Israelite people live in booths when I brought them out of Egypt. I am *Adonai* your God.** □

**From the
Tradition**

Hoshanah Rabbah, or the great *Hoshanah*, is the name of the seventh and last day of Sukkot. It got this name because of the many *hoshanot* recited on this day and is known because of the beating of the willow branches. From the thirteenth century onward, it was believed that the verdict of the individual as passed on Yom Kippur is "sealed" on Hoshanah Rabbah. Our commentator Nachmanides felt that this was related to the notion that during the festival of Sukkot, the world is judged as to whether water would be received (*Rosh Ha-Shanah* 1:2). Water thus becomes a symbol for redemption. □

Perush: Explaining the Teaching

Our teacher draws a connection between Sukkot and Creation by calling our attention to the end of the verse as completed by *Midrash Rabbah*. The "first day" of our verse now also refers to the first day of Creation, Yom Kippur. And this then is the reason why one would take the *etrog*: to make atonement for the first sin, eating the forbidden fruit, which is unspecified in the Bible, and must therefore have been an *etrog*. Since we know that one uses the *etrog* on Sukkot, our teacher establishes a parallel between Sukkot and Creation and invests the festival with its own level of repentance. □

Background Kol Kol Yaakov is a collection of writings by Yaakov Hamburger (1826–1911). He was a German rabbi and scholar who served as rabbi in Neustadt near Pinne, Poland, and Mecklenburg-Strelitz in Russia. □

(94) Be-Har: Beginning with Trust

The Teaching
from Chatam Sofer

What does the Sabbatical year have to do with Mount Sinai? [In Hebrew, the juxtaposition of Mount Sinai with the Sabbatical year is considered a paradigm non sequitur, as, for example, in English, "But what does that have to do with the price of tea in China?"]

Rashi: Why does Scripture feel compelled to state specifically that this commandment of all the commandments was spoken on Mount Sinai? Were not all the commandments given at Sinai?

Why does Scripture specify that the Sabbatical year of all things was given on Sinai?

One possible answer is that this →

Scriptural Context

Both the Sabbatical year and the Jubilee year are discussed in detail and frame the essential aspects of this portion. They provide us with the idealism of the biblical period in terms of our ancestors' yearning to build a just and fair society. □

From the
Tradition

The Sabbatical year takes place every seven years. At the end of seven Sabbatical cycles, the Jubilee was to be observed. According to the Talmud, the Jubilee did not come on its own. The *bet din* (rabbinic court) had to officially proclaim it and sound the *shofar* at its commencement. Thus, it began on Rosh Ha-Shanah. □

Targum: English Translation
Leviticus 25:1-7

1) *And God spoke to Moses on Mount Sinai, saying:* 2) *Speak thus to the Israelites, "When you enter the land that I am giving you, the land shall observe a Sabbatical year of Adonai.* 3) Six years you may sow your field and for six years you may prune your vineyard and gather in the yield. 4) But in the seventh year the land shall have a Sabbath of complete rest, a Sabbath of Adonai: you shall not sow your field or prune your vineyard. 5) You shall not reap the aftergrowth of your harvest or gather the grapes of your untrimmed vines: it shall be a year of complete rest for the land. 6) But you may eat whatever the land produces during its Sabbath – you, your male and female slaves, the hired and bound laborers who live with you, 7) and your cattle and the beasts on your land may also eat all its yield." □

Perush: Explaining the Teaching

Here in this section of Torah text, Mount Sinai is specified as the location of the giving of the instruction Moses is to give to the people of Israel. In other cases, Mount Sinai is not mentioned. It is assumed that all of the commandments were given to Moses by God on Sinai. What is the text, therefore, trying to teach us? The Chatam Sofer quotes Rashi's somewhat rhetorical comment on this text. By asking the question, Rashi is stating the obvious. However, the Chatam Sofer argues that the mention of Mount Sinai in this context emphasizes that the Sabbatical year and the Jubilee year are both concepts from heaven. Since they are unusual, he maintains that human beings could not have derived them on their own. That had to come from God – therefore on Mount Sinai. □

Background While one might argue that the Torah text attempts an apologetic for slavery, emphasizing that the Sabbatical and Jubilee years provided for manumission, the operative text in regard to slavery is that from Deute-ronomy 15:15: "You should remember that you were a slave in the land of Egypt." But the Torah goes on to teach us, "You are now slaves of God who redeemed you from Egypt" (Leviticus 25:55). □

The Teaching (*continued*)

weekly Torah portion that deals with the Sabbatical year offers instruction regarding the Torah, which came from Heaven. How would it be possible for mere human beings to know for sure: "And I ordained my blessing for you in the sixth year so that it shall yield a crop sufficient for three years" (Leviticus 25:1). This is a matter surely beyond the natural order, and yet it is possible to trust its veracity. □

(95) Be-Har: Strangers on Earth

The Teaching
from Rabbi Baruch ben Jehiel of Medzibezh

Since "you are but strangers," the children of Israel should always regard themselves as only strangers in this world. And for this reason therefore they are "residents with Me." They are considered in the eyes of God as residents (of heaven).

In other words, the measure by which one feels oneself distant, alien, and strange in this world of lies, by that very measure does one feel close to heaven. And the opposite is also true. □

Perush: Explaining the Teaching

For Baruch of Medzibezh, reality is measured by one's proximity to heaven. All else (the material world, in particular) is illusion. The Sabbatical and Jubilee years were ordered to remind us of this principle. The further we are from the material world, claims our teacher, the closer we are to God. Thus, to be a "stranger" is a term of endearment, not of insult. To be a stranger on earth is to be a resident with God – and that is the goal of *teshuvah*, of return. □

Scriptural Context

Concentrating on the Sabbatical year and the Jubilee year, our text focuses on the impact of these laws on the land itself. □

Targum: English Translation
Leviticus 25:23–24

23) *But the land must not be sold beyond reclaim, for the land is Mine; you are but strangers, residents with Me.* 24) **Throughout the land that you hold, you must provide for the redemption of the land.** □

From the Tradition

The Sabbath of the Land is treated extensively in a tractate of the *Mishnah* and the Palestinian Talmud called *Shevi'it* or "seventh year." At one time, it may have had a practical application in order to let the land lie fallow. This prevented an exhaustion of the soil. It was meant to be a unique Sabbath for the land, unparalleled in the ancient Near East. Such a Sabbath of the land allows us to recognize who truly is the Owner of the land, namely, God.

All material possessions are limited by time. Thus, in Hebrew, we say "*yesh li*" ("there is to me" – for a limited time while it is in my possession) rather than "I have" or "I own." Only God *has*! □

Background Baruch ben Jehiel of Medzibezh (1757–1810) was the grandson of the Baal Shem Tov, Israel ben Eliezer, founder of modern Chasidism. While he officiated from 1780 to 1788 in Tulchin, he returned to Mezbezh after encountering opposition in the former city. Regarding himself as heir to chasidic leadership, he felt that the *tzaddik* could save and lead the entire world. He taught that the duty of the individual was to leave his evil impulses (*yetzer ha-ra*) and abandon his desires. While he preached asceticism, he himself maintained a luxurious lifestyle. □

(96) Be-Har: Buy Low, Sell High

The Teaching
from Ha-Derash ve'Haiyyun

[Noting a grammatical irregularity in the Hebrew, the commentator wonders] why is "sell" written in Hebrew in the plural [timkeru] but "buy from the hand of" is written in the singular [kanoh]? Why not just write it in the plural [tiknu]?

We have here an allusion to a law in the *Shulchan Aruch* (*Choshen Mishpat* 227:9): If the seller sells his merchandise cheaply because he is hard pressed, there is no issue of extortion, because the notion of extortion only applies in routine matters of business [not in such extreme circumstances].

But in regard to buying, there is always the possibility of extortion, even when a buyer does so due to pressure. [If someone needs to sell, that's →

Perush: Explaining the Teaching

As would be expected, our teacher

Targum: English Translation
Leviticus 25:13–17

13) **In this Jubilee year, each of you shall return to his holding.** 14) *When you sell [Hebrew, plural] property to your [Israelite] neighbor, or buy [Hebrew, singular] from [Hebrew, singular] your neighbor, you shall not extort one another.* 15) **In buying from your neighbor, you should deduct only for the number of years since the Jubilee; and in selling to you, he shall charge you only for the remaining crop years. 16) The more such years, the lower the price; for what he is selling you is a number of harvests. 17) Do not wrong one another, but fear *Adonai*. I am *Adonai*, your God.** ☐

Scriptural Context

The Sabbatical and the Jubilee years comprise the focal points of this Torah portion. In addition to allowing the land to lie fallow and the remissions of debts (called *shemitah* in Hebrew), the Sabbatical year also provides provisions for the manumission of slaves. Following every set of seven Sabbaticals, that is, the fiftieth year, a Jubilee is pronounced. This Jubilee includes provisions beyond the Sabbatical.

Relevant to the Jubilee, our text is taken from a section that concerns the return of property (held to fulfill a debt obligation) to its original owner. ☐

From the Tradition

In *Bava Metzia* 4:3, we are told that this principle applies to all transactions: we must not take unfair avantage of one another in business or in any dealings with our fellows. ☐

notes the irregularity of moving in the same text from plural to singular. Why not simply write it all in the plural?

Noting a text from the *Shulchan Aruch*, he suggests that these texts are related to one another because of the question of extortion and the distinction there (in the *Shulchan Aruch*) between buyer and seller. Thus, "do not wrong one another" (extortion) when the possibility of extortion exists. ☐

Background Joseph Caro compiled the *Shulchan Aruch* (literally, "the prepared table"), the Code of Jewish Law. It is similar in nature to Jacob ben Asher's *Arbaah Turim* (Four Rows). However, Caro is concerned with being concise without citing sources. The *Shulchan Aruch* may be described as a halachic synopsis of Caro's own *Turim*, called *Bet Yosef*. While it is based on the works of Maimonides, Isaac Alfasi, and Asher ben Jehiel, in cases of disagreement Caro offers the opinion of the two who are in agreement with each other.

It is divided into four major sections: 1) *Orach Chayyim*: daily *mitzvot*, *Shabbat*, and festivals; 2) *Yoreh De'ah*: various subjects such as dietary laws, monetary interest, ritual purity, and mourning practices; 3) *Even Ha-Ezer*: marriage and divorce; and 4) *Choshen Mishpat*: civil and criminal laws. The *Shulchan Aruch* was first printed in 1565 and today usually appears with glosses by Isserles and later commentaries. ☐

The Teaching (*continued*)

business. But if someone needs to buy, you cannot take advantage of his or her straits for that would be extortion.]

And just this is the allusion, "When you sell [Hebrew, plural] property to your neighbor," as with most sales, [whether or] not from pressure – "or buy [Hebrew, singular] from your neighbor," when this happens individually, even when the buyer is hard pressed to buy, "you shall not wrong one another." □

(97) Be-Chukotai: Learning to Do

The Teaching
from the Rabbi of Modzitz

Leviticus Rabbah 35:7 reads: "Rabbi Yochanan said, If one learns with the intention of not doing, it would have been better for him had the placenta been placed over his face and he had not come out into the air of this world."

Why give such a horrible curse for specifically this? The reason is given by our sages in *Niddah* 30b: "While the one to be born is still in the belly of its mother, they teach it the entire Torah, the whole thing. →

Perush: Explaining the Teaching

Our teacher faces the challenge of intellectualizing Judaism, that is, learning about it but not doing it. In order to drive home his point, he cites a text from the *Midrash* regarding Rabbi Yochanan's opinion about the creation of the human being. In order to mitigate this harsh teaching, the rabbi of Modzitz comes to teach us that in the womb a child is taught Torah only to forget the whole thing at birth. Why? In order to learn Torah to do Torah. Learning is for the sake of doing. From this we learn that our study of Torah shall direct us toward doing Torah. □

Targum: English Translation
Leviticus 26:3–5

3) *If you walk in My Laws and keep My commandments and do them,* 4) **I will [then] give you rain in the proper season and make the earth yield its produce and its trees bear fruit.** 5) **Your threshing [grain harvest] will [be abundant and] overtake the vintage [time] and your vintage [time] will overtake [and occupy you until] sowing [time]. You will eat your fill of bread and live securely in your land.** □

Scriptural Context

Some scholars argue that chapter 27 of Leviticus is really an appendix since it contains supplementary laws after the previous statutes and ordinances have been given some closure in chapter 26, from which our text has been taken. Thus, this portion (especially at its beginning) puts a kind of sacred imprimatur on the laws that preceded it. God tells us that if we observe that which has been commanded, we will be blessed. □

From the Tradition

An alternative interpretation from *Mishnat Yisrael*–Rashi: "If you walk in My statutes. . . ." You might think that this means doing the commandments, but then the text goes on to say, "and keep my commandments, and do them." But if doing the commandments is specified later, what does "walking in My statutes" mean here? It must be an allusion to the passage in *Midrash Sifra* that says, "You shall work hard in Torah."

Our revered rabbi and teacher, Rabbi David of Kotzk, interpreted the saying of our sages, their memory is a blessing, as recorded in *Megillah* 6b.

Rabbi Isaac said: If a person says to →

Background from *Mei-Otzar Ha-Chasidut*

A different understanding of the same text: According to the author of *Chiddushei Ha-Rim*, Isaac Meir Rothenberg Alter of Ger, each Jew was created to repair one special thing, which no one else can fix. This is the meaning of the teaching in *Pirke Avot* 1:14, "If I am not for myself, who will be for me. . . ."

Thus also at each hour there is a special thing that can be mended *only* then and which it would be impossible to repair at any other time.

This is the meaning of the next phrase in the teaching, "If not now when?"

Nevertheless, once a person has repaired each specific thing that it was intended for him to repair, still he must bring himself into the community of Israel. And this is why the teaching continues, "When I am only for myself, what am I?" because the basic idea is that a person lose awareness of himself and his service into the larger community of Israel. □

The Teaching (*continued*)
And at the moment it comes into the air of this world, an angel comes and slaps it on its mouth, whereupon the child forgets the whole thing!" But this makes no sense; why would they make an infant forget the Torah?

Perhaps it is because while in the belly of its mother the Torah learned by the child can have no possibility of being fulfilled or done. Obviously this is learning that is not for the purpose of doing, therefore, as soon as it comes into the air of this world they cause it to forget this primordial Torah to demonstrate that one who learns without the intention of doing does not really learn.

Only through being in the atmosphere of this "world of doing" can a human being begin anew to learn for the sake of keeping, doing, and fulfilling.

And this is the explanation for Rabbi Yochanan's strange saying that "if one learns with the intention of not doing, it would have been better for him had the placenta been placed over his face and he had not come out into the air of this world." It is because such learning—not for the sake of doing—was done while the child was in the belly of its mother. There would be no gain for the child to come out into the air of this world if it had not learned for the sake of doing. □

From the Tradition (*continued*)
you, I have labored and not found, do not believe him. If he says, I have not labored but still have found, you may believe him. If he says, I have labored and found, you may believe him. This is true with regard to gaining enlightenment in words of Torah, but with regard to business, all depends on the assistance of heaven. And even for words of Torah, this is true only of penetrating their meaning, but for remembering what one has learned, all depends on the assistance of heaven.

When the understanding of a bit of Torah comes to you after working at it, you may be sure that you have discovered its essence, that it has been fulfilled through you. But when Torah wisdom comes without struggle, don't believe that you have fulfilled its teaching. For as it came, so it will depart.

And this is the meaning of Shammai's teaching in *Pirke Avot* 1:15: "Make your study of Torah a fixed routine." Toil and struggle in the study of Torah, for in that way Torah will be permanent for you. □

(98) Be-Chukotai: Speaking of Pain

The Teaching from Mignazay Tzadikim

[It happened] during the days of the youth (עלומיו, alumav; literally, his hiding), of Rabbi Menachem Nachum of Chernobyl, when he was near the Baal Shem Tov. On the *Shabbat* when we read the תוכחה, the great scolding, which is euphemistically בלשון סני נהור (literally, "in language filled with light, or blind") referred to as the Sabbath of Blessing, he was called up to the Torah. At first he felt bad because they had assigned to him of all portions, this one!

Behold, the Baal Shem Tov himself was reading the Torah, and when he began the reading of the portion, Rabbi Menachem Nachum felt he was a person who knew the sick and the burden of different pains, because with the reading of each verse from the great scolding, the pain of another limb was sent away and departed. So it went from one limb to another, until by the completion of the reading of the *parashah*, his entire body was healed. □

Scriptural Context

Following the detailed listing of all of the laws and ordinances as stipulated by God, the text concludes with an appeal to obey these laws. If not, a terrible punishment, known in the tradition as *tochechah*, or reproof, will be delivered by God. □

From the Tradition

Rebuke is common in the relationship between individuals. The rabbis argued that we rebuke neighbors to confront them with personal grievances in the hope of getting them to change their ways. □

Targum: English Translation Leviticus 26:14-17

14) *If you do not obey Me and observe all these commandments,* 15) *if you reject My laws and spurn My statements, so that you do not observe My mitzvot and you break My covenant* 16) *I will then do this to you: I will wreak havoc on you— consumption and fever, which cause the eyes to burn and the body to suffer. You will sow your seed for naught and your enemies will eat of it.* 17) *I will turn My face against you. You shall be routed by your enemies and your foes shall overtake you. You will flee though you will have no pursuers.* □

Perush: Explaining the Teaching

This is a powerful text in which our teacher is relating a person's story of transformation as a way of explanation for the way the Israelites felt when chastised by God. Through hearing one's *rebbe* read of great misfortune, one can actually be healed from it. The *rebbe* is spiritually strong enough to take the pain upon himself without injury. This coupled with the notion of "speaking the fear," diminishes its power. This is the Divine power that Rabbi Menachem Nachum felt as the Baal Shem Tov read the words of Torah. □

Background A disciple of the Baal Shem Tov, Menachem Nachum settled in Chernobyl (in the Ukraine on the river Pripet) in the late eighteenth century. By founding a chasidic dynasty there, he made it a center of Chasidism. The Jews there suffered from pogroms, and the Soviet government destroyed religious life in the town. Yet as late as 1970 some 150 Jewish families lived there. □

(99) Be-Chukotai: The Cause of All Causes

The Teaching
from Rabbi Tzadok Ha-Kohen of Lublin

The foundation and the root of estrangement from God and the source of all sins comes from saying that God does not supervise creation and that everything is only due to chance, without reckoning, without purpose.

The author of *Degel Machaneh Ephraim* [Baruch ben Yechiel of Medzibezh] teaches concerning this verse that one who says that it is only an accident is ritually unclean, and if one says, concerning no matter what occurred, that it is only chance, such a one is unclean and his root is in defilement.

The first premise of faith is to believe with perfect faith that there is no such thing as chance. "And God alone →

Scriptural Context

This portion really acts as the conclusion of the Book of Leviticus, primarily because chapter 27 serves as an appendix to the entire book. *Tochechah*, retribution or rebuke, frames the central message of our text. □

Targum: English Translation
Leviticus 26:23-28

23) *And if these things fail to discipline you for Me, and you remain hostile to Me,* 24) *I too will remain hostile to you: I in turn will smite you sevenfold for your sins.* 25) **I will bring a sword against you to wreak vengeance for the convenant; and if you withdraw into your cities, I will send pestilence among you, and you shall be delivered into enemy hands.** 26) **When I break your staff of bread, ten women shall bake your bread in a single oven; they shall dole out your bread by weight and, though you eat, you shall not be satisfied.** 27) **But if, despite this, you disobey Me and remain hostile to Me,** 28) **I will act against you in wrathful hostility; I, for My part, will discipline you sevenfold for your sins.** □

From the Tradition

(1) The mystical tradition is personified by the personal prayers of individual *rebbes* who yearn for communion with God. In this well-known prayer Levi Yitzchak of Berditchev, known for his challenge of heaven (*chutzpah klappei malah*), seeks an intimate relationship with God: "Lord of the world, I do not beg You to reveal to me the secret of Your ways—I could not bear it! But show me one thing; show me what this,

Perush: Explaining the Teaching

God is the Source of all things in the universe. There are no accidents in the verse. God runs it all! When one feels estranged, distant from God, it is because that person does not acknowledge God's centrality in the world. To suggest anything else is considered hostile behavior, an affront to God; hence, the text "if you remain *hostile* to me." In response, God will wreak havoc; God will offer *tochechah*, "rebuke": "I will remain *hostile* to you." □

which is happening at this very moment, means to me, what it demands of me, what You, Lord of the world, are telling me by way of it. It is not why I suffer that I wish to know, but only whether I do so for Your sake."

(2) The powerful theme of rebuke (*tochechah* in Hebrew) is discussed by Jewish teachers throughout history. It is one area in which the biblical notion of God is epitomized. The covenant is wonderful. However, once you have accepted →

Background Rabbi Tzadok Ha-Kohen of Lublin (1823-1900) was a disciple of Mordechai Leiner of Izbica. He had a particular interest in the philosophy of history. While he illuminated *halachah* with mystical elements, his knowledge of *halachah* enriched his chasidic teachings. The author of numerous volumes, he is best known for his *Tzidkat Ha-Tzaddik.* □

The Teaching *(continued)*

did everything, just as God does everything and will do everything." Every detail, small or great, they are all from the Holy One.

And this is the meaning of "you remain hostile to Me," that is, that everything is just chance. Then, "I too will remain hostile to you." I will certainly hide my face from you; you will not see Me as the cause of all causes. And then there will be no one to whom you can turn in times of distress. □

From the Tradition *(continued)*

responsibility for its maintenance, you cannot simply walk away from it. It is yours to keep – forever. If you choose not to do so, you will indeed incur the wrath of a vengeful God. □

NUMBERS

(100) Be-Midbar: Places of Power

The Teaching
from Chiddushei Ha-Rim, Isaac Meir Rothenberg Alter of Ger

Parashat Be-Midbar is always read immediately preceding Shavuot. This is because we read in *Be-Midbar*, "each person under his banner" (Numbers 1:52), which is to say that each person will be in his proper place. And this is the reason for the commandment of "setting bounds" just prior to the giving of the Torah. □

Perush: Explaining the Teaching

While the complexities of the Hebrew calendar confound even the most schooled among us (there are twenty-nine different Hebrew years in relation to the Gregorian calendar), Isaac Meir Rothenberg of Ger, the founder of the Ger dynasty, is amazed that this portion always falls as the assigned weekly portion just prior to Shavuot, which celebrates receiving Torah at Sinai. Here the search for meaning transcends the text itself, and is found in the interface of the lectionary cycle and the calendar. As he examines a seemingly innocuous →

Scriptural Context

After fleeing Egyptian slavery, the Israelites are in the second year of their desert journey, on the road to Canaan. In this portion, God speaks to Moses in the *Ohel Mo'ed*, the wilderness Tent of Meeting. God asks him to take a census of the people, tribe by tribe, taking one representative from each tribe as an elected assembly. □

Targum: English Translation
Numbers 1:47–54

47) However, the Levites were not to be counted among them [the Israelites] according to their ancestral tribe. 48) *Adonai* had said to Moses: 49) "Do not count the tribe of Levi; do not take a census of them among the Israelites. 50) [Instead] you should put the Levites in charge of the *Mishkan* and all its furnishings and accoutrements. It is they who should tend to it, watch over it, and camp around it. 51) During the journey, the Levites will be responsible to take down the *Mishkan* and put it up; any outsider who encroaches upon it shall be put to death. 52) The Israelites should make camp in divisions, *each person under his banner.* 53) The Levites, however, will make camp around the *Mishkan* so that harm will not come to the Israelites; they [the Levites] will guard the *Mishkan.*" 54) The Israelites did just what *Adonai* had instructed Moses; they did it [all]. □

From the Tradition

From *Divrei Yechezkel*: It is possible to say that another reason why our sages set the reading of *Parashat Be-Midbar* just before Shavuot is found in Rashi. He says that on account of God's love, God counted them all every hour (Rashi on Numbers 1:1). The Rambam comments on this verse, "God brought them out according to the number of their hosts, God called all of them by name." This is because the name of everything contains its essence and the innermost root of the thing. Therefore, because Israel is Holy, they prepared themselves for the chosen place, they needed to bind themselves in the place of their →

Background Israel Meir Rothenberg (Alter), 1787–1866, was the founder of the Ger dynasty. His father, Rabbi Israel, was a disciple of Levi Yitzchak of Berditchev and rabbi of Ger. A disciple of Simchah Bunem of Przysucha and Menachem Mendl of Kotzk, he became the acknowledged leader of the Kotzker *chasidim* following Menachem Mendl's death in 1859. His work, *Chiddushei Ha-Rim* (1875), from which this selection is taken, as well as his brief works on several tractates of Talmud and the *Shulchan Aruch*, became basic study texts and remain classics to this day. □

Perush: Explaining the Teaching (*continued*)

phase, he reasons that we have to be standing where we are supposed to be before the Torah will be given to us. If we try to be somebody else (and therefore be someplace else), the truth of Torah will only elude us. The process of receiving Torah, although epitomized by Matan Torah, is lifelong. In this sense, for the Gerer *rebbe*, the giving of Torah becomes the ultimate expression of knowing who we are. The minute we are who we are, we are able to be changed and grow. What keeps us from realizing ourselves is trying to be someone whom we are not. Somehow, as we grow up, we are contaminated by outside influences as to who we should be and what makes us happy. What we must do, therefore, is find out who we are, keep telling ourselves the truth. The source of our individuality is what we share with everyone else. God is that source. God is the only one who can give us the clue as to who we really are – for God created us. When we fulfill our obligations as Jews, we are able to know who we are. ☐

From the Tradition (*continued*)

origin – with the names of their holy tribes and the princes of Israel, the righteous of the generation, and only afterward would they be able to attain the goal of receiving the Torah. ☐

(101) Be-Midbar: *Tzaddik* Drinking Coffee

The Teaching
from Otzar Ha-Machshavah shel Ha-Chasidut

The author of *Degel Machaneh Ephraim* said, in the name of the Baal Shem Tov, that sometimes a *chasid* comes to the *tzaddik* in order to learn by watching how the *tzaddik* behaves. But the *tzaddik* is in a state of spiritual smallness. The *chasid* copies this way of being from his master without realizing that he must know when to exercise caution to protect his soul.

In this way it happened once that a *chasid* came to Rabbi Nachman of Bratzlav and saw him drinking coffee while he was dressed in his *tallit* and *tefillin*. The *chasid* returned home and began to do the same thing!

Our verse hints at just such a warning. "But let not [the Kohathites] go inside and see. . . ." means that they should not come to the *tzaddik* in order to see how the *tzaddik* behaves →

Perush: Explaining the Teaching

For the individual Jew, the *rebbe*, his *rebbe*, embodies Torah. As a result when we are in the *rebbe*'s presence, we are inspired. Because we may not have yet attained the level of spiritual greatness as has the *tzaddik*, however, if we naively copy everything the *tzaddik* does, we may injure ourselves. Even *rebbe* enter states of spiritual smallness, behaving inappropriately – drinking coffee while still wrapped in *tallit* and *tefillin*. At such times, the *tzaddik*'s spirituality is small, or "covered up," and we may fall from whatever level of spirituality we have achieved and symbolically die. Thus, our teacher reasons from this verse that we must allow our *rebbe* privacy and permission to tell us when it is "safe" to learn by emulation. □

Scriptural Context

The census of individual tribes has been taken and the responsibilities of the Levites have been outlined. All tribes are directed where to camp, each under his tribal standard. Finally, the assignments of divine service are made and an additional census is taken related to service in the Tabernacle. The section from which this comment is taken focuses on the separate census taken of the Kohathites, from among the Levites [Kohath was a son of Levi]. They had the responsibility of caring for the most sacred of the objects. □

From the Tradition

Traditionally, there are three classes of Jews: the priestly *Kohen*, the assistant priest or Levite, and the masses, the Israelites. While most liberal Jews reject this class distinction, it has survived the destruction of the Second Temple in various customs and observances, particularly regarding the order in which individuals read the Torah (priest, Levite, then Israelite).

Targum: English Translation
Numbers 4:17–20

17) **Adonai spoke to Moses and Aaron thus: 18) Do not let the Kohathites be cut off from the [rest of the] Levites. 19) (Instead) do thus with them to make sure that they will live and not die when they approach the sacred objects: Aaron and his sons should go in and assign a task to each one [of the Kohathites], 20)** *because they [the Kohathites] should not go inside and see the holy things as they are being covered and die* [as a result]. □

Background From *Bet Aharon*: Each person in Israel is obligated to know and consider that he is unique in the world. There has never been another like him, for if there were another like him, then there would be no need for him to exist. Indeed, each person is an utterly new thing in creation. Each person needs to realize this uniqueness and his Torah – which depends on his soul, and whereby the world will be repaired. □

The Teaching *(continued)*

and naively act the same way. "And . . . see when the holy things are covered . . ." means that it may be that the *tzaddik* is in a state of spiritual smallness, because the holiness has been covered and is concealed. " . . . lest they die" means that the people might then fall from whatever spiritual levels they had attained.

For this reason a person needs to be especially prudent to learn only during times of spiritual greatness. ☐

(102) Be-Midbar: The Place of the Tabernacle

The Teaching from Or Ha-Chayyim

When Scripture mentions the place, it says first, "in the wilderness of Sinai"; it employs a general expression. Afterward it says "in the Tent of Meeting," an expression of precise detail.

In contrast to this, when it mentions the date, first it says the specific, "on the first day of the second month," and afterward the general, "in the second year after they had gone forth." What is going on here?

The explanation may be that indeed even with regard to the place, the specific is mentioned first and afterward the general!

Our sages have taught with regard to the verse in Exodus 33:21, when God is speaking to Moses, "Behold, there is a place with Me." This means that "the Place" of God is attached to God. God is the very Place of the world but the world is not the →

Scriptural Context

The Israelites have left Egypt and are thirteen months into the forty-year transformative desert journey that will forge them from an enslaved multitude into a free people, ready to direct its own destiny – in covenant with the Almighty. □

Targum: English Translation
Numbers 1:1-4

1) **Adonai** *spoke thus to Moses in the wilderness of Sinai in the Tent of Meeting on the first day of the second month in the second year after they had gone forth out of Egypt:* 2) **Take a census of the entire Israelite community by the clans of the ancestral houses, listing the names of every male, head by head.** 3) **You and Aaron shall record them by their groups, from the age of twenty years up, all those in Israel who are able to bear arms.** 4) **Associated with you shall be a man from each tribe, each the head of his ancestral house.** □

From the Tradition

The oldest name for this book of the Torah is "The Fifth of the Musterings" (*Chumash Ha-Peku-dim*) because it begins with the fifth census that Moses takes of the people. Later, it came to be known by the fourth word in the opening line of the Hebrew "*Be-Midbar*," "In the Wilderness." This name provides a locus of time and place to what happened to the Israelites during thirty-eight of their forty years in the desert. The name Numbers itself comes to English through the Greek translation of the Torah known as the Septuagint. □

Perush: Explaining the Teaching

Our teacher takes note of the way the Torah distinguishes between the general and the particular. In the beginning of the phrase, the text speaks generally in the wilderness of Sinai and then specifically in the Tent of Meeting. Yet, in referring to the date of this encounter, the text starts out specifically by saying, "on the first day of the second month." The Or Ha-Chayyim teaches that there really is not a disparity in the way the Torah speaks. Both in fact (place and time) go from specific to general. In the case of the date, it is obvious. In regard to the place, while not so obvious, an elegant theological explanation is offered. Borrowing an understanding from Exodus 33:2, our teacher reasons that God is the place of the world but the world is not the place of God. Thus, the Tent of Meeting, that is, "God's Place," is the general place of the whole world whereas even the vastness of Sinai is merely a local particularity. □

Background Chasidic tradition suggests that Torah was given in the wilderness of Sinai rather than anyplace else specifically because it was such a wasteland. From the depths of their desert experience, the Jewish people could take their Torah to the lowliest on earth and together raise them to spiritual heights. □

The Teaching *(continued)*

place of God (*Genesis Rabbah* 68:9). Thus we understand that the Tent of Meeting is the general place of all the world, while the whole wilderness of Sinai is but a local particularity. □

(103) Naso: All from God

The Teaching
from *Akeidah*

The matter of the priestly benediction raises many fascinating questions. First of all, what is the benefit of this commandment [to Aaron and his sons], that the priests should bless the people, doesn't God do that already; what can the priest add? And then what is the meaning of "And they shall set My Name on the Israelites?" What is meant by this "setting" and what is its benefit? And finally, what is the meaning of "and I shall bless them?"

All of these questions can be explained thus: The foundation of faith is that a person know that everything, the good things, the successes, and all the bad occurrences and the good ones, in general and in specific, flow from the Holy One (even the Name is blessed). There is no event and no one can say, "By my strength and by my power alone has this come to pass."

Scriptural Context

In this portion, the laws of holiness are explained to the people. Immediately preceding our selection is the description of the Nazirite, who has pledged certain abstinences for himself for religious purposes. Our selection contains the well-known threefold priestly benediction. □

Targum: English Translation
Numbers 6:22–27

22) *Adonai* spoke to Moses thus: 23) *Speak to Aaron and his sons. Tell them thus: you shall bless the Israelites.* Say to them 24) *May* Adonai *bless you* and keep you. 25) *May* Adonai *cause Divine light to shine on you* and be gracious to you. 26) *May* Adonai *lift Divine countenance on you* and give you peace. 27) *So they shall put My Name on the Israelites and I will bless them.* □

From the Tradition

Duchan(an), which literally means "(elevated) platforms," is a term used to describe the place where the Levites sang in the Temple, the place where the priests stood and offered their priestly blessing over the people, and the place and ritual regarding the blessing of the congregation in the synagogue by the descendants of the priesthood. It also refers to the platform where teachers sat while teaching children. □

And the priests, precisely because they are the instruments of God's compassion, need to demonstrate to the people that everything is from God, "May *Adonai* bless you; may *Adonai* cause Divine Light to shine on you; may *Adonai* lift His Divine countenance upon you," because the blessings and the lights, the favors and the tribulations, they are all from God. →

Perush: Explaining the Teaching

Our teacher is puzzled by the peculiar instructions that God offers the Israelites through the agency of Moses and Aaron. He reasons that God wants to impress upon the Israelites the insight that everything flows from God, the Source of all Being. The commentator argues that there must be a reason for everything, since beyond the mystery of the Divine lies only meaninglessness and suicide. □

Background *Akeidat Yitzchak*, or the *Akeidah*, whose name is taken from the Binding of Isaac in Genesis 22, was written by Isaac ben Moses Arama (ca. 1420–1484), a Spanish philosopher, rabbi, and preacher. While his work is not sys- tematic and is written in the form of scriptural homilies, it greatly influenced Jewish thought. He had a particular knack for integrating the metaphysical problems of his day within a lit- erary framework. □

The Teaching *(continued)*

"So they shall set My Name on the Israelites," they shall impress the seal of God on the Israelites, on their way of life, their meditation, and on their occupation. And thereby, they shall come to recognize that everything is "My Name," except for the actual blessing itself, "and I will bless them." □

(104) Naso: The Name of Love

The Teaching from Rabbi Judah Loew ben Bezalel of Prague

From this we conclude that the Torah gives permission to erase God's Name, because by means of this erasure, peace is created between husband and wife. And between husband and wife dwells the presence of God. But this is no expulsion of God's presence; on the contrary, it is an invitation to the Divine presence. Indeed, "peace" is another name for the Holy One, so there is no expulsion here, only changing God's Name into another form. □

Perush: Explaining the Teaching

Puzzled by the permission the Torah gives to even the priest, our teacher searches out the peculiar *sotah* water ritual for meaning for our time. *Shalom bayit*, a peaceful home (good relations between husband and wife), is so important that the Name of God is →

Targum: English Translation Numbers 5:16–23

16) The priest should bring her forward to stand before *Adonai*. 17) Thus the priest should take consecrated water in an earthen vessel; taking some of the soil that is on the floor of the Tabernacle, the priest should put it in the water. 18) After the priest has made the woman stand before *Adonai*, the priest should uncover the woman's head and place in her [cupped] hands the meal offering of remembrance, which is the meal offering of jealousy, while in the priest's hands should be the bitter waters that induce the spell. 19) The priest should adjure the woman and say unto the woman, "If no man has slept with you, if you have not gone astray in defilement while married to your husband, be immune to these bitter waters that induce the spell. 20) But if you have gone astray while married to your husband, and have defiled yourself, if a man other than your husband has slept with you—" 21) Here the priest administers to the woman the curse of adjudication and further says to the woman—"May *Adonai* make you a curse among your people so that *Adonai* makes your thigh [sexual organs] sag and your belly distend. 22) May this water that induces the spell enter your body and cause your belly to distend and your thigh to sag." And the woman shall respond, "Amen, amen." 23) *And the priest shall write these curses in a book and rub it off under the water of bitterness.* □

Scriptural Context

This portion contains laws of holiness that do not appear to have much to do with one another. They include the exclusion from camp of ritually unclean individuals and priests who receive offerings from robbers who have confessed of their crimes. Our text is taken from the procedure that is to be followed when a woman is accused of adultery by her husband. All of these requirements share in common a recognition of the presence of God and thereby a demand to the community to be pure and holy. □

From the Tradition

From Aharet Torah: According to *Midrash Sifrei*, "In order to make peace between a husband and a wife, God says, a book written in holiness will be rubbed out into water."

In the morning version, the *Shemoneh Esrei* concludes with the →

Background Judah Loew ben Bezalel was also known as the Maharal (c. 1525–1609). Before going to Prague, he was *Landesrabbiner* of Moravia in Mikulou from 1553 to 1573. He remained in Prague until 1588 when he went to Moravia and then back to Prague. In the year 1592, he went to Posen to become chief rabbi before returning once again to Prague where →

Perush: Explaining the Teaching *(continued)*

allowed to be erased. Why? Because we know that God dwells in the relationship of husband and wife. [The *Midrash* teaches: no man without woman. No woman without man. And neither without the *Shechinah*.] So the Torah is really not permitting God's Name to be erased; it is merely encouraging the changing of God's Name to another form. □

From the Tradition *(continued)*

prayer for peace that begins, "*Sim shalom*, Grant peace," whereas in the evening liturgy, the concluding prayer for peace commences, "*Shalom rav*, Great peace." Why?

If during the daytime while a person is at work with many different people he needs to pray for peace one way, how much the more so, by evening when he returns home, does he need to pray for "*shalom rav*, great peace." This is because even the slightest matter could overturn the peace of the house. □

Background *(continued)*

he remained until his death. Known for his great scholarship, he also dabbled in alchemy. Legend attributes to him the creation of a Golem, a lump of clay brought to life by inscribing the Name of God on its forehead. □

(105) Naso: By the Grace of God

The Teaching

from *Akeidah* from *Degel Machaneh Ephraim*:

Rashi: [Citing a *midrash* in Sifre] suggests that "be gracious" means "And God will give you favor."

According to our sages, in *Numbers Rabbah* 11:6, after the Israelites (according to the preceding phrase) have already been blessed with the light of Torah and the light of the Divine Presence, what further "good favor" could they possibly need?

One explanation may be according to what is written in the commentary *Or Ha-Chayyim* on Genesis 39:21, "*Adonai* was with Joseph; God extended kindness to him and the chief jailer was *gracious* to him." In other words, the grace with which a person is blessed is a supernal kindness, for it is private and exclusive and beyond one's own power, nor is any person capable or fit to understand this special treasure of grace.

Now it happens sometimes that the spiritual being and character of another person is the opposite of the one who →

Scriptural Context

This section of the Torah portion focuses on the priestly benediction, the pinnacle of the Temple cult and its celebration. It helps to establish the authority of the priesthood and the centrality of the Temple. Focusing on the priests and their holy service, our text is taken from the priestly benediction, used to bless the people. □

Targum: English Translation
Numbers 6:22–27

22) ***Adonai*** **spoke to Moses:** 23) **"Speak to Aaron and to his sons saying, 'Thus you shall bless the Israelites.' Say to them** 24) **'May *Adonai* bless you and keep you.** 25) *May* Adonai *make divine light shine on you and be gracious to you.* 26) **May *Adonai* turn to you and give you peace.** 27) **And they shall set My Name on the Israelites, and I will bless you.'** " □

From the Tradition

According to the idiom of the Bible, a king shows his subjects favor by giving them an audience ("light of his face") and smiling at his subjects ("to lift one's face"). But this king offers his subjects not merely the simple absence of hostility but full contentment, that is, peace. The priestly benediction was part of the priestly cult and has been translated to the synagogue in the form of *duchanan*, ("to deliver the priestly blessing") the Yiddish expression pronounced with their hands uplifted. In response, the congregation responds: "Praised be *Adonai, Eloheinu*, the God of Israel, to all eternity" (*Sotah* 40b). □

Perush: Explaining the Teaching

This text appears to be redundant or, at least, in descending order of importance. If God has shone Divine light on you, then why would God also need to be gracious unto you. Divine light should be quite enough. Our teacher begins to explain this textual problem by first citing a teaching of Rashi. But Rashi seems only to make the question more difficult. Good favor seems less significant than "be gracious." Yet, our teacher explains that this grace – like the kind extended to Joseph in the dungeon – is supernal, beyond the kind that an individual is capable of understanding. To understand the kind of grace offered in this blessing is to understand the special kind of grace historically bestowed on Israel throughout its wanderings. □

Background In the *Kabbalah*, the mystics emphasized the unfathomable nature of God by applying such names as "the hidden of hidden" *temira de-temirin* and the "ancient of ancients," *atika de-atikin*. From the phrase in Proverbs 30:4, "What (*mah*) is His Name," they determine that God's name has forty-five letters in it, the numerical equivalent of the Hebrew word *mah*. □

The Teaching (*continued*)

has [been given this supernal] grace; then there is a high mountain between them and they do not understand one another.

Grace is [such a subtle] matter of taste. For each person has his or her own taste, and there needs to enter into the heart of the chief jailer a special perspective in order that he understand "the grace" of Joseph. [The grace that God gives with the priestly blessing is allowing others – who may have profoundly different dispositions – to see that Israel has grace.]

And just this is the meaning of "be gracious unto you," that others would understand the very special grace that has been bestowed upon Israel. □

(106) Be-Haalotecha: Craving a Craving

The Teaching
from the Sefas Emes, Yehudah Aryeh Leib of Ger

Rashi: If only we had meat . . ." Didn't they already have meat? Hasn't it already been said [in Exodus 12:38], "Moreover a mixed multitude went up with them, and very much livestock, both flocks and herds"? And if you say, "But they already had eaten them,"

I can reply, is it not also stated [in Numbers 32:1, at a later period that] "the Reubenites and the Gadites owned cattle in a very great number . . . ." [The explanation therefore must be →

Perush: Explaining the Teaching

In this text, our teacher sees the individual who is constantly looking for the opportunity to prove to God how worthy he is. This individual even goes so far as to set artificial temptations and tests for himself to prove himself so righteous that he can overcome even the temptations and tests he has set before him. The Sefas Emes teaches us that God is not really interested in such self-induced aggrandizement. Thus, the Israelites, that is, the riffraff among them, wanted most to show God how they could withstand the temptations. Simply serve God and stop playing games, teaches the Sefas Emes. □

Scriptural Context

At this point in the narrative, the Torah changes its focus and spends about ten chapters on the desert sojourn. The theme of rebellion is constant, and here, in our text in particular, the people are dissatisfied and bored. This eventually leads Moses to realize that he needs help in leading the people. □

Targum: English Translation
Numbers 11:1-6

1) **The people bitterly complained to *Adonai*. *Adonai* heard and was angry. A fire of *Adonai* broke out and ravaged the outskirts of the camp. 2) So the people cried out to Moses and Moses prayed to *Adonai* and the fire died down. 3) That place was called Taverah because the fire of *Adonai* had broken out against them. 4)** *The riffraff in their midst felt a gluttonous craving; and then the Israelites wept and said, "If only we had meat to eat!"* **5) We remember the fish we ate freely in Egypt, the cucumbers, the melons, the leeks, the onions, and the garlic. 6) Now our bodies are wasting, there is nothing at all [to eat] except this manna to stare at.** □

From the Tradition

You caused the east wind to set forth in heaven. And by your power You brought on the south wind. You caused flesh to rain upon them like dust. And winged fowl as the sand of the seas. And you let it fall in the midst of their camp. Near their dwellings, So they ate and were satiated. And You gave them exactly what they craved. They had not distanced themselves from Your cravings. Their food was still in their mouths. When the anger of God went up against them. And slew the lustiest among them. And smote the young men and women of Israel.

Psalm 78:21-23 □

Background Ger Chasidism placed Torah and its study at the center of spiritual life. While its form takes its direction primarily from Jacob Isaac of Przysucha and Menachem Mendl of Kotzk (and the philosophy of Judah Loew ben Bezalel of Prague–the Maharal), the principal part as established by Isaac Meir diverged radically. Instead of withdrawing (like Menachem Mendl), its leaders were heavily involved with the day-to-day problems of the people. It was similar to the Kotzk approach in that it emphasized profundity in the pursuit of truth. The work of the Sefas Emes was known for its lucidity and clear exposition of text, in contrast to the *pilpul* method of his grandfather (Isaac Meir). □

179

The Teaching (continued)

that] they were seeking an excuse. . . ." (Midrash Sifrei).

Sefas Emes: Just before [our text] it is written, "התאוו תאוה, hitavu taavah, literally, 'and they craved a craving.' " Indeed, Israel did not crave meat, for [after Sinai] they were already free from the evil impulse. Rather, they craved a craving, they yearned to have a [physical, bodily] craving.

It seemed to them that it would be preferable to come under the power of craving meat and [be able to demonstrate] that they could withstand the temptation, and that they could eat the meat in holiness and purity, and thereby bring pleasure to God.

But their way was not proper in God's eyes, for no person needs to make a test for himself, even if by means of this, he merits to attain a very high rung. For this way [of self-contrived testing necessarily] involves conniving [deception] and self-importance [self-injury, arrogance].

A person who indeed loves God is more satisfied when he is simply [able to] serve – without [any] mental games of craving and temptation. □

(107) Be-Haalotecha: Secretly Following Orders

The Teaching
from Menachem Mendl of Kotzk

Rashi: To make known the praise of Aaron; he did as he was commanded without making any change.

One could not discern in the holy service of Aaron any outward fluctuation or modification.

This was a matter of the innermost heart.

All the great things have as their central idea something that is hidden and concealed in the heart – with no outward manifestation whatsoever! □

Scriptural Context

Our portion first describes the lighting of the golden candlestick in the Tabernacle and then focuses on those who serve there, the Levites and their responsibilities. □

Targum: English Translation
Numbers 8:1–3

1) *Adonai* **spoke thus to Moses: 2) Speak to Aaron and say to him, "When you mount the lamps, let the seven lamps give light at the front of the lampstand."** 3) **Aaron** *did so; he mounted the lamps at the front of the menorah, as* **Adonai** *had commanded Moses.* □

From the Tradition

The Gerer *rebbe* taught: "The central desire of a worthy person should be to receive the ability to serve God without thought of a reward. If one prays for this wholeheartedly, he may be assured that he will be granted all necessities as well, the lack of which would prevent his service from being pure. □

Perush: Explaining the Teaching

In a manner most typical of our teacher, Menachem Mendl of Kotzk, he sees a profound message in what appears to be a straightforward text. God tells Moses what to tell Aaron to do. Moses then tells Aaron what to do, according to what God had told him. And Aaron does what he had been told to do by God through Moses. According to Menachem Mendl, when one does precisely what is asked of him – in service to God – it is done with a full commitment of heart. This was what made Aaron fitting for the holy service of the priesthood. It is only when one "creatively" modifies the *mitzvah* that there is doubt as to the "*mitzvah* doer's" intention. □

Background Rabbi Nachman of Bratzlav said: "The one who influences others for good erects a Holy Temple to God and builds an altar upon which is offered to God the goodness which he has awakened." He also said: "Even though your fellow human being may not pay attention to you, you will have benefitted yourself. By reproving others, your own higher impulses are awakened more than by the effort of self-admonition." □

(108) Be-Haalotecha: This Light Is Forever

The Teaching
from She'arit Menachem

Rashi: Why is the section about lighting the *menorah* next to the section about the Tabernacle dedication offerings of the princes of Israel [which concludes the preceding *parashah, Naso*]? Because when Aaron saw the dedication offerings, he became troubled that neither he nor his tribe were listed among those giving gifts. But God said to him, "By your life! You are greater than all of them for you will get to prepare and kindle the *menorah!*"

Nachmanides, in his commentary on the Torah, raises a similar problem. Why did God comfort Aaron with the kindling of the lights and not with offering incense or with all the sacrificial offerings and priestly services of Yom Kippur and the light that could not be religiously acceptable unless performed by a priest? →

Scriptural Context

Our text is taken from the beginning of the Torah portion that focuses on the Levites and their status in the hierarchy of service in the tabernacle. □

Targum: English Translation
Numbers 8:1–3

1) *Adonai* **spoke thus to Moses: 2)** *Speak to Aaron and say to him, when you set up the lights, seven lamps shall give light in front of the menorah.* **3) Aaron did so; he mounted the lamps at the front of the lampstand, as** *Adonai* **had commanded Moses.**

From the Tradition

Judah Tzvi Stretiner instructs us: "Within each individual Jew is an element of the Messiah, which the individual is required to purify and mature. The Messiah will come when Israel has brought *mishichut* (messiah-ness) to the perfection of growth and purity within themselves. □

Perush: Explaining the Teaching

Light, one of the symbols of redemption, becomes the salient element of our teacher's lesson. He builds his argument very carefully. First, he ascertains the relationship between the themes in the Torah portion, noting Rashi's view of the relationship between the dedication of the princes of Israel and the lighting of the *menorah*. Aaron is troubled that he and his tribe are not among the gift givers. God comforts Aaron, telling him, in essence, that his life of service is indeed a gift.

Nachmanides sees a similar problem. While acknowledging that God comforted Aaron in this way – by allowing him to kindle the *menorah* – he wonders why this means of holy service was chosen over the other possibilities. Citing various rabbinic *midrashim*, Nachmanides notes that in this act God is anticipating the future. The Temple sacrifices (which could have been one of the means of holy service chosen) would end when the Temple was eventually destroyed. Yet, the lights of the Menorah will always need to be kindled. →

Background The students and followers of a chasidic *rebbe* approached their spiritual leader with a complaint about what they perceived as an increase in the amount of evil in the world. They asked their teacher to guide them, to help them to drive the forces of darkness from the world. The rabbi suggested that they take brooms and try to sweep the darkness from the basement. They did as they were told – but their efforts came to naught. Then they were told to take sticks and beat vigorously at the darkness. Again, they followed their teacher's guidance. Again, they failed. Next, they were told to go back down to the basement and shout against the darkness, vociferously urging it to leave. When this, too, failed, the *rebbe* said, "Let each one take a candle and light it against the darkness." They went down to the basement, each with his lit candle and beheld that indeed the darkness had been driven out. □

182

The Teaching (*continued*)

He comes to his conclusion on the basis of various *midrashim*. The intention was to anticipate the dedication (Chanukah) of the Hasmoneans and their descendants in the Second Temple. From the seed of Aaron, it would be established, even after the destruction of the First Temple. And in *Numbers Rabbah* we read that the Holy One said to Moses, "Go, say to Aaron, 'Don't be afraid. You are destined for something greater than this. The sacrifices will be offered all the time that the Temple is in existence. But the lights will shine forever!' "

We can also say that Aaron was anxious that the princes merited participation in the dedication of the Tabernacle, according to the interpretation of Rashi, because the princes of Israel had endured Egyptian oppression, whereas he and his tribe had not. The tribe of Levi was not included in the bondage, and Aaron feared that on account of this they were not worthy to be included in the dedication ceremonies.

The Holy One said to him, "They have given their lives and their blood in exile and no trace remains of anything that was, and no one offers praise for a miracle that happened outside of the Land of Israel. But you are greater than all of them, for you will prepare and kindle the lights. You will kindle the light of Israel. You and your tribe will face the head of the rebellion and you will declare who is for God. [Perhaps this an allusion to the Korach rebellion.] And through your power the Kingdom of Israel will be readied and rebuilt. And just this will serve as an eternal symbol; it will last forever. □

Perush: Explaining the Teaching (*continued*)

Aaron was still worried. He and his tribe had not endured Egyptian slavery. He was fearful that he was therefore not worthy of redemption. Again, God told him not to fear, for although the Israelites endured the bitterness of slavery in Egypt, they were in exile outside of the Land of Israel. The light for which Aaron is responsible is Israel's light (from the Land to the rest of the world). These lights will usher in *"meshiach-zeit"* (the time of the Messiah) and actually a symbol of hope and promise for that time to come. What loftier responsibility could Aaron have hoped for? □

(109) Shelach Lecha: Women Who Love the Land

The Teaching
from Ephraim Solomon ben Aaron of Luntshitz

Rashi: Why does God say, "Send for yourself...," and not simply "Send"? The "yourself" implies that this is not a Divine command but that what you do here will be according to your own judgment. If you want to do so, send them.

Now why indeed would the Holy One desire that Moses not send men to scout out the land?

Our sages explained that the men despised the land and said just give us permission and we will return to Egypt. But the women loved the land and said, "Give us an inheritance." [Perhaps a reference to Numbers 27:1 where the daughters of Zelophehad, who had no sons, ask Moses to grant them an inheritance.] For this reason the Holy One said, since I am able to see the future, it would be better to →

Scriptural Context

Finally, the first opportunity to enter Canaan! Since the possibility of a military confrontation was considered probable, scouts were sent into the land. But the reports of the spies differed considerably one from another. □

Targum: English Translation
Numbers 13:1-3

1) So *Adonai* spoke thus to Moses: 2) *"Send for yourself men to scout the Land of Canaan,* which I am giving to the Israelites; send one person from each of their ancestral tribes, each one a tribal leader." 3) So Moses according to God's [direct] command, sent them out from the wilderness of Paran, all the people who were heads of the Israelites. □

From the Tradition

Rabbi Nachman of Bratzlav taught: The Book of Ezekiel commences with his mystical vision of the chariot. "The heavens opened and I saw visions of God...." (Ezekiel 1:1). The first letter of each of the five words in Hebrew are the letters of the word for "faith," *Emunah.* When you believe, you see. □

Perush: Explaining the Teaching

Our teacher wants to understand why the Hebrew construction is such that the text does not just say "send" (*shelach*) but says "send for yourself" (*shelach lecha*). Quoting Rashi, he learns that the Torah implies that God did not actually instruct Moses to send out scouts. Rather, God gives Moses permission to send out the scouts and says to him, if you want to send them, it's all right with me, but use your own judgment. And so Ephraim Solomon wonders, why wouldn't God want to send out scouts? He reasons that it was not that Moses wanted to send out scouts that troubled God. Rather, it was the fact that Moses wanted to send out men, while God—recalling their ambivalence in the past—knew the kind of report these men would bring back to Moses. Now had Moses wanted to send women—who loved the Land—that would have been another story! □

Background Ephraim ben Aaron of Lunshitz (Leczycea) is usually referred to as Ephraim of Lunshitz (1550-1619). He was a circuit preacher until he took his first permanent rabbinical post as head of the *yeshivah* in Lemberg, but he was already well past the age of fifty. In 1604, he became president of the rabbinical court in Prague and *rosh yeshivah* there. In his sermons, he spoke out against the wealthy whose high regard for money inhibited their desire to provide funds for the community poor. He also rallied against their aspirations to equate their spiritual status with their financial success. Likewise, he chastised the poor for taking advantage of the gifts of the wealthy while not attempting to help themselves. His commentary of the Torah, *Kelei Yakar* (Lublin, 1602) is included in many editions of *Mikraot Gedolot*. □

The Teaching (*continued*)

send the women who love the land and would not fabricate calumnies.

But I understand that according to the way you yourself see matters, you think that these men are worthy and that the land is loved by them, so, "Send for yourself men. . . ." □

(110) Shelach Lecha: Hard Truth

The Teaching
from Menachem Mendl of Kotzk

Did the spies lie? Did they fabricate from their hearts words that were not [true]? Behold, they spoke as they saw [it]. So how did they sin?

But not everything that is not a lie is truth. A person who is not a liar is not [automatically] a person of truth. The truth is not sometimes as it appears; it gushes from the depths of the heart, from the sources of faith. Truth and faith →

Perush: Explaining the Teaching

The Kotzker, known for his relentless pursuit of truth, is puzzled by this text because it seems that the "spies" who assumingly told the truth were punished. What is it, the Kotzker ponders, that they did wrong? Apparently, the Torah text here contains a different concept of truth. Only Joshua and Caleb bring back an optimistic report on the land. For the Israelites, →

Scriptural Context

This portion presents the Israelites with their first opportunity to enter the Promised Land. So Moses, the aging leader whose leadership was brought into question in the previous portion, forced to share his authority with others, sends out scouts to explore the land. The majority correctly report that while it is a good land, its inhabitants are insurmountable giants! Only two judge conquest possible. □

Targum: English Translation
Numbers 13:25–32

25) They [the spies] returned from their forty-day scouting patrol of the land. 26) They went to Moses and Aaron, to the entire assembly of Israelites to the desert of Paran, to Kadesh; there they brought back word and showed them the land's bounty. (27) They [the spies] told him [Moses] thus, *"We came to the land, where you sent us, and indeed it is flowing with milk and honey; this is its fruit. 28) But the people who inhabit the country are powerful;* the cities are greatly fortified and [by the way], we saw the Anakites there. 29) Amalek dwells in the southlands; the Hittite, Jubusite, and Amorite all inhabit the mountains; and the Canaanite lives by the sea, alongside the Jordan [River]. 30) [Sensing its anxiety], Caleb calmed the people for Moses by saying "Let's go there immediately and take it over." 31) But his scouting colleagues confronted him: "We are unable to go against the people [there]; they are stronger than we are." 32) They proceeded to tell their side of the story to the Israelites, "The land, the very one which we recently traversed, is a land that consumes its inhabitants, and these are real men too!" □

From the Tradition

In connection with the report of the spies, in Daghestan at Gruzia (Republic of Georgia), the doorposts of the house of bride and groom are smeared with butter (milk) and honey. □

Background Menachem Mendl of Kotzk taught that truth could only be reached in the context of total freedom from both conformity and outside pressures. While he did not preach asceticism, he did suggest that we often have to go against ourselves and society in order to find that truth. His disciples actually practiced this by leaving their studies, their homes, and their families in order to live in Kotzk to search for truth. Unlike other *chasidim*, he taught that →

186

The Teaching (*continued*)

are locked arm and arm; no person acquires truth easily or with attention to the superficial, but with toil and effort, with wisdom and understanding.

And the spies did not strain for the truth of the word of God. They were not wise enough to stand on the secret of God. They stopped [stood] with their vision limited and contracted and false against God's assurance, [which] is the absolute truth – and this was the great sin. □

Perush: Explaining the Teaching (*continued*)

the Land is the future. If *Adonai* were to show the people what the conquest would be like, they might not muster the inner strength and courage to move forward. This is the perspective of the other scouts on their reconnaissance mission. Only Joshua and Caleb had faith in their future. For the Kotzker, faith in one's self and faith in God are related. For him, what God was doing, namely, bringing the Israelites into a land, albeit inhabited by powerful peoples in fortified cities (cf. Numbers 13:28–29), had to look good. □

Background (*continued*)

the search for truth could only be realized in study – of Torah and Talmud. Yet, that study, while the safest way to travel for the Jew, is indeed dangerous, nonetheless. Menachem Mendl took his own teaching to the extreme when he "left the world" twenty years before his death and locked himself in a room near the house of study. Food was passed to him and he was rarely seen by anyone, except for close friends and family. He used to say, "I don't want you to sin, not because it is wrong, but because there isn't enough time." □

(111) Shelach Lecha: How Do I Look?

The Teaching
from Menachem Mendl of Kotzk

This was one of the sins of the spies. "And we were in our own eyes like grasshoppers"; this is a reasonable reaction.

But when we say, "And so we must have appeared to them," what is going on? What possible difference could it make for you [to know or even care] how you appear in the eyes of others! □

Perush: Explaining the Teaching

Like so many of our teachers, the Kotzker is attempting to determine what the sin of the spies was. On the surface it appears that they did exactly what they were asked to do: go and scout out the

Scriptural Context

Finally, the Israelites are provided with their first opportunity to enter the Promised Land. Moses sends out spies and they bring back conflicting reports of what they saw. Our text reveals the perspective of those who brought back negative reports. □

From the Tradition

The image of a large cluster of grapes on a carrying frame, depicting the fruits that Caleb and Joshua had brought back from their reconnaissance mission, has become a symbol of modern Israel. It also is a logo for Carmel wine and the Israeli Ministry of Tourism. □

Targum: English Translation
Numbers 13:30–33

30) Caleb quieted the people before Moses and said, "By all means, let us go. We shall gain possession of the land; we shall surely overcome it." 31) But the men who had gone up with him said, "We cannot attack the people for they are stronger than we are." 32) Thus they spread rumors among the Israelites about the land that they had scouted: "The country that we traversed and scouted is one that devours its settlers. All the people that we saw there are of great size; 33) *And there we saw the Nefilim [demi-gods or giants], descendants of Anak of the Nefilim. And we were in our own eyes like grasshoppers, and so we must have appeared to them.*" □

land. They brought back the reports of what they saw, so what was the sin? Menachem Mendl teaches that their sin was one of ego and self-centeredness. They were told to evaluate the land and came back and said we were like grasshoppers compared to the *Nefilim*, those giants. That was to be expected. But when they said: *We must have appeared* that way to them, Menachem Mendl argues, "What do you care what you appeared like to them?" You were sent out to do a holy job and you were worried about your own appearance. That is your sin!

A harsh statement but a warning: When you are sent on a holy mission, don't worry about how you look. Instead, pay attention to what you are looking for – in life, as well. □

Background The *Nefilim* were said to be a race of giants who dwelt in pre-Israelite Canaan. In Genesis 6:1–2, we note that "sons of gods" that is, angelic beings, took mortal wives. Then the *Nefilim* appear (according to verse 4). In the Apocrypha the angels are depicted as rebels against God who had been "felled" (from the Hebrew *nafal*) by the charms of women, defiled their heavenly purity, and introduced all wickedness and sinfulness on earth. Their giant offspring were wicked and violent. □

(112) Korach: Every Man for Himself

The Teaching
from Tzvi Hirsch Kalischer

Why is the verb *took*, referring to what Korach, Datan, and Abiram, all did, written in the singular and not in the plural?

Because each and every one of them was in this battle only for himself. □

Perush: Explaining the Teaching

Our teachers note that the verb *he took* is written in the singular where one would expect the plural, in its reference to Datan and Abiram, and On. Tzvi Hirsch Kalischer suggests that these were not real *leaders*; they were merely challenging the leadership of Moses and Aaron on their own personal behalf, selfishly trying to fulfill their own self-serving agendas. □

Scriptural Context

This portion focuses on the rebellion of Korach, Datan, Abiram, and On. Our text, taken from the beginning of the *parashah*, introduces these rebels. □

Targum: English Translation
Numbers 16:1–3

1) *Now Korach, son of Izhar, son of Kohat, son of Levi, took himself, along with Datan and Abiram, sons of Eliab, and On, son of Pelet–descendants of Reuben* 2) **to rise up against Moses along with 250 Israelites who were community leaders, representatives of the assembled, men of good repute.** 3) **They conspired against Moses and Aaron and said to them, "You have gone too far [this time]! The entire community is holy and** *Adonai* **dwells among it. Why do you persist in raising yourself above** *Adonai's* **community?"** □

From the Tradition

From the Sefas Emes, Yehudah Aryeh Leib of Ger: According to the Aramaic translation of Onkelos, ויקה קרה, "Now Korach . . . took," means ואתפלג קרח, "Now Korach divided (himself)."

And our sages make the following point: a person is obligated to ask, when will my deeds touch the deeds of my parents?

Rabbi Simchah Bunem of Przysucha explained this means that in the deeds of every Jew there must be continuity with, cleaving, bonding, and attainment of the awesome deeds of one's parents, for only in this way can we insure the linkage of the generations.

And just this was the son of Korach, ויקח קרח, "Now Korach . . . took," ואתפלג קרח, "Now Korach divided (himself)." He took for himself another way, which had no bond with the past. He severed himself from the root of his parents. □

Background Tzvi Hirsch Kalischer, who lived in the nineteenth century, was one of the early proponents of the Zionist idea, spending much of his time advocating the settlement of *Eretz Yisrael*. He spent most of his life in Thorn, Poland, serving as an unpaid acting community rabbi. He was more preoccupied with the problems of his day than with the esoterica of tradition, although a strict adherent to the observance of religious precepts. He did not believe that "suddenly God would come down from the heavens or suddenly send His Messiah." Instead, he contended that salvation would be brought about through human actions, in contradistinction to his rabbinic colleagues. □

(113) Korach: The Mouth of the Earth

The Teaching
from Harei Ba-Shamayim

Why was Korach punished this way?

Our sages, their memory is a blessing, interpret Job 26:7, "God suspends the earth upon restraint," according to *Chullin* 89a, "the world exists only on account of [the merit] of one who restrains himself during a quarrel."

But as for Korach and his band, it was not enough that they merely be able to restrain themselves; on the contrary, they fanned the flames of the argument [with Moses], and the earth was simply unable to exist beneath them. So "the earth opened her mouth and swallowed them up." □

Targum: English Translation
Numbers 16:31–33

31) He [Moses] had scarcely finished speaking all these words when the ground under them burst open 32) *And the earth opened its mouth and swallowed them up with their households, all Korach's people, and their possessions* 33) They went down alive to Sheol, with all that they owned. The earth closed over them and they vanished from the congregation.

Scriptural Context

This *parashah* represents the most serious challenge to Moses' leadership during the entire desert journey. God aids the chosen leaders by destroying the antagonists, dooming the uprising to failure. While this portion is usually identified with Korach as the leader of the rebellion, the text shifts its focus throughout the narrative to Datan and Abiram. Perhaps two uprisings are joined together within the folk tradition of our people. □

From the Tradition

Pirke Avot 5:17 asks: "What is an example of a battle that is not for the sake of heaven? This is the battle of Korach and his band." According to *Yaarut Devash*, the text should logically read, "the battle of Korach and Moses." But in the very midst of Korach's dissenting band itself there was dissent. Each and every one of them was only in it for his own glory. And from this we can conclude that their intention was not for the sake of heaven. □

Perush: Explaining the Teaching

The punishment of Korach seems severe. It extended beyond him to his children, their families, and possessions. Our teacher explains that God did not simply kill Korach and his clan by forcing the earth to swallow them up. Rather, Korach did nothing to restrain himself. He provoked an argument and the earth could not sustain itself (in reference to the cited text from *Chullin*). Thus, the earth's foundations "temporarily failed." Therefore, Korach and his folk were engulfed by the earth itself; they were absorbed back to the source. □

Background According to Simchah Bunem of Przysucha, Korach was extraordinarily blessed. He came from the best family, he was a *talmid chacham*, a brilliant student, he was wealthy and bright, indeed, he was even probably destined to be a leader of the Jewish people. Why was the authority not given to him? Because "he took himself" (Numbers 16:1), he could not wait until they brought him the crown of leadership. Instead, he tried to take it by force. And that is why he never got it. □

(114) Korach: Overcompensation

The Teaching
from Sefas Emes, Yehudah Aryeh Leib of Ger

Rabbi Simchah Bunem of Przysucha said that from this verse one could understand how the opponents of the *tzaddik* [a *rebbe*] chose to speak to him and to shame him precisely by the very instruments of his own self-improvement. They [like Korach] would say, "Why do you raise yourselves . . . ?" despite the fact that Scripture testifies that "this man, Moses, was a very humble man" (Numbers 12:3).

It is possible to explain his words in this way: Moses was humble in his personality and his very being; there was no sense whatsoever of any feeling of arrogance. Therefore he conducted himself in so many ways in a manner like this that someone might be able to say that there was here a little arrogance. But in reality there was no arrogance whatsoever, and for this reason Moses' humility was unintelligible to the common people. □

Scriptural Context

Of the many challenges to Moses' leadership and God-appointed authority, the rebellion of Korach and his companions is perhaps the most striking. This dramatic coup d'etat ended with the earth swallowing up the challengers. Our text is taken from the midst of this rebellion. □

Targum: English Translation
Numbers 16:1–3

1) Now Korach, son of Izhar, son of Kohath, son of Levi, took himself along with Datan and Abiram, sons of Eliab, and On, son of Peleth – all descendants of Reuben – 2) in order to rise up against Moses, together with 250 Israelites, chiefs of the community, chosen of the assembly, people of repute. 3) *They gathered themselves against Moses and Aaron and said to them, "You have gone too far! For all the community are holy, all of them, and Adonai is in their midst. Why do you raise yourselves above Adonai's congregation?* □

From the Tradition

Korach's sin was that he, unlike Moses, sought leadership for personal gain, not for the sake of Heaven (see *Pirke Avot* 5:20). He was consumed by the jealousy he felt for Moses. According to the Talmud, once while Rabbah bar Bar Chanah was traveling in the desert, a local Bedouin showed him the place where Korach and his companions had been engulfed by the earth. Bar Chamah placed his ear to the crack and heard voices crying, "Moses and the Torah are true and we are liars" (*Bava Batra* 74a). □

Perush: Explaining the Teaching

Simchah Bunem's comment is incredibly insightful. From his understanding of Korach's rebellion, he suggests that a lot of people behave in a particular way because they are afraid that they will behave in the opposite way. Jung called this overcompensation. A person who is really arrogant becomes humble. Korach thought he saw this in Moses and so he rebelled. That was his wickedness. □

Background The chasidic teachers suggest that Korach seized authority himself – and that is not the way to achieve greatness in this world. Only God is capable of bestowing greatness on a human being. □

(115) Chukat: The Torah Is Like a Cow

The Teaching
from David of Tolnye

This is surprising. What does Torah have to do with a cow? Only perhaps that just as the cow defiles and makes pure, so too does the Torah.

And our sages say in *Mishnah Yadayim* 3:5, "All the sacred Scriptures render the hands unclean. . . ." For one who learned and thereby made himself a sage and a teacher and subsequently became arrogant, such a person the Torah has defiled. Whereas if a person does not think that he is important at all, the Torah likens him to water [the instrument of purification] for about such a one it is said in Ezekiel 36:25, "And I shall sprinkle upon you pure water." And he will be cleansed from all his impurities. As our sages →

Perush: Explaining the Teaching

David of Tolnye is not trying to figure out the ritual, but rather to teach us about our own relationship to the Torah. The cow, like the Torah, has the potential to both defile and purify the one who originally came into contact with a dead body. The Torah can likewise defile one who uses its wisdom for self-aggrandizement and can likewise "purify" an individual who studies and practices its words. □

Targum: English Translation
Numbers 19:1–3

1) *Adonai* **spoke thus to Moses and Aaron.** 2) *"This is the law of the Torah, which* **Adonai** *has commanded saying, 'Speak to the Israelites and they shall take for you a red cow, perfect and unblemished and upon which no yoke has been laid."* 3) **Give it to Elazar the priest. It should be taken outside the camp and slaughtered in his presence.** □

Scriptural Context

The Red Heifer is the most mysterious ritual in the Torah. It is the only time in which an entire sacrificial animal is turned to ashes on the altar. (Usually, only the inedible pieces are burned, and the remainder is given to God through the office of the priests.) Following this sacrifice, the ashes of the heifer are sprinkled over an individual who has come into contact with a dead body and therefore has become ritually impure. □

From the Tradition

Jehiel Michael of Zloczow began his teaching on this verse with something he learned from studying Rashi. Rashi taught that according to *Pesikta Rabbati* and *Yoma* 67b, since "the adversary" (Satan), and the nations of the world taunt Israel with "What is this commandment and what is its purpose?" therefore the Torah writes it is as a law, a decree from God. You are not permitted to question it.

Why do the nations of the world taunt Israel just about this commandment (*davka*)? Aren't there more than enough other commandments without any apparent reason?

One explanation for the reasoning behind the commandment of the Red →

Background Tolnye is a city in the Kiev oblast. The height of its Jewish population was reached in 1897 when approximately 5,400 Jews (57 percent of the total population) lived in the city. Rabbi David (David of Tolnye) Twersky (1808–1882), son of Mordechai of Chernobyl and grandson of Menachem Nachum ben Tzvi of Chernobyl, lived there. He was probably the most influential of the Twersky dynasty of his generation. Thousands of *chasidim* from around the Ukraine followed him (and later his sons). It is said that he sat on a silver throne inscribed with the words "David King of Israel lives forever." He was held under arrest by the Russian authorities for a long time. He loved singing and music and was often visited by popular Jewish singers and musicians. His writings are spiced with parables and references to the secular world. □

The Teaching (*continued*)

have said in *Tehillim Rabbah* 1:18, "Just as water covers the nakedness of the sea, the words of Torah cover the nakedness of Israel." □

From the Tradition (*continued*)

Heifer may be as Rashi offers in the name of Rabbi Mosheh HaDarshan – that it comes in order to make atonement for the sin of the Golden Calf. But I can reply that the nations of the world, wanting to remind everyone of our sin with the calf, and, by means of this, to arouse the accuser against Israel, would be quick to request a reason for (*davka*) this commandment.

For this reason, God fixed this commandment without any reason, precisely so that Israel would not be obliged to respond to the nations of the world. It is simply a law without reason. You have neither permission to question it nor to answer. □

(116) Chukat: Breaking Vessels

The Teaching
from Menachem Mendl of Kotzk

Rashi: The Torah here is speaking of an earthenware vessel, which does not receive uncleanness by [an unclean thing touching] its exterior but only by [the unclean thing] inside it.

Impurity attaches itself to a thing of importance because it is drawn from the dimension of holiness. Therefore, in *Pirke Avot* 5:5, our sages enumerated "the ten miracles that were performed for our ancestors in the Temple . . . [one of which was that] no fly was ever seen in the slaughterhouse. . . ." According to *Berachot* 61a, a "fly" is an allusion to the human impulse to do evil. This must be the miracle that is mentioned, that in the Temple, the center of holiness, neither the evil impulse was seen nor could the power of impurity take hold.

With a metal vessel, whose value is intrinsic, to itself, the impurity is drawn from its importance. Therefore the impurity remains outside [the vessel]. But an earthenware vessel, which has no intrinsic value of its own and all its importance is only a function of what it is able to contain, receives impurity only from its contents, instead of its own worth. Only then would the impurity effectively take over the vessel.

For this reason there is no way to purify earthenware vessels except through breaking them, for the impurity penetrates to their innermost core where there can be no repair save through "the breaking of the vessel." □

Scriptural Context

This section of the Torah portion discusses the unintentional contamination through contact with a corpse. It extends the rules regarding home and community to tents and the wilderness. □

Targum: English Translation
Numbers 19:14–16

14) *This is the ritual: When a person dies in a tent, whoever enters the tent and whoever is in the tent shall be unclean seven days* 15) *and every open vessel with no lid fastened down shall be unclean.* 16) **And anyone who touches a person out in the open field, who was killed [literally, "by a sword"] or died of natural causes or [just] human bones or a grave shall [also] be unclean for seven days.** □

From the Tradition

Kelim, "vessels," is the first tractate of the *Mishnah* order of *Tohorot* and includes vessels of all kinds, with instructions for purification. The last statement in the tractate deals with glass (a waterclock) that does not receive impurity. Thus, the tractate ends on a note of cleanness, as a result of which Rabbi Yose exclaimed, "Blessed are You, O *Kelim*, for you enter in uncleanness but go out in cleanness." □

Perush: Explaining the Teaching

Our teacher learns by an analogy to the rules of kashering different kinds of pots. First citing Rashi, he notes the different kinds of vessels of which the Torah text might be speaking and how they may become contaminated. Menachem Mendl seems to wonder whether or not impurity is intrinsic or extrinsic to the person just as it is with pots. In a worthless vessel, the impurity is contained by the vessel's walls, but in a vessel of worth, the impurity can contaminate the vessel and its walls. □

Background The tractate of the *Mishnah* called *Kelim* (vessels), in the order called *Tohorot* (purity), addresses the various questions concerning the purity or impurity of different kinds of vessels. From this extensive legal material, the rabbis draw various analogies about the condition of being human. The best summary of the entire text is offered by Rabbi Yose, who wrote; "Praised are you, O *Kelim*, for you entered in uncleanness but have gone forth in cleanness." □

194

(117) Chukat: The Sin of Sharp

The Teaching from Yad Yosef

According to Moses Maimonides, the main sin of Moses and Aaron was in the language with which they spoke to Israel: "Listen, you rebels."

To be sure, many of the prophets of Israel spoke with sharpness in similar language.

But here it was inappropriate since the children of Israel sought water, incontestably an urgent matter of life and death for a person. There was no reason to speak to them harshly. □

Perush: Explaining the Teaching

This is the sin of Moses. For this, he was unable to lead the people into Canaan. He had to stop at its borders. But what actually was this sin, so significant that it prevented Moses, the one who had led Israel so far, to lead the people home? Maimonides claims it was in the language. Moses spoke too sharply to the people. Our teacher tries to understand Maimonides' comment. Yad Yosef suggests that Moses had no reason at all to speak to the people in the manner he did. They were thirsty – at the brink of death – they simply sought to restore themselves. □

Scriptural Context

Our text follows the mysterious Red Heifer and the laws of purification. This passage brings us near the end of the desert wanderings. Here we learn the fate of Israel's leaders since the generation of slavery has died out and a free Israel has been born. The people are thirsty and complain of their thirst, and God directs Moses to coax water from the rock. According to the text, Moses does not do precisely as he was told and is therefore prohibited from entering the Promised Land with the people he had led through the desert. □

From the Tradition

The *Zohar* (ii, 47a) teaches: "The acts of the leader are the acts of the nation. If the leader is just, the nation is just; if he is unjust, the nation too is unjust and is punished for the sin of the leader." □

Targum: English Translation
Numbers 20: 6–12

6) Moses and Aaron came away from the congregation to the entrance to the Tent of Meeting, and fell on their faces. God presented God's Divine Self to them. 7) And God spoke thus to Moses: 8) You and your brother Aaron should take the rod and assemble the community. Before its very eyes order the rock to issue forth its water. Thus, you shall produce water for them from the rock and provide drink for the congregation and their beasts. 10) *Moses and Aaron assembled the congregation in front of the rock and he said to them, "Listen, you rebels, shall we get water for you out of this rock?"* **11) Moses raised his hand and twice struck the rock with his rod. Out came abundant of water, and the community and its beasts drank. 12) But** *Adonai* **said to Moses and Aaron, "Because you did not trust Me enough to affirm my sanctity in the sight of the Israelite people, you shall not lead this congregation into the land that I have given them."** □

Background According to Maimonides, a leader should not lose his temper. Thus, Moses and Aaron's behavior was considered reprehensible in divinely appointed leaders. □

(118) Balak: Balak's Forty-Two Sacrifices

The Teaching
from Birkat Avraham

Of the fifty-four *parshiyot* in the Torah, only five are named after the people: Noach, Yitro, Korach, Balak, and Pinchas.

Scripture testifies concerning Noach, in Genesis 6:9, that "Noach was a righteous man."

Jethro augments one *Parashah* as we read in the Torah in Exodus 18:21, "You shall provide out of all the people, men of ability. . . ."

Sanhedrin 110a comments on Numbers 16:2, which describes Korach and his band: "chosen in the congregation, men of repute. . . ." The sages explain that "chosen in the congregation" can also be read as "chosen for the appointed times," which means →

Scriptural Context

This Torah portion chronicles the struggle between Israel and those who would curse her. Balak engages the sorcerer Balaam to lay a curse on Israel but, feeling the spirit of God upon him, Balaam blesses Israel instead. The divine messenger is seen only by Balaam's donkey, who speaks to the sorcerer. □

From the
Tradition

According to the *Tanchuma* (Balak), Balaam counseled Balak as to how to destroy Israel. This act caused the departure of the holy spirit from the Gentile peoples and saw that the prophecy was preserved in Israel alone. □

Targum: English Translation
Numbers 22:2–6

2) *Balak, son of Tzippor, saw all that Israel had done to the Amorites.* 3) **Moab was alarmed because that people was so numerous. Moab dreaded the Israelites, 4) and Moab said to the elders of Midian, "Now this multitude will clean out our surroundings just as an ox licks up the field." Balak, son of Zippor, who was king of Moab at that time, 5) sent messengers to Balaam, son of Beor, in Pethor, which is by the Euphrates, in the land of his kinfolk, to invite him, saying, "There is a people that came out of Egypt; it hides the earth from view, and it settled next to me. 6) Come and put a curse on this people for me, since they are too numerous for me; perhaps I can thus defeat them and drive them out of the land. For I know that the one you bless is indeed blessed and the cursed one is cursed."** □

Perush: Explaining the Teaching

Our teacher is puzzled by the honor bestowed on Balak by a having a Torah portion named in his honor, shared only by four others. Why would one who attempted to curse Israel be honored in such a way? Birkat Avraham reasons, taking his cue from *Sotah* 47a, that Balak did offer forty-two sacrifices. In return for this, Ruth was issued from his seed because the sacrifices were not offered on his own behest. And Ruth issued David and Solomon – the line of the Messiah. □

Background The Bible reiterates the journey of the Israelites to remind us that it is our journey as well. We share in the historical memory of the Jewish people as our journeys become part of the collective journey of the Jewish people. Our ancestors' journey through the desert is our journey as well. As they travel, each time we read of it in Torah, we travel with them. The distance between us of time and space collapses and we are there together, escaping slavery, leaving Egypt, wandering through the desert, receiving Torah, and entering the Promised Land. □

The Teaching *(continued)*

they were skilled in intercalating the year and fixing the new moons, and the phrase, "men of repute," means they were famous throughout the world. (Other commentators on the Torah suggest a further praise of Korach by noting that the last letters of the phrase in Psalm 92:13, צדיק כתמר יפרח, "the righteous will blossom like a date palm," spell קרח, Korach.)

Pinchas, "zealous for the passion of God and the sanctification of the Name of Heaven," is also equated with Elijah [cf. *Pirke de Rabbi Eliezer* 47k; Rashi on *Bava Metzia* 114b; *Song of Songs Rabbah* 2; *Yalkut Shimoni* 7 on Pinchas].

But by what merit does Balak deserve to have a *parashah* named after him? We read in *Sotah* 47a: "Rab Judah said in the name of Rab: Always a person should occupy oneself with Torah and commandments even though it be not for their own sake. One comes to do so for their own sake, because as a reward for the forty-two sacrifices which Balak, king of Moab, offered, he merited that Ruth should issue from him, and from her issued David and Solomon. . . ." So the merit of David and Solomon and even of the Messiah of the House of David was accounted to Balak. ☐

(119) Balak: Treasuring Amorite Words

The Teaching
from Magen Avraham

Read it: "Everything that Israel had done to *emorai*, My words." [Balak saw] how the children of Israel were able to elevate the words of a person to the highest level, how they sanctified them with the Torah and through prayer, adorned them, cherished them, protected them. As we read in Numbers 22:3, "And Moab dreaded the people." A people like this, one should fear.

And even from the simple ones of the people (the word for people, עַם, *am*, evokes the image →

Perush: Explaining the Teaching

Our teacher reads the text from Numbers 22:2, and the word *emorai* jumps out at him. While it literally refers to the Amorites, its con-

Scriptural Context

Our text comes from the very beginning of the Torah portion. Balak, king of Moab, seeing how the Israelites had destroyed the Amorites, vows to find a way to retaliate and curse the Israelites. His plans come to naught as his hired sorcerer, Balaam, instead praises Israel. □

From the Tradition

The Talmud uses the term *darkei Ha-Emori* (ways of the Amorites) to refer to heathen practices, generally superstitions, that did not have a specific prohibition. Only those things that are done for medicinal purposes were not prohibited. □

Targum: English Translation
Numbers 22:2-6

2) *And Balak, son of Tzippor, saw everything that Israel had done to the Amorites.* 3) **Moab was alarmed at the size of the Israelite [nation]. Moab dreaded the Israelites [afraid that they would do the same to Moab as they had done to Amora].** 4) **So Moab said to the elders of Midian, "This mob will clean out our community just as an ox eats clean the grass in the field." Balak, who was then king of Moab,** 5) **sent messengers to Balaam of Beor in Petor, by the Euphrates, in the land of his kinsfolk, with this invitation: There is a people that has come out of Egypt [so numerous] it hides the earth from view and it has settled near me.** 6) **Come now and put a curse on this people for me since it is so unwieldy. Perhaps I might then be able to defeat them and drive them out of here. I know that the one whom you bless is blessed and the one you curse is indeed cursed.** □

struction lends itself to a wordplay. One would normally expect to read *Amora'im*. But Magen Avraham suggests that this peculiar word could also be read *emorai* – "my words." Balak saw not what Israel had done to defeat the Amorites. Rather, as Magen Avraham reads it, Balak saw how Israel had taken the words (and deeds) of people and through a relationship with Torah, elevated them, causing them to soar heavenward. Magen Avraham pushes the image further by reading the following verse, Numbers 22:5: "Moab dreaded the people [all the people]." So devoted are the people of Israel that even after a long day of work, still they hurry to prayer and the recitation of divine words. □

Background *Magen Avraham* was prepared by Polish Rabbi Abraham Abele ben Chayyim Ha-Levi (c. 1639–1683). Following the Chmiel-nicki massacre, he left his city of birth, Gombin, and eventually became the *rosh yeshivah* and *dayyan* of the *bet din* in Kalisz. The *Magen Avra-ham*, his best-known work, is actually a com-mentary of the *Shulchan Aruch*. His main purpose in preparing the book was to establish a com-promise between the decisions of Joseph Caro and Moses Isserles, but it upholds the opinion of the latter when a compromise cannot be reached. □

The Teaching *(continued)*

of נחלים עוממות, *gahalim omammot*, dying embers).

As Abba Mieri said in the name of the Baal Shem Tov: For even one who is occupied in his business and worldly pursuits all day, when the time arrives for the *Minchah*, afternoon prayer, he hurries, sighing and praying with a broken heart, and his sigh pierces the heavens. ☐

(120) Balak: Beware of Good News

The Teaching
from Toledot Yaakov Yosef, Yaakov Yosef of Polnoye

What is the difference between a true prophet and a false one?

The true prophet can be identified in most cases by their scoldings. They point out the blemishes and defects and want to break the measure.

The false prophet flatters the people with sweet talk and sees none of the low land. "Peace, Peace, everything's fine and there's no need for correction." →

Targum: English Translation
Numbers 24:5–7

5) *How goodly are your tents O Jacob, your dwelling places, Israel.*
6) **Like palm groves that stretch out; like gardens beside a river; like aloes planted by** *Adonai;* **like cedars beside the water.**
7) **Their boughs drip with moisture; their roots have abundant water. Their king shall rise above Agag; their nation shall be exalted.** □

Scriptural Context

Balaam is sent by Balak, the king of Moab, to curse Israel. Things don't happen the way Balak had planned. Instead of a curse, Israel receives a blessing. Balaam feels the presence of God and recites a well-known blessing from which this text is taken. □

From the Tradition

An evil eye, a haughty spirit, and a proud soul are the marks of the disciples of wicked Balaam (*Pirke Avot* 5:22). □

Perush: Explaining the Teaching

We are told that Balaam senses that his words pleased God and once again claimed to be speaking on God's behalf. But our teacher wonders how one determines the veracity of his message. How do we know that he speaks for God and is therefore a true prophet? This question has concerned our teachers for generations. Yaakov Yosef of Polnoye says the key is in the nature of the message itself. Tough love. If a prophet merely bestows compliments on Israel, we can know that such a prophet is false for he does not encourage Israel to reach higher. To do so, a true prophet scolds. He wants the people to reach higher, to ascend the rungs of the ladder toward heaven. □

Background *Toledot Yaakov Yosef* was prepared by Yaakov Yosef of Polnoye. This work embodies the first systematic exposition of chasidism in written form. It contains many of the sayings, interpretations, and traditions of the Baal Shem Tov, which Yaakov Yosef continued to teach in his subsequent works. Polnoye was an important commercial and spiritual center in the second half of the eighteenth century. Both Yehudah Aryeh Leib and Yaakov Yosef, in succession, held rabbinical posts there. Located in the Ukraine, in the Kamenets-Podolski oblast, it is not clear when the Jewish community of Polnoye developed.

During the Chmielnicki massacres (1648) it was regarded as one of the most important cities in Volhynia. When the Cossack armies reached the town, 12,000 Jews found refuge in its fortress. Along with the Poles, they defended themselves against the enemy. When the Cossacks finally overcame the Jewish opposition, they came upon 300 Jews who had gathered in the *bet hamidrash*, led by the mystic Rabbi Samson Ostropoler. They had wrapped themselves in their *tallitot* and met death with a prayer still clinging to their lips. Ten thousand Jews had been killed. Following that disaster, Countess Lyubomirskaya granted Jews the right to build houses in one of the town's quarters, and they were granted exemption from military service, except in the general mobilization after an attack by an enemy. The area became an important printing center and over ninety works came from the town, mostly kabbalistic in nature. □

The Teaching (*continued*)

[An allusion to Jeremiah 6:14, 8:11: "They offer healing offhand for the wounds of my people; say, Peace, Peace, when there is no peace."]

But true prophets (*davka*), genuine lovers of the people, they scold.

Balaam, however, does not sing from any great love of Israel, even though he has many songs and praises for Israel. On the contrary, he intends to entice Israel so that they will not do anything, so that they will no longer yearn to ascend higher and higher up the ladder.

They are absolutely perfect; they are blessed with every good quality. And just this is the difference between him and the prophets of Israel. □

(121) Pinchas: Accidental Zeal

The Teaching
from Divrei Sha'ul, Rabbi Joseph Saul Nitnazon

The story is told in the Tosefta, *Pe'ah*, chapter 13, of a certain *chasid* who was informed that he had forgotten a sheaf of barley in the field. The *chasid* was so happy over this that he ordered that a sacrifice be brought. They said to him, why do you prefer to be happier with fulfilling this commandment than with any other in the whole Torah?

Replied the *chasid*, all the other *mitzvot* were by my own will and →

Perush: Explaining the Teaching

Our teacher, Rabbi Joseph Saul Nitnazon, wants to understand how Pinchas acted so spontaneously. He didn't consult Moses and he certainly didn't consult God. Through a story, our teacher suggests that *mitzvot* must be spontaneously undertaken without any ulterior motive but to serve God. Divrei Shaul wants us to understand that Pinchas's earnest and quick response actually prevented the destruction of the entire people of Israel. ☐

Scriptural Context

On the way out of the desert, at Shittim, the last stop, the Israelites get involved with Moabite women, and are seduced into following their idolatrous practices. One Israelite is caught in the act with a Midianite woman. Both are murdered by the zealot Pinchas for which the latter is rewarded with the priesthood. ☐

Targum: English Translation
Numbers 25:10-13

10) *Adonai spoke thus to Moses* 11) *Pinchas, son of Eleazar, son of Aaron the priest, has turned back My wrath from the Israelites by being zealous with my jealousy, so that I did not wipe out the Israelite people in My passion.* 12) **Therefore, say "Behold I give you a treaty of nonaggression.** 13) **This shall stand for him and his descendants, an agreement for the priesthood for all times because he took up the cause of an impassioned God, this making expiation for the Israelites."** ☐

From the Tradition

Regardless of Pinchas's unauthorized zeal, the rabbis accord him great merit. He is chosen to accompany the Israelites in their campaign against Midian – in order to complete what he had started by slaying the Midianite woman (*Numbers Rabbah* 22:4). He also does this, according to the rabbis, to avenge his grandfather Joseph who had been sold into slavery by the Midianites. ☐

Background (1) Y. Eiger taught: Two *parshiyot* are before *Parshiyot Pinchas, Chukat*, and *Balak*, and two are after it, *Mattot* and *Masei*. In most years, they are joined and read as doubled portions. (In fact, only in the exile [where the liturgical calendar varies slightly from the one used in the Land of Israel] are portions *Chukat* and *Balak* never joined.) But *Parashat Pinchas* is always read alone. This is because Pinchas was a fanatic, and fanatics must live alone. And if there were many fanatics, everyone would go along in his or her own way, according to his own opinion.

Woe to a generation when the fanatics are all joined together!

(2) There are fifty-four weekly Torah por-

tions. One is read each *Shabbat*. The only exception is when a holiday, which has its own (i.e., independent of the regular weekly cycle) Torah reading, coincides with a *Shabbat*. In such a case, the regular weekly portion is simply postponed until the next nonholiday *Shabbat*. This means that, depending on the liturgical calendar, some years will need fewer weekly *Shabbat* Torah portions than others. And, since we must complete reading the entire Torah each year by Simchat Torah, seven portions (*parshiyot*) can be doubled, or read as one portion. They are *Va-Yakhel-Pekudei, Tazria-Metzora, Acharei Mot-Ke-doshim, Be-Har-Be-Chukotai, Chukat-Balak, Matot--Massei, Nitzavim-Va-Yelech.* ☐

The Teaching (*continued*)

intention, but this *mitzvah, davka,* is done not on purpose and inadvertently; it comes by itself.

And behold, Pinchas did not ask Moses our teacher how to act – if it was appropriate for him to risk his life for this particular *mitzvah*. And furthermore, if he had asked, he would not have been answered, for behold this is the law and there are no teachers here.

And if Zimri had killed him, there would have been no one to demand his blood. Pinchas did all this by himself, without any consultation or self-reflection, without preparation and without intention, only from some inner impulse. This is the real praise of Pinchas, and the verdict is that he shall receive his reward. □

(122) Pinchas: Deserving Priesthood

The Teaching
from the Sefas Emes, Yehudah Aryeh Leib of Ger

What kind of justice is this? The children of Israel were already overcome with great shame and remorse on account of the action of Zimri. As we read in Numbers 25:6, "And, behold one of the children of Israel came, and brought to his brothers the Midianite woman, in the eyes of Moses and all the congregation of the children of Israel, who were weeping at the entrance of the Tent of Meeting."

Pinchas brought their thoughts from potential to action. This is the primary task of the priest; they are our messengers, translating the yearnings of the heart of the people of Israel from potential thought into deed. In this way Pinchas's reward of the priesthood was justly deserved, measure for measure. □

Scriptural Context

The Israelites are at Shittim, their last stop along their desert journey, and get involved with Midianite women—following their idolotrous practices. One Israelite actually flaunts the moral code and is executed by Pinchas, Aaron's grandson. Pinchas, for whom this portion is named, is rewarded for his zealous act by a decree issued by God as a *brit* (covenant) not only for him but for all his descendants as well. □

From the Tradition

Pinchas is connected with the identification of Elijah because they were both distinguished by the zealousness with which they completed their mission. His angelic transformation (as one of the spies sent by Joshua to Jericho) according to the rabbis is prefigured in Malachi 3:1, 23. As such, he is a forerunner to the Messiah. □

Targum: English Translation
Numbers 25:10–13

10) *Adonai* **spoke thus to Moses.** 11) **Pinchas, son of Eleazar, son of Aaron the priest, has turned back My wrath from the Israelites by being zealous with my jealousy, so that I did not wipe out the Israelite people in My passion.** 12) *Therefore, say, "Behold I give to him My covenant of peace.* 13) **This shall stand for him and his descendants, an agreement for the priesthood for all times because he took up the cause of an impassioned God, thus making expiation for the Israelites."** □

Perush: Explaining the Teaching

The Gerer *rebbe* is troubled by the Divine justice that was meted out by God through the agency of Pinchas. The people of Israel were ashamed; surely that was punishment enough. What Pinchas did, to prove that he deserved his eventual election to the priesthood, was not ugly zealotry, but a translation of the yearnings of the people, to heal the rift with God, into actions. In fact, says Yehudah Aryeh Leib, this is the function of all priests. Thus, his reward was according to his merit. □

Background The rabbis debated whether Pinchas had acted with or without the approval [permission] of Moses. They wondered in this regard, whether a disciple could act in an emergency without the guidance of his teacher (*Sanhedrin* 82a). Since the act had unquestionable biblical approval, they determined that its legitimacy could not be questioned. □

(123) Pinchas: Fingers in Their Ears

The Teaching
from Shnei Luchot Ha-Brit

Rashi: I say that this is really the family of Etzbon [mentioned in Genesis 46:16].

What is the relationship between Ozni [which in Hebrew means, "ears"] and Etzbon [Hebrew for "finger"]?

Our sages said in *Ketubbot* 5a–b: "Bar Kappara also expounded, 'What is the meaning of Deuteronomy 23:14, "And you shall have a peg among your implements"? Do not read, "Your implements [Hebrew, *awzen*]", but "upon your ear [Hebrew, *ozen*]"; this means that if one hears an unworthy thing, one must plug one's fingers into one's ears.' "

Targum: English Translation
Numbers 26:16

16) *Of Ozni, the family of Oznites.* . . . ☐

Scriptural Context

The zealous Pinchas has done what he felt he had to do and God brought to a halt the plague God had caused to sweep through the Israelite encampment. Our text is taken from the midst of the census taken of Israelites, generally a metaphor for Israel taking stock of itself following a major challenge to its faith. ☐

From the Tradition

"Do not permit the ear to hear anything to which it is not able to listen" (*Tehillim Rabbah* 1:4). ☐

Behold, the tribe of Gad resided near the tribes of Reuben and Simeon, who had wicked people among them: Datan, Abiram, and the 250 people from Korach's congregation, all from the tribe of Reuben. Zimri and his friends were from the tribe of Simeon. Nevertheless the children of Gad did not learn from their wicked ways or listen to them.

For this reason they are called Etzbon [Hebrew, "finger"], an allusion to the fact that they put their fingers in their ears.

But now, after the wicked have departed and all of them have returned in repentance, they have removed the fingers from their ears and are called Ozni [Hebrew, "ears"], as we read in Proverbs 15:31, "One whose ear heeds the discipline of life, lodges among the wise." ☐

Perush: Explaining the Teaching

Who is this Ozni? And who are the Oznites that Ozni needs to be identified in this manner? Rashi identifies him as one of Etzbon, one of Gad's sons, mentioned in Genesis as one of the descendants of Jacob who sojourned in Egypt. So our teacher asks (since all names are related to the essence of the individual and their spiritual journeys): what is the relationship between Ozni (ears) and Etzbon (fingers)?

First comes a relationship established in the Talmud by Bar Kappara. He teaches us that if we hear wicked things in our ears, we should put our fingers in them. The tribe of Gad dwelled near the tribes of Reuben and Simeon. It was these two tribes that had wicked people, namely, Datan, Abiram, and 250 of Korach's folk. Alluding to the fact that they must have put their fingers in their ears, since they were not persuaded by Korach's wickedness, they were called Etzbon. Here they are called Ozni because the wickedness has departed from their midst, and they no longer need to have fingers in their ears. They have all repented. ☐

Background According to the *Zohar* (iv, 123a), there are two levels of penitence. If a person repents of his evil deeds and ceases to do them again, that person achieves the lower level. If a person repents of his evil deeds, however, and then strives to perform good deeds, his penitence is of the higher type.

(124) Matot: The Power of Holy Words

The Teaching
from the Sefas Emes, Yehudah Aryeh
Leib of Ger

Rashi: [Noting that the word for "break" (*yakhel*) is etymologically related to *kehallel* (to secularize) suggests that "he shall not break" means] he shall not secularize his word.

From this we may infer that the power of the spoken word is holy. And the children of Israel were worthy of it by the power of the Torah [for it told them how to speak]. And throughout the forty years that Moses, our teacher, was busy with them, he infused in them the power of the voice and the Hebrew language. For this reason they were commanded regarding the guarding of their utterances.

And the paragraph that includes "he shall not break his pledge," immediately follows the paragraph which speaks of the "continual sacrifices and the additional sacrifices," implying that the words of prayer can take the place of sacrifice, as it is written in Hosea 14:3, "We will offer cows with our lips."

And also with regard to the Torah our sages taught in *Menachot* 110a, "This is the Torah of the burnt offering . . . all who occupy themselves in the Torah are as if they had offered a sacrifice."

And this is the real meaning of Genesis 27:22: "The voice is the voice of Jacob . . ." – the sound of the study of Torah and prayer, and the inheritance of Jacob is the →

Scriptural Context

The beginning of this portion focuses on vows specifically to women. As a result, this section offers a great deal of insight into the biblical perception on the status of women. Our text first establishes the parameters for a man's oath to be followed later in the Torah by a different set of requirements for oaths taken by women. □

Targum: English Translation
Numbers 30:2–3

2) **Moses said this to the heads of the Israelite tribes: 3)** *If a person makes a vow to* **Adonai** *or takes an oath imposing a prohibition on himself, he shall not break his pledge; he must carry out all that has come out of his mouth.* □

From the
Tradition

The Bible provides no legal sanction for oaths. Punishment was left to God. The divine sanctions were personified as demons.

A person who takes false oaths not only desecrates the name of God (Leviticus 19:12) but he may not have access to God's holy places or their blessings (Psalm 24:4). □

Perush: Explaining the Teaching

The Gerer *rebbe*, one who surely understands the spiritual potential inherent in carefully crafted language, is particularly sensitive to the power of the oath as articulated in Numbers 30:3. What one says is what one is. Rashi offers us an interesting wordplay on the word *yakhel* ("to break"), which is related to *kehallel*, ("to make secular"). Our teacher moves us beyond Rashi. He deduces that if to break a pledge means to secularize it, then the words of the oath must be holy in themselves. God made the world with words: "Let there be. . . ." Words make reality. Uttering the words themselves implies an action. When these words are spoken in distress, they can be redemptive. When these words are infused with the words of Torah, they provide us with inner strength. □

Background Euphemisms are often found in the context of oaths. Often the rabbis changed the biblical text when referring to it on religious grounds. Likewise, less offensive words were substituted for offensive or disparaging ones. One reason for this: One should not open one's mouth to Satan (*Berachot* 19a). □

The Teaching (*continued*)

annihilation of distress. Therefore [the law of] this paragraph pertains to times of distress. For by means of the voice one is able to get out of straits, as it is written in Psalm 118:5, "In distress I called on God."

And just this was the intention of our sages who would utter vows during times of distress. Therefore, when one is in distress it is good to fortify oneself with the words of Torah and prayer. □

(125) Matot: Escape Route

The Teaching from Torah Temimah

They surrounded him on all four sides.

Rabbi Nathan said, quoting *Midrash Sifrei*, God gave to them [an open] quarter, in order that they would flee. In other words, God arranged that anyone who wanted to flee would have a place.

And the Rambam, Moses Maimonides, in his *Mishneh Torah*, "The Laws of Kings and Their Wars" (chap. 6, law 7), wrote that when you attack a city to seize it, you must never →

Perush: Explaining the Teaching

It would seem that our teacher is concerned with the wholesale slaughter that is described in our *parashah*. However, what really disturbs the commentator is an apparent contradiction. The text seems to imply that the Israelites surrounded the Midianites on all four sides and slew the entire male population – leaving no room for anyone to escape. Yet, *Midrash Sifrei* states that God arranged for one side of Midian to be left open. This would allow people to "run for their lives" in retreat when a city is under seige. This more humane approach to war is →

Scriptural Context

This chapter focuses on Moses' last armed struggle: the military campaign against the Midianites. Pinchas (instead of Joshua) is placed in command. Once the battle is over, the first permanent settlement takes place. □

Targum: English Translation
Numbers 31:1–7

1) **Adonai thus instructed Moses. 2) Avenge the Israelite people on the Midianites; then you can return to your kin. 3) Moses spoke thus to the people: Let us pick from among you men to form an army, and let them fall upon Midian to take *Adonai*'s vengeance on Midian. 4) You shall dispatch one thousand men from each tribe for the military campaign. 5) So one thousand from each tribe were handed over from the divisions of Israel, twelve thousand for the military campaign. 6) Moses sent forth on the military campaign one thousand from each tribe, with Pinchas, son of Eleazar serving as priest, equipped with the sacred vessels and the trumpet for sounding the attack. 7) *They took the field against Midian, as* Adonai *had commanded Moses, and slew every male.* □**

From the Tradition

In Numbers 35:13 and Deuteronomy 19:9 we have the six cities assigned by Moses as cities of refuge. There the manslayer would be free from the blood avenger to live a normal life. Scholars were permitted to take their students with them and a student was entitled to have his teacher brought to him (*Makkot* 10a). They were restricted from certain trades. Later, the additional forty-two cities allotted to the Levites were added as cities of refuge. All roads to these cities had to be kept in good repair, straight, and level. The manslayer would present himself to the elders of the city at the city gate. They would try him and determine whether the murder had been premeditated or not. If it had been, then he would be executed. Otherwise, he would be given refuge. □

Background Best known for his *Torah Temimah*, Baruch Ha-Levi Epstein was a Russian talmudic scholar who lived from 1860 to 1942. Unlike other scholars, he declined rabbinical positions in Pinsk, Moscow, and Petrograd in order to work in a bank, devoting his spare time to his study. The *Torah Temimah* is a classic compendium of quotations from the oral law arranged according to scriptural verses and annotated by his commentary. □

The Teaching (*continued*)

surround it on all four sides, but only three. You must leave a place for escape so that anyone who wants to escape can escape with his life. As it is said, "They took the field against Midian, as *Adonai* had commanded Moses. . . ." We have it on oral tradition that this was commanded.

But the language is not clearly explained, "We have it on oral tradition that this was commanded," nor are we told how this oral tradition was obtained. Furthermore, just where did Rabbi Nathan get this novel idea?

One possible explanation may depend on *Shevi'it* J. 6:1, which says that "Joshua sent three announcements before he entered the Land of Israel, and one of them was for anyone who wanted to flee to safety." And it seems that Joshua learned this from the way Moses waged war: "They took the field against Midian as *Adonai* had commanded Moses. . . ."

And this is the intent of the language "We have it on oral tradition that this was commanded," which is to say that Joshua learned that the custom was originally commanded to Moses. □

Perush: Explaining the Teaching (*continued*)

corroborated by Rambam in his *Mishneh Torah*. While the *Torah Temimah* discounts the possible explanation of the Yerushalmi, our teacher reasons that there must be an oral tradition to support both Rabbi Nathan and the Rambam. He comes to this by understanding "as *Adonai* commanded Moses" thus: "We have it on oral tradition that this was commanded." □

(126) Matot: Cleaning Your Brain

The Teaching
from Menachem Mendl of Kotzk

Why are the children of Israel commanded concerning the purification of objects only after the war with Midian? Why was this commandment not given immediately after the war with Sichon and Og, for surely then there were forbidden objects?

The reason is that in the battle with Sichon and Og the thought process of Israel was not contaminated, and therefore the commandment of purification was not given. But the Midianites defiled the thinking of Israel, as we read in Numbers 25:18: "They assailed you by the trickery they practiced against you, because of the affair of Peor and the affair of their kinswoman Cozbi, daughter of the Midianite chieftain. . . ."

For this reason the commandment regarding purification is renewed for the children of Israel; there is in it something of a hint: to relinquish everything that has been assimilated, which is to say, all impure thinking. □

Scriptural Context

While the entire chapter from our Torah portion deals with Moses and his final military undertaking, the section from which our text is taken focuses on the various regulations that govern the behavior of those involved in an armed struggle. □

Targum: English Translation
Numbers 31:21–24

21) Eleazar the priest said to the troops who had taken part in the battle, "This is the ritual that *Adonai* has instructed Moses to do." 22) Gold and silver, copper, iron, tin and lead, 23) *Any object that can withstand fire, these you shall pass through fire and they shall be clean* and they must be cleansed with the water of lustration; all others that cannot be passed through fire should just be passed through water. 24) On the seventh day, you should wash your clothes and be purified. After that you may return to camp. □

From the Tradition

Just as you can be made unclean by coming into contact with ritually impure things, you can be made holy by coming into intimate contact with holy things—like the altar. Even the vessels became holy once they had come into contact with God's presence. □

Perush: Explaining the Teaching

In this text, the Israelites are told how to purify a specific set of objects that had been defiled, presumably through contact with the dead. Always looking for inner consistency, Menachem Mendl is puzzled as to why this regulation is imposed, when it had not been imposed during the battle with Sichon and Og. He reasons that the physical cleansing must represent a spiritual cleansing as well. In the former battle Israel's thought processes had not been contaminated, but in this battle, as indicated in Numbers 25:18 (*Parashat Pinchas*) the Israelites' minds (and moral reasoning) were contaminated and needed to be purged. □

Background   Purity is a religious ideal. It is one of the steps on the way to the spirit of holiness (J. *Shekalim* 3:3). Purity and holiness are complemented by repentance and good deeds. Just as water purifies from ritual impurity, so does Torah purify the impure from his impurity (*Song of Songs Rabbah* 1:2, no. 3). □

(127) Masei: On the Road

The Teaching
from Ha-Shelah, Isaiah ben Abraham Ha-Levi Horowitz in *Shnei Luchot Ha-Brit*

The "wanderings" are a hint at exiles and pardons.

Every person who embarks on a long and tiring walk to learn Torah and, as we read in the name of Rabbi Nehorai in *Pirke Avot* 4:14, "wanders afar to a place of Torah," [should know that] this wandering is the very source. As the text implies: "The wanderings of the children of Israel at the command of God [or literally, 'were toward the mouth of God']." Thus these Jews were the first who wandered far from their homes to find a place of Torah. And your sign will be: "Go and learn." □

Scriptural Context
This portion, the last weekly portion of the book of Numbers, reviews the wanderings of the Israelites and projects the settlement boundaries for the eventual conquest of the Land. Eventually, how to deal with the native population, as well as self-government procedures are also established. □

Targum: English Translation
Numbers 33:1–2a

1) *These are the wanderings of the children of Israel who set out from the land of Egypt, troop by troop, in the charge of Moses and Aaron.* 2) **Moses recorded the starting points for each of the wanderings as instructed by** *Adonai.* □

From the Tradition
Some chasidic teachers traveled from village to village according to the principle of *Nedudei Galut*, the wanderings of exile. Their travels symbolically expressed their identification with the wanderings of the *Shechinah*, God's presence. □

Perush: Explaining the Teaching
There are those who believe that the Israelites could not have reached the exalted spiritual state in the land of Canaan without first experiencing slavery and exile in Egypt. But to get to the land of Israel, you must make a spiritual journey. Thus, Ha-Shelah comes to teach us that not only is this an introduction to the spiritual journeys (wanderings) of the Israelites but that the text (as hinted at in *Pirke Avot*) implies that such a spiritual journey (wandering) can only be achieved through the study of Torah. □

Background Isaiah ben Abraham Ha-Levi Horowitz (c. 1565–1630) was called Ha-Shelah Ha-Kadosh, the Holy Shelah from the initials of his most famous work *Shnei Luchot Ha-Brit* ("Two Tablets of the Covenant"). Born in Prague, Horowitz moved to Poland with his father, who was his first teacher. Later studying with various teachers including Meir of Lublin (the Maharam), he gained a reputation even while still a young scholar. In 1597 he published his father's *Emek Berachah* and included his own glosses. There his early influence by *Kabbalah* is already easily discernible. Holding several important European posts (*av bet din* of Dubno; *av bet din* and *rosh yeshivah* of Ostraha; *av bet din* of Frankfurt-am-Main), he moved to *Eretz Yisrael* and settled in Jerusalem in 1621 following the

death of his wife. Active in building up the Ashkenazi community there, he was imprisoned by the pasha and held for ransom. He died in Tiberias and is buried near Maimonides.

His chief work was first published in Amsterdam in 1649. It consists of two parts. The first contains laws according to the festival calendar and the second summarizes the 613 commandments as they appear in the Bible. Further subdividing the work, Horowitz included the reasons for the *mitzvot* according to *Kabbalah*, and *musar*–ethical precepts that emanate from the *mitzvot*. The laws for every day of the year are arranged in the framework of tractates, and he includes rules for hermeneutics.

Horowitz believed that *Kabbalah* was the teaching of "sages of truth who entered →

Background *(continued)*

the secret of *Adonai* received in unbroken tradition by word of mouth from Moses at Sinai." He contended that the time had come to reveal the secret wisdom of the *Zohar* in preparation for redemption, which was imminent. Since redemption was close at hand, such public study was permitted, for those studying would not fall to error. □

(128) Masei: Places to Hide

The Teaching
from the Sefas Emes, Yehudah Aryeh Leib of Ger

Behold, [for] one who murders someone even unintentionally, the very earth is cut out from beneath his feet. As we read in Numbers 35:33, "The land can have no expiation for blood that is shed on it, except by the blood of the one who shed it." Such a person would have no place in God's world were it not that the Holy One, from great love, gives this person a place to which he can flee.

In Moses Cordovero's *The Palm Tree of Deborah*, the idea is suggested that this great Divine love designates a place for "the destroyer" who kills someone. And this is the meaning of Exodus 21:12–13: "[He who fatally strikes a man ... unintentionally ...] I will assign you a place [to which you can flee]." The Holy One gives him a place, as we read in Deuteronomy 4:41, 43–44: "[Then Moses set aside three cities ...] *Betzer*, in the wilderness ... [and this is the Torah that Moses set before the children of Israel]." This gives him some strength [*Betzer*] and power, when he is "in the wilderness:" in his isolation, without habitation, all alone with himself, with only a broken heart [for company].

[Another interpretation is:] One who finds a refuge in the Torah, as our sages have taught in *Makkot* 10a: "Rabbi Yochanan asked, from where can we learn that the study of Torah provides asylum? From the passage in Deuteronomy 4:43, 'Then Moses set →

Scriptural Context

While most people attribute the importance of this Torah portion as a result of its mention of the Levitical towns that served uniquely as cities of refuge, these cities of refuge add to the complex understanding of the Levites. While part of scholarly debate, these cities apparently took the place of local altars that had previously served as places of refuge in the case of (unnatural) death. □

Targum: English Translation
Numbers 35:9–12

9) *Adonai* said to Moses 10) Speak to the Israelites and tell them when you cross the Jordan into the land of Canaan, 11) *You shall provide yourselves with places to serve you as cities of refuge to which a manslayer who has killed a person unintentionally may flee.* 12) These cities will serve you as shelter from the blood avenger until he has stood for justice in front of the [people's] court. □

From the Tradition

Moses assigned six cities as cities of refuge and set these aside in Transjordan while Joshua sanctified the other three west of the Jordan after the conquest of Canaan. If a person in need of refuge were a scholar, he was entitled to take his school with him. If a student, he could request that his teacher be brought. □

Perush: Explaining the Teaching

Quoting another teacher, the Sefas Emes wants to understand both the physical and spiritual levels of the cities of refuge as designated by the Torah text. He employs a wordplay from the city Betzer to "in the narrow place." This type of wordplay – which many teachers use – provides another mode of learning. On one level, God, out of Divine mercy, provides even the manslayer with a refuge. The refuge may be in Torah (according to Yochanan in *Makkot* 10a) or it may be an actual place. But if God is providing such refuge, however interpreted, then why might the manslayer be eligible for an avenging death if he goes beyond the boundaries set for him? Because if he leaves those boundaries, says the Sefas Emes, it is as if he has no blood (and is already dead).

For the rabbis who lived under the government of Rome, biblical Edom was merely a euphemism for Rome in their writings. □

The Teaching (*continued*)

aside three cities . . . Betzer, in the wilderness. . . .' And following it in verse 4:44, 'and this is the Torah which Moses set before the children of Israel.' " [In other words, Betzer is Torah.]

But if, as we read in Numbers 35:26: "However, if the manslayer ever goes outside the boundary of the city of refuge to which he fled . . . ," that is, he crosses the boundary that they drew for him, then the words of Numbers 35:27: ["And the avenger of blood find him outside the boundary of the city of his refuge, and the avenger of blood kill the manslayer,] he has no [shall not be guilty of] blood." As Rashi explains it, the blood avenger "is as though he had killed a dead man, one who has no blood."

And this is the intention of our sages in *Makkot* 12a: "Resh Lakish said that the prince [guardian angel] of Edom [cruel Rome, Esau] is destined to make three errors, as it is written in Isaiah 63:1, 'Who is this that comes from Edom with dyed garments from Botsrah?' [This alludes to a time when Rome's cruelty and murder of so many innocents will be punished.] He will err [first], because only Betzer affords asylum but he will go to Botsrah; he will err [again], as asylum is afforded only to slayers in error, but he slays with intent; and he will err [yet again], as asylum is afforded only to man, but he is an angel!" □

(129) Masei: Brains before Beauty

The Teaching
from ancient sources compiled in *Itturei Torah*

Rashi: Here it enumerates them according to their superiority over one another in years, for they were married in the order in which they were born. But everywhere else in the Bible it enumerates them according to their intelligence. [In Numbers 27:1, they are listed in the following order: Machlah, Noah, Choglah, Milkah, and Tirtzah.] This tells us that they were all equal.

The wife of Rabbi Saul of Amsterdam, as a young woman, was famous as a genius. After her marriage, when she was overburdened with the responsibilities of nursing children, her studies were interrupted.

They asked her, "What is the reason for this [enumeration]?"

She replied, "Throughout Scripture, the daughters of Zelophechad are enumerated according to their intelligence, but in →

Scriptural Context

Our text from this portion, near the very end of the book of Numbers, focuses on the family heads of the clan of Gilead, descendants of Manasseh, who ask Moses to rectify what appears to be an oversight in the allotment of land to the tribes. It seems that Zelophechad's land is to be divided among his daughters but if they marry outside the tribe, their portion will be transferred to the new tribe (of her husband). Moses tells them to marry within the tribe of the father and no land will be lost. □

Targum: English Translation
Numbers 36:10–12

10) **The daughters of Zelophechad did as** *Adonai* **had commanded Moses. 11)** *Machlah, Tirtzah, Choglah, Milkah, and Noah, Zelophechad's daughters, were married to sons of their uncles,* 12) **married into the clans of the descendants of Manasseh, son of Joseph, so that their portion remained in the tribe of their father's clan. □**

From the Tradition

Zelophechad died in the wilderness without sons, only five daughters. His daughters claimed that he did not deserve the punishment of dying "with the destruction of his name." Yet, there is no real indication as to what his desert sin was. Moses knew that Zelophechad was forgiven (for whatever sin he had committed) because the *Zohar* records God as speaking of him by name. The daughters requested from Moses that they be recognized as heirs to inherit their father's land. The case was settled by Divine decree, which led to the ruling regarding what becomes of the property of a man who dies without a male heir. □

Perush: Explaining the Teaching

Sensitive to even the slightest nuance, our unnamed teacher questions why the daughters of Zelophechad are listed in one order here in Numbers 36:11 and in a different order in Numbers 27:1. Citing Rashi, he reasons that in one place they are listed according to chronological age (the order also of their marriage), but elsewhere they are listed according to their intelligence. But the teacher reasons they are, in fact, listed according to the criterion of intelligence in both cases. Their intelligence changed because after they were married, they were burdened with housewifery and husbands! □

Background As in this passage, we are often able to sense the tension the tradition feels with regard to women, especially as readers view the tradition through a modern lens. Few women's voices are heard in the text, and therefore they must be searched out. Yet here there is a dichotomy established between intelligence prior to marriage and after it. The tradition attempts to establish a compromise between what it knows as an equality of intelligence with a desire to maintain distinctions between the roles distinctly assigned to men and women. □

The Teaching *(continued)*

our passage, according to when they were married. Why? Because when they were married, they were given millstones around their necks. So they forgot their intelligence, and therefore they are reckoned here only according to when they were married." □

DEUTERONOMY

(130) Devarim: You Hear Who You Are

The Teaching
from Simchah Bunem of Prszysucha

The word that Moses spoke depended *on all* Israel, to each one according to his or her character and age, his or her understanding and level of perception, each one according to his or her measure. □

Perush: Explaining the Teaching

Our teacher, Rabbi Simchah Bunem, is fascinated by the relationship between speaking and hearing. How could Moses use the same words to speak to everyone? Like all words, each individual can only hear them based on personal experience, ability, and wisdom. □

Scriptural Context

This portion begins the Book of Deuteronomy. It is a low-key introduction to the retelling of the story of the Israelite journey, playing down the hills and valleys of Israel's past. □

Targum: English Translation
Deuteronomy 1:1–5

1) *These are the words that Moses spoke to all Israel on the other side of the Jordan,* through the wilderness in the Aravah, near Suph, between Paran and Tophel, Laban, Chazerot, and Di-Zahav. 2) It is eleven days from Chorev to Kadesh Barnea by way of Mount Seir. 3) It was in the fortieth year, on the first day of the eleventh month, that Moses spoke to the Israelites according to the instructions given by *Adonai.* 4) After he had defeated Sichon, the king of the Amorites who dwelled in Cheshbon and Og, king of Bashan, who dwelled at Ashtarot [and] Edrei, 5) On [this] side of the Jordan in the land of Moab, Moses began explaining this Torah saying. . . . □

From the Tradition

According to the *Midrash* (*Exodus Rabbah* 47:15), the angels were jealous of the role God had entrusted to Moses on bringing Torah to human beings. Thus, they voiced suspicions that Moses might add his own ideas. God tells the angels that Moses would not do so but that he could nevertheless be trusted to reflect the Divine will. □

Background Rabbi Yishmael maintained that the Written Torah spoke in the language of humans but he regarded each word as divinely inspired. Even God's speaking at Sinai was heard differently by all 600,000 Jews assembled at the foot of the mountain. □

(131) Devarim: *Teshuvah* before Torah

The Teaching
from *Maor Ve-Shemesh* (Light and Sun)

[Why does it say in the fifth verse, "He began" explaining? Because he "began" explaining] the connection to the preceding verses, "These are the words . . ." (Deuteronomy 1:1) [which, according to Rashi] are words of reproof, scolding [for he enumerates all the places where the people provoked God].

Now it is possible to explain this connection [between scolding and Torah] according to the teaching of Jacob Isaac, "The Seer of Lublin" (1745–1815): "One needs to make *teshuvah* [turn in repentance] before one begins to study. Otherwise, God forbid, [one might become like the "wicked child" of the Passover *Haggadah*]. "God →

Scriptural Context

In this portion Moses retells the story of the journey of the Israelites. Moses reviews his own role in the journey in the wilderness, especially disclosing his own disappointment at not being able to enter the Promised Land. □

Targum: English Translation
Deuteronomy 1:1–5

1) **These are the words which Moses spoke to all Israel on the other side of the Jordan. Through the wilderness in the Aravah, near Suph, between Paran and Tophel, Laban, Chazerot, and Di-Zahav. 2) It is eleven days from Chorev to Kadesh Barnea by way of Mount Seir. 3) It was in the fortieth year, on the first day of the eleventh month, that Moses spoke to the Israelites according to the instructions given by Ado-nai. 4) After he had defeated Sichon, the king of the Amorites who dwelled in Cheshbon and Og, king of Bashan who dwelled at Ashtarot [and] Edrei 5)** *On [this] side of the Jordan in the land of Moab, Moses began explaining this Torah saying. . . .* □

From the Tradition

God urges Israel to repent and not be ashamed to do so because a child is not ashamed to return to one's loving parent (*Deuteronomy Rabbah* 2:24). Furthermore, God says to Israel, "My children, open for Me an opening of repentance as narrow as the eye of a needle and I will open for you gates through which wagons and coaches can pass" (*Song of Songs Rabbah* 5:2, no. 2). □

Perush: Explaining the Teaching

Our teacher is intrigued by the words "he *began* explaining" since our text is taken from the fifth verse of the chapter. Should not such a phrase appear at the beginning of the chapter (and Book of Deuteronomy)? What he began to explain, suggests our teacher, is the connection between the previous verse "These are the words" that refers to the words of rebuke and the phrase "this Torah." One must make repentance before study. Thus, Moses wanted the Israelites to do *teshuvah*, to return, before he explains Torah to them so that they may study its words. The act of study here is understood as the ultimate act of communion with God. □

Background Kalonymus Kalman of Cracow Epstein (d. 1823) became noted for the ecstatic mode of prayer he adopted. In 1875, he organized groups of *chasidim* in Cracow and arranged *minyanim* who prayed with bodily movements. Opposed by the establishment, he was excommunicated but continued to flourish nonetheless. His *Maor Ve-Shemesh* is a fundamental work on Chasidism. Published by his son Aaron, it contains a great deal of information on the history of the *chasidim*. □

The Teaching (continued)

says to the wicked one, 'What is it to you to recount My statutes.' "

Even meditating on the possibility of *teshuvah* (repentance) is enough. Accordingly our sages taught in *Kiddushin* 49b, "[If a man says to his bride under the *chuppah*, Behold] you are consecrated unto me [as my wife], on the condition that I am righteous,' she is still betrothed. For even if he is found to be wicked, he may have meditated on making *teshuvah* [and that would have been enough]."

And just this is what is hinted at in the juxtaposition of the verses. "These are the words . . ." (Deuteronomy 1:1), [which Moses] spoke, words of reproof and scolding, in order to get the people to return in *teshuvah*. And why? Because [only now, five verses later, do we read that] "Moses began explaining this Torah . . ." (Deuteronomy 1:5). So we conclude that first he wanted to get them to return in *teshuvah*. □

(132) Devarim: Sichon and Og

The Teaching
from Sefas Emes, Yehudah Aryeh Leib of Ger

My teacher, Isaac Meir of Rothenberg Alter of Ger, the author of *Chidusshei Ha-Rim*, said that before this, Moses was unable to get his words to penetrate the hearts of the children of Israel, for Sichon and Og were great and terrible *kelippot*, "broken shards."

Indeed so it is alluded to in the →

Perush: Explaining the Teaching

In the beginning of the Book of Deuteronomy, Moses addresses the people and the text tells us that the address took place after the battle of Sichon and Og. Why at this point, asks the Sefas Emes? He reasons

Scriptural Context

The first portion of the last book of the Torah provides the setting for what follows. Unlike the later chapters it presents mostly details with little emotion. □

Targum: English Translation
Deuteronomy 1:1–5

1) **These are the words that Moses [used to] address Israel on the other side of the Jordan. Through the wilderness in the Aravah near Suph, between Paran and Tophel, Laban, Chazerot, and Di-Zahav. 2) It is eleven days from Horeb to Kadesh Barnea by the route of Mount Seir. 3) It was in the fortieth year, on the first day of the eleventh month that Moses addressed the Israelites in accordance with the instructions that** *Adonai* **had given him for them. 4)** *After he had defeated Sichon king of the Amorites, who dwelt in Cheshbon, and Og king of Bashan, who dwelt at Ashtarot and Edrei.* **5) On the other side of the Jordan, in the land of Moab, Moses attempted to explicate this teaching.** □

From the Tradition

Rabbinic tradition imagines Og as a giant. *Genesis Rabbah* 53:10 suggests: "When Og, who was present at the feast Abraham made on the occasion of Isaac's weaning, was teased by all the great men assembled there for having called Abraham a sterile mule, he pointed contemptuously at Isaac saying, 'I can crush him by putting my finger on him.' Whereupon God said, 'You mock the gift given to Abraham. By your life shall you look upon myriads of his descendants and *your* fate will be in their hands.' " □

that before this point, Moses would not have been able to reach the Israelites – in their hearts. Sichon and Og, according to the Sefas Emes, are really "broken shards."

This is an allusion to the Lurianic image of the source of evil. According to the *Kabbalah*, the universe is strewn with the debris of a cosmologic cataclysm and Sichon and Og are actually metaphors for this primoridal refuse. How does he know this? He deduces it from the passage in Exodus instructing us to wear *tefillin*. By wearing them, near our eyes and heart, God's Torah penetrates each individual. The metaphor of God's *tefillin* serves our teacher in a similar way for the entire people of Israel. It allows God to nullify all evil thoughts and evil influences that would potentially have the power to destroy Israel. □

Background Isaac Meir Rothenberg of Ger was known as Chiddushei Ha-Rim (the insightful writings of Rabbi Isaac Meir) or Itsche Meir as he was often called. As Gerer *rebbe*, he wrote, "Rabbi Simchah Bunem led with love and [Menachem Mendl of] Kotzk with fear. I shall lead with Torah." An interesting character, he once said, "I do not want a rabbi who will embrace me. I want one who would rend the flesh from my bones." While certainly the leader of the Gerer community, he remarked, "I am not a *rebbe*. I do not want money. I do not care for honor. All I want is to spend my years bringing the children of Israel nearer to their Father in Heaven." □

The Teaching (*continued*)

passage from Exodus 13:9 dealing with *tefillin*, "And this shall be for you a sign on your hand and a reminder between your eyes, in order that the Torah of God may be in your mouth."

This is because by means of wearing *tefillin*, the Torah of God is inculcated into the heart. Therefore the deed of laying *tefillin* with commitment enables one to recite the *Shema*. And just as in private, so with the entire community of Israel.

And just this is an allusion to *tefillin*, as it were, worn by the Master of the Universe. For just as the children of Israel dedicate their hearts, nullify all their thoughts and evil deeds serving the will of the Creator, so, as it were, God nullifies the power of the impulse to do evil and all [evil] influences only for the children of Israel. And this is the real meaning of the battle of Sihon and Og. □

(133) Va-Etchanan: The Reward of I Am

The Teaching
from Tzadok Ha-Kohen of Lublin

According to *Makkot* 24a, [the first two utterances,] "I am" and "You shall not have," were heard *Mi-Pi Ha-Gevruah*, directly from God.

The utterance "I am" precedes the utterance, "You shall not have." And upon careful reflection on the "I am, the *anochi*," – with sure faith in God's perfection – one is saved from [violating] "You shall not have" and protected from all kinds of impediments to the service of God.

Our sages taught in *Midrash Tanhuma* (on *Parashat Vayetze*) that for every commandment one fulfills, there is made for that person a guardian angel. Measure for measure. Israel received all the commandments through Moses, our teacher, an intermediary. And on account of this an angel was assigned to them to watch over them.

But the "I am" and the "You shall not have" Israel heard directly from God [without any intermediary, without any guardian]. And for this reason, [as] the reward for fulfilling the "I am" God, God's Divine Self protects a person from violating the "You shall not have." □

Scriptural Context

In this Torah portion, Moses moves from a relatively simple summary of the past to the essential covenant requirements of what the God of Israel requires of the people of Israel. With this, the second discourse, the former stammerer, who had previously hesitated in responding to God's request to speak to Pharaoh, rises to the height of master orator. □

Targum: English Translation
Deuteronomy 5:6–10

6) *I am* Adonai, *your God who brought you out of the land of Egypt, out of the house of bondage.* 7) *You shall have no other gods besides Me.* 8) **You shall not make any graven images, any likeness of the heaven above or the earth below, or the waters that flow beneath the earth.** 9) **Don't bow down or serve them. I** Adonai, **your God, am an impassioned God visiting the guilt of the ancestors on their descendants, upon the third and fourth generations of those who reject Me.** 10) **But I show kindness to the thousandth generation of those who love Me and keep my** *mitzvot.* □

From the Tradition

Rabbi Simlai taught that 613 commandments were revealed to Moses on Mount Sinai. Three hundred and sixty five prohibitions are equal to the solar days, and 248 mandates correspond to the number of bones in the body. (*Makkot* 23b). The number 613 is usually referred to in the Hebrew mnemonic TaRYaG. □

Perush: Explaining the Teaching

Reflecting on the verses "I am *Adonai*" and "You shall have no other gods," the Tzadok Ha-Kohen of Lublin recalls that according to *Makkot* 24a, these utterances were actually heard directly from God, while the rest of the Divine commandments were heard through Moses. He reasons that since "I am" precedes "You shall not have," the text implies that awareness of the Divine self (I am) prevents you from going astray (You shall not have). The reason for belief, therefore, is that God Godself protects/prevents you from going astray by way of the *mitzvot.* □

Background According to the mystics, commandments are integrated into the general system in relation to two basic principles: a symbolic view according to which everything in the world, as well as all human acts – especially religious acts – are a reflection of the Divine process; and a reciprocal influence between the upper and lower worlds, which are not separated from one another but do impact one or the other. □

(134) Va-Etchanan: Your Money or Your Life

The Teaching
from the Sefas Emes, Yehudah Aryeh Leib of Ger

Rashi: [citing *Midrash Sifrei*]: You have people whose money is more precious to them than their bodies, [they could easily suffer great pain rather than part with their money] and it is on account of this that scripture adds, "with all your might." [That is to say, you must love God with your money as much as you love God with your life.]

At first glance this seems odd. How could there be someone whose wealth is more precious to him than his body? Perhaps the answer is this: the goal of human life is that we repair our deeds and return "this which has been lent on deposit" to its original owner. [Traditional logic is that we return our bodies to God.]

Our sages [after all do] explain in *Berachot* 8a that Psalm 32:6, " 'For this let every one that is godly pray unto You in the time of finding.' . . . Rabbi Nachman ben Isaac said that 'in the time of finding' refers to [the finding of] death." →

Scriptural Context

This portion contains the second discourse of Moses. With it, his oratory rises to a level that truly reflects the character of Deuteronomy. In this presentation, Moses' instructions are not only substantiated by God's concerns but they are also actually linked with Divine promises for Israel. □

Targum: English Translation
Deuteronomy 6:4–7

4) **Listen Israel. Adonai is our God. Only Adonai. 5) And you shall love Adonai, your God, with all your soul, and with all your might. 6) And these instructions that I give you today 7) Teach them to your children and when you are at home or away, on rising, and on lying down** [to go to sleep]. □

From the Tradition

In the morning liturgy, we ask God to unify our hearts to love and fear (revere) Your name. Love and fear of God–and the tension that exists between these two feelings–are the primary motivations for serving God. Yet, we are reminded to act out of love, for the Torah makes a distinction between one who acts out of love and one who acts out of fear. □

Perush: Explaining the Teaching

The Sefas Emes wants to understand why the text has placed this important part of the *Shema*'s blessings as heart, soul, and then might. Citing Rashi, who in turn is citing the *Midrash Sifrei*, he suggests that it is to teach us that one should love God with substance– for those whose money is exceptionally precious to them–as much as their life. The Gerer is not persuaded by the argument since he knows that both body and substance (not soul) are simply lent to us by God during our earthly sojourn. Perhaps therefore the text refers to our time of death when our souls realize what they have yearned for all our life–to be with God. But the text has a more profound message, says the Gerer. The one who loves God with his money and thereby causes his body discomfort (through depriving himself of "creature comforts") is loving God with his body as well. □

Background Simchah Bunem of Przysucha taught: It is possible to surmise from what our sages said concerning the verse in Genesis 3:16, "In pain you shall bear children . . .," that [it means] with the measure of "all your soul." [They said that] when a woman is in childbirth, she is forty-nine parts dead and one part alive.

But if "in pain" is [categorized as] forty-nine parts [death!] what could it possibly mean to "love the Lord, your God . . . with all your soul"? From this we begin to learn just how far one needs to go to arrive at the "love of God." □

The Teaching (*continued*)

We also have in the book, *Duties of the Heart* [Bachya ben Joseph ibn Pakuda, 11th century] that righteous ones [*tzaddikim*] yearn to leave the prison of the body [so you could easily think that giving one's body away would be the goal]: "Therefore, those who punish themselves with the love of God, punishing their souls with a whole heart, will be rewarded with the knowledge and understanding that this is the beginning of truth."

But [for] one who hands over his money in order to dwell in distress and hardship, and the misery transports him on behalf of their Creator – a test like this is harder than risking his life. □

(135) Va-Etchanan: Public and Private

The Teaching
from the Sefas Emes, Yehudah Aryeh Leib of Ger

The Book of Deuteronomy, or the *Mishneh Torah* [meaning "the retelling, or recapitulation of the Torah," not to be confused with Maimonides' fourteen-volumes of law by the same name] is like the *tefillin* worn on the hand [whose box has only one compartment], while the four other books (of the Five Books of Moses) are like the *tefillin* worn on the forehead [whose parchments are rolled individually and set in four separate chambers].

And, in the same way, everything that has been said in the preceding four books is contained in the *Mishneh Torah*, so, all the biblical passages are [rolled into a single scroll contained] in the one "house" of the *tefillin* worn on the hand.

For this reason, the book is called *Devarim* [words], words of rebuke [as we find in *Parashat Ki Tavo*, Deuteronomy 28] whose aim is to draw the children of Israel near and bind their hearts to the Torah – just like the *tefillin* of the hand, which is "bound" upon the forearm directly beside the heart. In contrast, the *tefillin* of the head are close to the brain.

Our sages said in *Berachot* 6a, "And all the people of the land saw that the Name of God has been called upon you." This refers to the *tefillin* worn on the head [since it is public and always in view]. →

Scriptural Context

Moses' second discourse opened with a restatement of the Decalogue. In the section of our portion, he elucidates the second commandment and articulates what becomes the Shema and its blessings. □

Targum: English Translation
Deuteronomy 6:8–9

8) *You shall bind them as a sign on the hand and they shall be for frontlets between your eyes.* **9) Inscribe them on the doorposts of your house and on your gates.** □

From the Tradition

The wearing of *tefillin* is designed to induce a serious frame of mind and prevent levity (*Berachot* 30b). The kabbalists developed a meditation (*kavvanah*) to create this context: "You have instructed us to lay the *tefillin* on the head as a memorial of Your outstretched arm, opposite the heart to indicate the duty of subjecting the longings and designs of our heart to Your service, and on the head over against the brain to teach the mind whose seat is the brain together with all senses to subject it to Your service." □

Perush: Explaining the Teaching

While the Sefas Emes is commenting on verses later in Deuteronomy, he is reflecting on the subject of the entire book. He believes that just as the *tefillin shel yad* has one compartment, while the *tefillin shel rosh* has four compartments, it is more concentrated, so to speak. What is said in Deuteronomy is a recapitulation of what had come before in the prior four books, but in a more pointed manner.

This book is called *Devarim* (literally, "words"), words that are considered words of rebuke. Such words bring the individual closer to God, just as *tefillin shel yad* are drawn closer to the heart. Through this sign (cf. Deuteronomy 6:8) the Israelites bind themselves to God. Our teacher reasons that the *tefillin shel yad* is actually hidden from view, but the *tefillin shel rosh* is open for all to see. The sequence of the text suggests that we bind ourselves (*shel yad*) before we share our relationship with others and make it visible to the public (*shel rosh* – as frontlets). We also put the *tefillin* on our hand before placing it on our head in the morning ritual sequence. □

Background According to a *baraita*, it was permissible for *tefillin* to be worn by women. "Michael, the daughter of a Cushite, wore *tefillin* and the sages did not protest (*Eruvin* 96a). □

The Teaching (*continued*)

And this also was the way things were for the people of the wilderness generation; it was a time of revelation, with revealed miracles [everywhere]. But the *Mishneh Torah* represents the way things were for the Jewish people after they had entered the Land of Israel – [for now, all the miracles were] in concealment.

As it says in *Menachot* 37b, " 'And it shall be for you a sign upon your hand,' implying that the sign shall be for you but not for others [because it is worn on the arm, concealed from view by one's clothing]."

And I have heard from the mouth of my elder teacher, his memory is a blessing (the author of *Chiddushei Ha-Rim,* Isaac Meir Rothenberg Alter of Ger) that [of all the five books] the children of Israel had the most intimate relationship with the *Mishneh Torah,* for through the power of the *Mishneh Torah* they bound themselves to the whole Torah.

[The sequence is precisely the way] we read in Deuteronomy 6:8, [first] "You shall bind. . . ." And only after this is it written, "And they shall be for you for frontlets. . . ." □

(136) Ekev: Spiritual Hunger

The Teaching
from Mendl of Rymanov

What possible purpose could God have had to starve us in the wilderness? Normally when a person wants something to eat, once it is put into his hand, even if he refrains from eating it, his craving stops.

But in spiritual matters, no matter how much one tries to quench one's thirst, the yearning continues. And just this was the virtue of the *mannah*: Even though it was given to them every day, and in a measure appropriate to each person's needs, a measure per person, nevertheless, despite all this, they were hungry and yearned for the *mannah*, and it did not satisfy their [yearning] at all. □

Perush: Explaining the Teaching

Knowing that God's plans are for our eventual benefit, Mendl of Rymanov wonders why God would

Scriptural Context

This portion focuses on Moses' attempt to help the people realize the profound benefit of God's gifts to Israel. It is only through God's benevolence that Israel continues to enjoy good fortune – as the people did during their desert sojourn. The Israelites are told that the land that they will inherit is a good land but that they will enjoy its produce only if they do not fall prey to vain pride. □

From the Tradition

According to the *Tanchuma* (Exodus 66), each day *mannah* fell sufficient to sustain the Jewish people for two thousand years. This spared the Israelites the need to carry it throughout their wanderings. Receiving a new supply every day made the Jews turn to God constantly for daily bread (*Yoma* 76a). □

Targum: English Translation
Deuteronomy 8:1-6

1) **You should observe all of the *mitzvot* that I offer you so that you might live well and take advantage of the land that *Adonai* promised your ancestors. 2) Remember the journey that *Adonai* your God led you on these past forty years in the desert so that you might be tested by difficulties to learn what is [truly] in your hearts, whether you would [really] observe the *mitzvot* [or not]. 3) [God] afflicted you and starved you and fed you *mannah* that neither you nor your parents had known, so that you might learn that human beings do not live only on bread, but that men [and women] might live on anything that *Adonai* arranges. 4) Your clothes did not wear out, nor did your feet swell these forty years. 5) Keep in mind that *Adonai* your God disciplines you in the same way a parent disciplines a son [or daughter]. 6) Go observe the *mitzvot* of *Adonai* your God; walk in [holy] ways and revere [God].** □

want to starve the Israelites in the desert only to provide them with *mannah* to eat. Unlike regular food, which allays the craving to eat – even before it is eaten, once it is provided on your plate – *mannah* did nothing to satisfy the spiritual yearning of the people. Thus, they continued to yearn for God's presence. Food feeds the body but not the spirit. Even communion with God cannot satiate our spiritual yearning. □

Background Menachem Mendl of Rymanov (also Rymanower), a pupil of Elimelech of Lyzhansk, was a *tzaddik* who was an ascetic. Legend suggests that he saw the battles of Gog and Magog manifest in the Napoleonic wars and prayed for the victory of Napoleon as a precursor for redemption. □

(137) Ekev: Leave Laughing

The Teaching
from Lev Same'ach (A Joyous Heart)

According to *Leviticus Rabbah* 11:7, the word ve-hayah, והיה ("and there will be," that is, "if you do these rules") connotes joy wherever it occurs in the biblical text. And it is by means of joy that you will come to such a point that "you will obey these rules and observe them carefully . . ."

According to *Pesachim* 31b, we learn that "money can only be guarded [by burying it] in the earth." *Mitzvot*, Divine commandments, likewise can only be guarded (or, kept) with *simchah*, joy.

Rabbi Hanoch of Aleksandrow (of the Przysucha school) used to teach that "if you depart in *simchah*, joy, you will be transported in peace." By means of joy, it is possible to leave every sorrow in peace. □

Perush: Explaining the Teaching

Our teacher senses several things at work with the word *ve-hahah* (and there will be). Drawing on *Leviticus Rabbah*, he concludes that it implies joy in connection with the performance of *mitzvot*. The joy that ensues from following God's way will sustain us through every sorrow. □

Scriptural Context

This Torah portion deals with the challenges the Israelites will face in the pagan world of the Canaanites. This will be the first time since leaving Egypt that the Israelites will be in such close contact with a foreign and potentially influential element. □

Targum: English Translation
Deuteronomy 7:12–13

12) *And if you do obey these rules and observe them carefully, then* **Adonai** *our God will maintain faithfully for you the covenant that God made an oath with our ancestors.* 13) **God will love you and bless you and make you numerous. God will bless the fruit of your womb and the fruits of [your labors on] the earth, your new grain, wine and oil, the calving of your herd and the lambing of your flock in the land God swore to your ancestors to give you.** □

From the Tradition

Rabbi Arthur Green, in *Seek My Face, Speak My Name* (Jason Aronson, 1992) wrote: "It is we who make this covenant, we who, in the person of Moses, dash half the blood of a sacramental offering over the altar—representing God—and pour the other half over ourselves, binding ourselves in an act of eternal commitment to the One of Sinai. In doing so, the Jewish people performs an act of eternal living commitment, forging a link between this event and all Jewish generations to come. It is in this sense that we continue to speak of Sinai as covenant. It is we who at Sinai declare our undying devotion to the universal ever-flowing and yet unchanging One. . . . Covenant is our willingness to be a channel, to serve as a conduit of God's presence to those with whom we live." □

Background According to the Baal Shem Tov, "Weeping is evil, for humans should serve God with joy. But if one weeps for joy, tears are commendable." □

(138) Ekev: A Joy to Serve

The Teaching
from the Sefas Emes, Yehudah Aryeh Leib of Ger

According to *Leviticus Rabbah* 11:7, the word *ve-hayah*, והיה, and there will be . . . connotes joy wherever it occurs in the biblical text.

According to the joy and a person's yearning for fulfilling the commandments, so one merits to hear, to attain, and fulfill them. "And it shall come to pass if you faithfully listen. . . ." If you receive the commandments in joy, by means of this you will listen to My commandments . . . to love *Adonai* your God and serve God with all your heart and with all your soul. . . ."

The reward of a commandment is a commandment. By means of the beauty and the joy of the commandment comes complete fulfillment of the commandment. And just this is the preparation for performing a commandment and the reason why we are commanded to recite a blessing before doing a commandment. □

Scriptural Context

In this portion, the rules for the occupation of Canaan are given to the Israelites. They are rather simple and straightforward. The instructions reflect a potential clash of cultures (not unlike our own times)—and eventually turn to the inner life of spiritual Israel. Our text is taken from the section of the portion that indicates to the people of Israel that if they do as God has instructed them, they will indeed be successful—in whatever they do in the Land. □

From the Tradition

According to *Mishnah Sukkah* 5:1, unless one witnesses the Water Drawing Festival, one has not experienced real joy. The Yalkut to Psalms went so far as to say, "The one who has seen something pleasant and not enjoyed it will be held guilty." □

Targum: English Translation
Deuteronomy 11:13–14

13) *And it shall come to pass if you faithfully listen to My commandments that I command you today to love **Adonai** your God and to serve God with all your heart and with all your soul.* 14) **I will grant the rain for your land in the appropriate season, the early and late rain. You shall gather in your new grain and wine and oil.** □

Perush: Explaining the Teaching

The Sefas Emes calls to mind a text from *Letivicus Rabbah* connecting *ve-hayah* with joy. But he takes it one step further, arguing that the level of joy with which one approaches the *mitzvot* is equal to one's ability to actually reach its level of (spiritual) fulfillment. Thus, the reward of the *mitzvot* is the joy of completely fulfilling your obligation and coming close to the One who offers the *mitzvot* in the first place. Hence, a blessing is recited prior to the performance of each of the *mitzvot*.

Background Rabbi Hanoch of Aleksandrow taught: "Do you wish to know how important it is to be full of joy at all times? Moses encountered a long series of crises (later in Deuteronomy 28) and then remarked (verse 27) because you did not serve *Adonai* with joyfulness and with gladness of heart." □

(139) Re'eh: All of One

The Teaching from Tzeror Ha-Mor

The verb, *to see*, in Hebrew is in the singular but its object, *before you*, is in the plural. The reason is to teach us an important principle of faith and the meaning of being a Jew.

For while the people of Israel are many, they are also effectively a singular corporate entity, for the root of their souls originates in the Only One of Being.

As Rashi has taught from the *Midrash*, commenting on Genesis 46:26: "Esau's family had only six [himself and five sons], and Scripture refers to them as "the souls of his house," in the plural, because they served many gods. Jacob's family had seventy souls [when he went down to Egypt] yet Scripture refers to them as "a soul" in the singular, for they worshiped One God.

Scriptural Context

This portion comes between the end of the second discourse and the beginning of the third, opening with the command to bless Mount Gerizim and curse Mount Ebal. Invoking God's name, the special laws of Deuteronomy are listed. □

Targum: English Translation
Deuteronomy 11:26–28

26) *See, I set before you today a blessing and a curse.* 27) **A blessing: if you obey the instructions of** *Adonai* **your God, which I offer you today.** 28) **A curse: if you do not regard the instructions of** *Adonai* **your God but turn away from the directions I have shown you today and follow other gods who you do not [really] know.** □

From the Tradition

According to the Book of Deuteronomy (27:4-8), the Israelites were instructed to build a stone altar on Mount Gerizim, to engrave on it all the words of the law. A blessing was to be placed on Mount Gerizim and a curse on Mount Ebal (Deuteronomy 11:29; 27:12–13). Both mountains rise above the city of Shechem. Gerizim is covered with trees while there is comparatively little vegetation on Ebal. □

For this reason we find in the Torah instances when Israel is referred to in the singular: "You shall not have other gods," and in the plural, "You shall not make for yourselves other gods," indicating Israel's excellence: for even when they are many they are nevertheless one, all of them a single unity.

For this reason our sages teach in *Pirke Avot* 3:6, "Ten who sit and busy themselves in Torah, the *Shechinah* dwells among them. . . and this applies even to five . . and this applies even to one," all in order to teach that even when they are many, they are one, and when they are one, they are many.

And the Holy One of Being joins with them, for God is the Only One of Being [the source of all unity] and, in the words of Psalm 24:2," The whole earth is full of God." □

Perush: Explaining the Teaching

Our teacher notes that the verb in the text is set in the singular while its object is written in plural form. Why the difference? It is written this way to teach us the essential Jewish lesson. While there are many Jewish people, our souls all originate from the "Only One of Being" and they represent a singular unity. In other places in the Torah where idol worship is mentioned, such a singular is not used. Only when the Torah is referring to the monotheistic faith of Israel is such a construction apparent. Even when there are many, there is only One. □

Background Serving the One God makes for the unity of people. While the serving of many gods fragments the individual. □

(140) Re'eh: The *Maskilim* and the Kotzker

The Teaching
from the Chasidic Anthologies

Many enlightened, free-thinking intellectuals (*maskilim*) would come again and again to the door of the rabbi of Kotzk. Some came with the pure intention of gleaning his sharp and deep words of wisdom; others came only to argue and annoy him.

To one of these *maskilim* from the former category the Kotzker once quoted Psalm 14:2, "'*Adonai* looks down from heaven on humanity to find a person of understanding [literally, "a *maskil*"] who seeks God.' The Holy One personally searches everywhere for a real person of understanding [*maskil*] who truly seeks God. Whereas *maskilim* who [think they can] find wisdom on the end of their noses are beyond counting."

A *maskil* from the second group once said to the Kotzker, "*Berachot* 56b–57a, teaches that 'if one sees an elephant →

Targum: English Translation
Deuteronomy 13:2–5

2) *If there appears among you a prophet or a dream-diviner and he gives you a sign or a portent* 3) saying, "Let's go worship another god that we will follow" – one whom you have not experienced – even if the sign or portent [somehow coincidentally] comes true, 4) do not heed the words of that prophet or dream-diviner. God is really testing you to see if you really love *Adonai* with all your heart and soul. 5) Follow none [other] but *Adonai* [who is your] God and revere none but God. Hold fast to God. □

Scriptural Context

This portion, which includes Moses' third discourse, begins with a discussion of the central sanctuary. In order to achieve this centrality, all other sacred sites and altars were to be destroyed. This raised other problems such as false prophets. This section is divided into three parts: the signs or warnings a false prophet might unintentionally give you to belie himself; things family members might do to lead you astray; and the devastation that will be wreaked on the community that follows a false prophet. □

From the Tradition

It was known that there were professional prophets and dream diviners in the ancient world. Joseph and Daniel were not considered dream diviners (false prophets) because they were asked ad hoc by foreign potentates to interpret dreams for them. They were amateurs, not professionals, so to speak. □

Perush: Explaining the Teaching

Chasidism had many detractors, most notably the *maskilim*, those who felt that the secular enlightenment offered the Jewish people a truth that the folk religion of the *chasid* was incapable of offering. Therefore, the *rebbes* were often in a position of defending their position.

Here the *rebbe* used the text to show that those who challenged the *rebbe's* authority were akin to those false prophets and dream diviners mentioned in the Torah.

This exchange was fairly typical of the style of the Kotzker *rebbe*. He was famous for his quick-witted, acerbic love of Jews and truth. He said to his challenger, Judaism is only transformational to the believer. If you don't believe, it will do you no good. So don't expect it. □

Background The Hebrew in Deuteronomy 13:5 uses the root *achar* (literally, "go after *Adonai*"). This root is only used when the object is far away. Our teachers wondered then, why would the text use such a word when the ultimate goal is to bring the individual close to God. They reasoned that it is only after one pursues *after* God that the individual can become close to God. □

The Teaching (*continued*)

[*pil*] in a dream, miracles [*pila'ot*] will be done for him . . and if one sees a myrtle in a dream, he will have good luck with his property [like a myrtle, which has numerous leaves].' Well, [sneered the *maskil*], I saw an elephant in my dreams and I saw a myrtle and no miracle happened for me and business didn't prosper at all."

Replied the Kotzker: "One who eats like a Jew and drinks like a Jew and sleeps like a Jew and lives like a Jew, dreams like a Jew. But if you gorge yourself like your enemy and you get drunk like your enemy and you sleep with animals like your enemy and you live like your enemy, do you expect that the interpretation of your dreams should then be like a Jew?" □

(141) Re'eh: City of Happiness

**The Teaching
from the Saba of Slobodka, "Der
Alter," Rav Nison Tzvi Finkel**

The Torah offers this commandment
with an explanation
for the reason right
beside it. It is the
commandment of
the second tithe. It
regards dedication
to holy service, for it
obligates every Jew
to separate a tenth
portion of his or her
produce and forbids
us from eating of it
in any place except
Jerusalem. But
why? "So that you
may learn to revere
Adonai, your God,
forever."

The idea seems to
be that from the
time of eating →

**Perush: Explaining
the Teaching**

The Saba of Slo-
bodka begins his
lesson by noting

Scriptural Context

If Israel is to become a holy nation, then
holiness must come from its adherence
to a higher set of standards and values
for communal liv-
ing. This section
of the portion fo-
cuses on food,
tithes, and equity
among socioeco-
nomic classes. ☐

**From the
Tradition**

For the Jew, Jeru-
salem is the center
of the world.
Among the ten mir-
acles wrought in
Jerusalem are, "No
person was stricken
in Jerusalem, no
person ever stum-
bled in Jerusalem,
no fire ever broke
out in Jerusalem,
and no building ever
collapsed in Jerusa-
lem" (*Avot de Rabbi
Natan* 35). ☐

**Targum: English Translation
Deuteronomy 14:23–26**

23) *You shall consume the tithes of
your new grain and wine and oil and
the firstlings of your herds and flocks,
in the presence of* **Adonai** *your God,
in the place where God will choose to
establish God's name, so that you
may learn to revere* **Adonai**, *your
God, forever.* 24) **If the distance is
too great for you and you are unable to transport them because
the place God has established the
Divine name is too far, because
God has blessed you** 25) **then you
may convert them to money.
Wrap up the money and take it to
the place** *Adonai* **has chosen** 26)
**and spend it on anything you
want—cattle, sheep, wine, or
other intoxicant, or anything you
desire. Then you should feast
there in the presence of** *Adonai*
**your God. Rejoice with your
household.** ☐

how our text gives us the reason for the commandment right next to the commandment
itself. He then offers a teaching about Jerusalem and the role of joy in serving God. Our
obligation is to try to live our lives in fulfillment of the *mitzvot* in a "Jerusalem" state of
mind, open to God's presence in our lives. If this is the case, however, why does the text
end in such self-abnegation? The teacher reasons that since Jerusalem is the joy of all the
land, we would diminish her joy with any personal sorrow. And thus, we are directed to
always rejoice before *Adonai*. ☐

Background Nison Tzvi ben Moses Finkel
(1849–1927) was born in Lithuania and raised
in his uncle's home in Vilna. While he was early
recognized as a rabbinic scholar, it was chance
meeting with Simchah Zissel ben Israel Broida
that profoundly affected him and opened up the
world of *musar* (or ethical pietism) to him. He
was overwhelmed by the charisma of Broida
and became one of his disciples. First he assisted
Broida at Bet Talmud in Grobina, which sought
to combine Talmud study with *musar*. After a
difference of opinion, Finkel left and found his
own *kollel* in Slobodka. Later, in 1892, he established a *yeshivah*, Keneset Israel, where hundreds
of scholars were educated. By 1897, he set up a
branch in Slutsk and helped establish major
yeshivot in Telz, Bransk, Stutsin, Shklov, Lodz,
and Grodno. When World War I broke out, the
Slobodka *yeshivah* was moved to Minsk and
then to Kremenchug (in the Ukraine). He later
established a branch in Hebron and in 1925 left
to follow its development in Israel. ☐

The Teaching (*continued*)

the tithe in Jerusalem, one's heart would be open to receive the fear of heaven in such an appropriate place, a place where the Divine Presence dwells, a place from whence holiness emanates throughout all Israel.

For this reason the way we normally understand that the fear of heaven would extend to us is that a person who goes to Jerusalem to learn to revere *Adonai* would be sunk in depression, sadness, and abstinence, [for simply being in the Holy city of] Jerusalem [his feelings] would be turned into mourning.

How surprised we are with our own self-abnegation at the end of the paragraph where we read, "And you shall spend [the money] on anything you want–cattle, sheep, wine, or other intoxicant, or anything you desire. Then you should feast there in the presence of *Adonai* your God. Rejoice with your household" (Deuteronomy 14: 26). "And rejoice"– what is this doing there?

Rejoicing with family, drinking rich drink, and all this is in order to teach you to revere *Adonai* your God? This is because Jerusalem is supposed to be joy of all the land, so that we must keep far from it any tinge of sadness or unpleasantness.

In *Exodus Rabbah* (*Pekudei*, end) we read that Rabbi Yochanan said: "There was a special counting house just outside Jerusalem where all accounts were gone into [by merchants], and anyone who wished to make up his accounts would go there so that he might not make his reckoning in Jerusalem and [perhaps] become distressed, [since one must not be grieved there] because it is 'the joy of the whole earth.'"

And for this reason, any imperfection in joy and gladness is a defect in revering God and in the life of Torah and therefore in the learning every Jew should do to revere God, it is where one learns to live and to rejoice before *Adonai*. ☐

(142) Shofetim: Leaders of the Time

The Teaching
from Simchah Bunem of Przysucha

Rashi: Even though he is not as eminent as other judges that have been before him, you must obey him – you have no one else but the judge who lives in your days.

Rabbi Simchah Bunem of Przysucha used to quote the Baal Shem Tov: The Besht said before his death that we are appalled by leadership until the advent of the Messiah. There are ten categories of shepherds appointed over Israel. And these are they: →

Perush: Explaining
the Teaching

In an amazing comment, Simchah Bunem focuses on the nature of Jewish leadership. He validates Jewish communal leadership of any given period in the words of the text "the judge who will be *in those days.*" He goes on to reveal his frustration over seeing quarreling among one's own community (read *chasidim*). This, he concludes, acknowledges the work of Satan in such quarrels and delays the advent of the Messiah. □

Scriptural Context

Detail after detail, the Israelites are presented with regulations for communal self-government. The section of the portion from which our text is taken reflects the establishment of a judicial system and peoples' court. □

Targum:English Translation
Deuteronomy 17:8-10

8)**If a case is too complicated for you to adjudicate, whether it is a controversy over a homicide, civil law, or assault – matters of dispute in your court – you shall quickly take it to the place where God has designated [for such disputes]. 9)** *And appear before the Levitical priests or the judge who will be in those days and present your problem.* **When the verdict has been announced, 10) you shall carry it out from the place** *Adonai* **chose, attending meticulously to the details of the decision.** □

From the
Tradition

The *rebbe* remains as the spiritual leader of the chasidic community. He is its guiding force and community members do little without seeking his advice. While in most cases the leadership of the early European communities was passed down through families, in some cases (such as in Bratzlav), so powerful was the love for the *rebbe* that he maintained his hold on the community even after his death, and no successor was appointed. □

Background Rashi: Even though he is not as eminent as other judges who have been before him, you must obey him – you have no one else but the judge who lives in your days.

When Menachem Mendl of Kotzk was a disciple [literally, "stood in the doorway of"] his teacher, Rabbi Simchah Bunem of Przysucha, there once came a *melamed*, a schoolteacher, to Przysucha to ask the counsel of the *rebbe* on behalf of his son. He was a handsome young man, diligent in his studies of Bible, *Gemara* and legal interpretations. He was considering for him marriage to the daughter of a very prominent and wealthy man who offered an enormous dowry; furthermore he would outfit the groom as was appropriate. Not only that, but the *melamed*, the father of the groom, would also receive a considerable sum of money, five hundred pieces of gold, enough so that he would never have to work as a schoolteacher. There was only one problem with the arrangement; the father of the bride was not a man who feared heaven.

Rabbi Menachem Mendl did not budge from the side of his teacher. He heard his teacher's approval for the marriage and remained silent, but once the *melamed* had left the presence of Rabbi Simchah Bunem, Rabbi Menachem Mendl ran after him and said that despite the approval of my teacher, his own opinion was against this marriage. The *melamed* was confused and didn't know whether to listen to the →

The Teaching (continued)

Prophets, judges or elders, kings, priests, *Taana'im* [mishnaic rabbinic teachers], *Amora'im* [talmudic rabbinic teachers], leaders, sages, rabbis, and the later teachers, they are called *tzaddikim*.

Satan asked the household of heaven: What characterizes a *tzaddik's* leadership [What is so special about a *rebbe*]? Aren't all Israel obligated to be *tzaddikim*, as it is written in Isaiah 60:21, "All your people are *tzaddikim*"? They replied to him: There will be schools of *chasidim* and each school will have its own head or leader, who will be called, "*tzaddik*," who will in turn instruct them in the ways of Chasidism and serving God.

Satan figured that this matter could serve him as a stumbling block. Satan said to himself, I will always give my powers to the prosecutor against the *tzaddikim* and deprive them of any rest and they will have no energy left to lead the generation. And this was Satan's plan: He would give the prosecutor permission to instigate quarrel and strife between chasidic schools so that there would be no unity among them, and every school would delight in recounting the disgraces of the leader of other schools, and shame the other leader and consider that their own leader had performed a *mitzvah* in such a way.

Rabbi Simchah Bunem of Przysucha concluded: The urge to quarrel in the heart of *chasidim* is the reason redemption is delayed. □

Background (continued)

advice of his rabbi or the advice of his great student. Ultimately the love of money prevailed and the *melamed* agreed to the marriage. The young man went to the home of his father-in-law and he lacked nothing. The *melamed* also received the money he had been promised from his son's father-in-law and he went into business and prospered.

After many years Rabbi Simchah Bunem died, and within several days the young man turned from his good fortune and the studies of Torah to irreligious books and departed from the path of God. Even the prosperity of his father began to decline little by little until he too was completely impoverished. The father journeyed to Kotzk, to Rabbi Menachem Mendl, and poured out the sadness in his heart, that he had come to begging for bread and that his son had forsaken the holy way, and though he was still rich, he didn't want to support his own father.

Rabbi Menachem Mendl said to him: But didn't I once tell you not to enter into this marriage? The *melamed* replied: But didn't your teacher Simchah Bunem agree to it? Said the rabbi of Kotzk: A *tzaddik* can only see for the time while he is alive, "the judge who will be in those days." Indeed, all the time that our teacher was alive no harm befell your son and your wealth did not diminish. □

(143) Shofetim: Rabbinic Security

The Teaching
from Shmelke of Nikolsberg

The following story is told about Rabbi Shmelke of Nikolsberg: When he served as rabbi in a community, he would always hang his walking stick and his knapsack on the wall of the synagogue.

When the officers of the congregation would ask him, "Rabbi, why do you do this?" he would reply, "I have no favorites; I don't bend the rules; and I don't show deference to anyone. [Punning on God's response to Moses, "I will be who I will be," but here in reference to the appropriate verdict,] it will be what it will be. Let the law pierce the mountain – let justice run its course.

"And if one of you is displeased, I am always prepared to resign as your rabbi, to pick up my staff and my knapsack, and to live as a wanderer – even if it means I must survive, God forbid! – begging from door to door." □

Scriptural Context

As the name of this portion implies, this section of the Torah is devoted to the establishment of a system of order for the settlement of Canaan – to be developed in the spirit of Torah. Our text is taken from the beginning of the portion. Here Moses is instructed to appoint *shofetim*, magistrates, to govern the people. □

Targum: English Translation
Deuteronomy 16:18–20

18) **Appoint magistrates and officials for your tribes, in all the settlements that *Adonai* your God is giving you. They shall govern the people with due justice. 19) *You shall not judge unfairly; you shall show no deference; you shall not take bribes*; bribes blind the eyes of the discerning and upset the plea of the just. 20) Justice, justice, justice, you shall pursue – that you may thrive and occupy the land that God is giving you.** □

From the Tradition

According to the Talmud (*Rosh Ha-Shanah* 16b), it is a person's duty to pay respect to one's teacher on festivals, New Moons, and on the Sabbaths. Thus, a visit to the *rebbe* was a major event in the life of the individual *chasid*. According to Rabbi Nachman of Bratzlav, those who travel to the *rebbe* are actually rewarded for their efforts. □

Perush: Explaining the Teaching

Often chasidic teachers offer parables as instruction, fulfilling the dictum to "be Torah." This modest story underlines Shmelke's sense of self and offers guidance to us all. He takes his work seriously, but not himself. □

Background Samuel Shmelke of Nikolsberg was a kabbalist who lived in Poland and Galicia (1726–1778). A disciple of Dov Baer, the *Maggid* of Mezerich, he did much to spread chasidism in Poland and Galicia as a rabbi in several towns before settling in Nikolsberg. Unlike other teachers, he was an ascetic, about whom many miracle stories are told. □

(144) Shofetim: Holiness Everywhere

The Teaching
from Rabbi Abraham Isaac Kook

Once a person accustoms himself or herself to hearing the voice of God issuing from everything, the supernal meaning now comes that has eluded the person, and this is spiritual wisdom.

For certainly, concealed and hidden spiritual wisdom contains divine meaning. Moreover by means of getting in the habit of paying attention to the voice of God issuing from everything, the voice of God is revealed now [even] in spiritual wisdom.

Until finally, in the spiritual wisdom itself, one finds the true appearance of God.

Scriptural Context

As the name of the portion implies, it deals primarily with the laws for providing a community structure for the Israelites. Such legal and ethical regulations are designed to ensure the quality of Israelite communal living as a "kingdom of priests" as they settle the Promised Land. □

Targum: English Translation
Deuteronomy 18:15–17

15) *Adonai* will raise up a prophet for you, just like me, from among your people. You will [likewise] heed him. 16) *This is just what you asked from* Adonai *your God at Horeb on that day of the assembly saying, "Let me not hear the voice of* Adonai *my God any longer or see this wondrous fire anymore, lest I die."* 17) Consequently *Adonai* said, "They have done well speaking this way." □

From the Tradition

"Every day a *bat kol* [heavenly voice] proclaims from Mount Horeb, 'Woe to those who slight the Torah'" (*Pirke Avot* 6:2). This teaches us that God's voice issues continuously, constantly guiding and instructing us. □

And everyone who continues to search and philosophize increases the holiness of faith and cleaving [to God] and the light of the holy Spirit. □

Perush: Explaining the Teaching

A peculiar request, senses Rav Kook. Why would the individual no longer want to hear the voice of God when one's life frames a yearning to seize the Holy Spirit? Our teacher seems to be suggesting that the phrase "let me not hear" is better understood, "let me not be aware that I am hearing." In other words, let me be so aware of God's voice in everything that I will not be self-conscious of hearing God's voice. Then I may really live – a life of the spirit – and not die. □

Background Abraham Isaac Kook saw a harmony between the individual and the world. Thus, he did not see a dichotomy between the sacred and profane seen by so many. All that was essential to human life was considered sacred. He contended that even the advances of science were part of the intellectual advance of humankind. He wrote, "The sacred and the profane together influence the human spirit, which becomes enriched through absorbing from each of them whatever is suitable." □

(145) Ki Tetze: Turning Captive Sins into Free Merits

The Teaching
from Isaiah ben Abraham Ha-Levi Horowitz, Ha-Shelah, in his *Shnei Luchot Ha-Brit*:

In the battle with the evil impulse, according to *Berachot* 5a:

"[Rabbi Levi ben Hanna says in the name of Rabbi Shimeon ben Lakish:] A person should always incite the good impulse to fight against the evil impulse."

"When you go out to battle against your enemy"— when you challenge the evil impulse to battle; "And *Adonai* your God, delivers him into your →

Perush: Explaining the Teaching

Our teacher sees in this verse not a military directive but rather a therapeutic technique for personal healing. In the internal struggle that resides within each individual, you must not wait to see whether the good impulse will triumph over the impulse to do evil. Thus, the individual (and his good impulses) must engage the evil impulse in battle. Only then will God assist you. In doing so, we capture the sins (which are in the possession of the evil impulse). However, by doing so, by capturing these sins, the very action (rather than a passive reaction), turns these sins into merit. Such is the power of *teshuvah*. ☐

Scriptural Context

Our text, which initiates this portion, sets the tone for the collection of divine laws that follow. These laws create a moral tapestry for the emerging Israelite community. While other laws may not have the same obvious moral foundations (such as the prohibition of *shatnez*), they all help to separate Israel out as a separate community (of God's people). ☐

Targum: English Translation
Deuteronomy 21:10-13

10) *When you go out to battle against your enemy, and* Adonai *your God delivers him into your hands and you take him captive* 11) and you see among the captives a beautiful woman whom you desire and want to take her as your wife 12) you must bring her into your home and trim [shave?] her hair and trim her nails. 13) Discard her garments of captivity. She should spend a month in your home mourning her father and mother. After that, you may come to her and possess her, taking her to wife. ☐

From the Tradition

Shneur Zalman of Liadi taught in his *Shem Mi-Shmuel*: Why here is the text "When you [singular] go out to do battle" followed immediately by "And *Adonai* your God delivers him into your hand . . .," whereas in *Parashat Be-Haalotecha* (Numbers 10:9) read, "When you [plural] go out to do battle in your land . . . you shall sound short blasts on the trumpets that you may be remembered . . . ," and then, "and be delivered from your enemies"?

And why here is it said in the singular and there in the plural?

The first problem is explained by the second. Because this which is said here in the singular, which is to say, when you go out like one person, with one heart in harmony and friendship, then "*Adonai* →

Background Isaiah ben Abraham Ha-Levi Horowitz was known as Ha-Shelah Ha-Kadosh or the Holy Shelah from the initials of his major work, *Shnei Luchot Ha-Brit*. Born in Prague (c. 1565), he moved to Poland with his father, who also was his first teacher. A kabbalist who published his father's work (with his own glosses), he was *av bet din* of Dubno in 1600, moving to assume the same role in Ostraha in 1602 where he also headed the *yeshivah*. While he served as *av bet din* in Frankfurt-am-Main from 1606, he left in 1614 when Jews were expelled, returning to his native Prague. Following the death of his first wife, he moved to Jerusalem, remarrying and becoming rabbi of the Ashkenazi community there. Imprisoned by the pasha with other scholars, he later lived in Tiberias, in 1630. ☐

The Teaching (*continued*)

hands"–when someone comes to purify himself, [Heaven] helps him; and even more than this, "And you take him captive,"–the captive that the evil impulse has captured by tricking you [that is, the evil impulse has "got you" by the sins you've committed–you effectively capture them back].

All the sins that are in your hand, you turn into merits, as our sages, their memory is a blessing, have said: "Great is *teshuvah*, for [through it] sins are transformed into merits." □

From the Tradition (*continued*)

you God delivers him into your hand."

According to what our sages, their memory is a blessing, said in *Leviticus Rabbah* 26:2, "The generation of Ahab were all worshipers of idols, yet since there were no informers among them, they would go out in battle and be victorious. But when they went out in battle, they were divided according to groups and congregations, [each] with different opinions, then they needed great love [for one another]." □

(146) Ki Tetze: Not from Vengeance

The Teaching
from Rabbi Avraham Shmuel Benyamin Sofer, Ketav Sofer

Why were Pharaoh, Amalek, and Haman punished, when all they did was carry out the Divine decree? The reason is that they never intended to fulfill God's wish, but rather, in their wickedness, they did what they did from hatred for Israel. For this reason it says, "Remember what Amalek did to you," even though, "you were tired and weary and did not fear God." In other words, the punishment came upon you (not from Amalek, but) from →

Perush: Explaining the Teaching

Our teacher is puzzled by the challenge to remember Amalek (and all the enemies of Israel). What exactly is it about them that we should remember, especially when you consider the fact that it appeared that they were doing what was asked of them? It was God who hardened the heart of Pharaoh, and furthermore, God is in control of everything. Our teacher comes to teach us, however, that while their action may have been decreed by God, the intent of the action came from a hatred of Israel that bubbled up inside of them. They did not fear God; they merely saw the Divine decree as an opportunity to exercise their hatred of Israel. We should learn, and continue to learn as we remember, that our actions, whatever they may be, should simply and always be in an effort to fulfill God's directives, nothing more, nothing less. When we blot out the memory of Amalek, we blot out his motivation (his lack of deference to God). □

Scriptural Context

We come to the end of this portion, which is a diverse array of social, legal, ethical, and ritual laws. Maimonides contended that 72 *mitzvot* (of the 613) are included in this Torah portion. While they seem unrelated, they are united by a concern for the stability of the community as a bastion for religious values and practices. □

Targum: English Translation
Deuteronomy 25:17-19

17) *Remember what Amalek did to* you **on your journey, after you left Egypt, 18)** how he surprised you **on your way,** *without any fear of God, when you were tired and weary* **and he cut down those who lagged behind. 19) Therefore,** when *Adonai* **your God provides you with a haven from all the enemies who surround you in the land that** *Adonai* **your God is giving you as an inheritance,** *you shall blot out the memory of Amalek* **from under heaven.** *Do not forget!* □

From the Tradition

The war with the Amalekites did not end with their defeat. The Israelites were instructed to always remember their dealings with the Amalekites. Amalek is the irreconcilable enemy of the people. It is, therefore, forbidden to show mercy foolishly to one wholly dedicated to the destruction of Israel.

Even more so, the attack of the Amalekites on Israel encouraged others to assault Israel, as well. The verse reminds us that those who smite Israel will in the end be smitten. Yet, the instruction to "remember" enjoins us to recall our actions – what the Amalekites forced us to do. □

Background The Schreiber rabbinical family (known as Sofer) are descendants of Moses Sofer. Rabbi Avraham Shmuel Binyamin Wolf lived from 1815 to 1871. He was the oldest son of Moses Sofer and succeeded his father in 1839 as rabbi and *rosh yeshivah* of Pressburg upon his father's death. Following his father's policies, he was an active organizer of the Hungarian Orthodox Jewish community who ultimately gave his approval to the split that developed among Hungarian Jews. He held this post for thirty-two years during which time he collected all his writings, which were later published under the name Ketav Sofer. □

The Teaching *(continued)*

heaven. And this is the reason why you shall "blot out the memory of Amalek." What comes with his memory—how his intention was (not to fulfill heaven's decree but) to do evil to you—you shall not forget. And in your battle with Amalek, be careful therefore that you yourself do not act from vengeance and hatred (as he did) but in order to fulfill God's command. □

(147) Ki Tetze: The Easiest *Mitzvah*

The Teaching
from Abraham Mordechai of Ger

Rashi: If, in the case of an easy commandment involving no monetary loss, the Torah says, "in order that it will go well for you and that your days be long" [which is an extraordinary reward], how much the more so should be the reward for fulfilling a difficult commandment. But indeed we have many more commandments that also do not require financial loss and are not called "easy" commandments. Why specifically is the commandment of letting the mother bird go free called an "easy" commandment? Because the fulfillment of this commandment requires no preparation. [In order to fulfill it first you must accidentally find a mother bird sitting on a nest.] And this is the law [spoken of in the preceding verse, Deuteronomy 22: 6, →

Scriptural Context

This Torah portion presents Israel with a variety of laws designed to make Israel a holy people, separate and distinct from surrounding cultures. According to Moses Maimonides, there are seventy-two *mitzvot* in this Torah portion. Our text is taken from a section that has become the traditional focus on God's justice. □

Targum: English Translation
Deuteronomy 22:6-7

6) **If, along the road, you happen upon a bird's nest, whether it is in a tree on lying on the ground, containing fledglings or eggs, and the mother is sitting over the baby birds or on the eggs, do not take the mother along with the young.** 7) *You must let [the mother bird] go free and take only the young, in order that it will go well for you and that your days be long.* □

From the Tradition

The Torah is concerned with preventing cruelty to animals, known in the tradition as *tzaar baalei chayyim*. [Later laws concerning the ritual slaughter of animals emanated from this early biblical concern.] Maimonides argued that if the mother is let go, she will not be pained by the sight of seeing her young ones taken away. He further argues that this will lead people to leave everything alone – since what might be taken is generally unfit to eat, in any case. Nachmanides suggested that the laws were written to teach people to be kind, in general, rather than a specific concern for animals. Jewish tradition wants human beings to imitate their Creator who practices loving acts of kindness to all creatures, large and small. □

Perush: Explaining the Teaching

Here our teacher is fascinated by the relationship between what the Torah requests of us and the reward: "that it will go well for you and that your days be long." Why would such a simple commandment allow for such a noble reward? Rashi suggests that if the reward is such for an easy commandment involving monetary loss, then why not for a difficult commandment. But our teacher points out that letting go of the bird is an easy commandment to fulfill. It requires no preparation, says Abraham Mordechai of Ger. □

Background Abraham Mordechai Alter (1866-1948) was called the "emperor of the *chasidim*" and Ger was the capital of his empire. He advocated a return to the meticulous observance of the *Shulchan Aruch* with an emphasis on Torah study. He was especially interested in young people and was fond of joking that "in Ger, there are 10,000 *chasidim* who eat on Yom Kippur [referring to children who are not required to fast]." He often traveled to Israel, taking different, often long and arduous, overland routes. He said, "Just as a *chasid* must visit his *rebbe* from time to time, I must visit the Land of Israel. I want to explore the different ways that lead to the Holy Land." □

The Teaching *(continued)*
"If, along the road, you happen upon a bird's nest . . ."] that excludes the possibility of preparation.

A *mitzvah* that requires no preparation is an easy *mitzvah*. □

(148) Ki Tavo: Returning to the Source

The Teaching
from the Sefas Emes, Yehudah Aryeh Leib of Ger

The *mitzvah* of first fruits was a preparation for Rosh Ha-Shanah, because obviously during the time from Atzeret (Shavuot) until Sukkot most of the first fruits were brought before Rosh Ha-Shanah.

In this way, by the end of the year, the people would bring back the first fruits to the Holy One, and thus the end of everything would be joined →

Perush: Explaining the Teaching

The Sefas Emes is responsive to the word used in the text to reflect "from every first fruit – *mei-reishit.*" It sounds similar to the first word of the Torah, *bereishit.* Our teacher reasons that the *mitzvah* of first fruits is completed prior to Rosh Ha-Shanah and the beginning of the year. Thus, first fruits that end the year connect us to the beginning (of the world and of the year). Hence, the word used is *reishit.* Furthermore, this *mitzvah* of first fruits provides us with the spiritual →

Scriptural Context

This portion continues the social and ritual subjects treated in the previous portion, including an emphatic instruction to observe the covenant. Our text is taken from the regulations concerning the parameters for Israel's conquest of Canaan. ☐

Targum: English Translation
Deuteronomy 26:1-3

1) **When you enter the land that** *Adonai* **your God is giving you as an inheritance, and you occupy and settle it,** 2) *you shall take some from every first fruit of the soil* **that you harvest from the land that** *Adonai* **your God is giving you. Put it in a basket and take it to a place that** *Adonai* **your God has chosen to establish the Divine reputation.** 3) **You should then go to the priest at the same time and say to him, "I acknowledge today before** *Adonai* **your God that I have entered the land that was promised to my ancestors to give to me."** ☐

From the Tradition

The *Mishnah* (*Bikkurim* 3:2-9) vividly describes the first fruit ceremony in the period of the Second Temple. The people gathered in the early morning hours in the open squares of district towns and began their journey to Jerusalem. They sang, "Arise and let us go up to Zion, to *Adonai* our God." They walked in a procession headed by an ox whose horns were adorned with gold and silver. The pilgrims were accompanied by musicians and they carried baskets of fruit, which they gave to the priests along with their offerings of *bikkurim.* When they reached the Temple, they were greeted by the Levitical choir singing Psalm 30. Then a confession was recited. ☐

Background Elimelech of Lyzhansk taught: A man goes down into his field and sees the first ripe fig; he ties a thread of reeds upon it as a sign and declares: Behold, this is the first fruit (Rashi on *Bikkurim,* chapter 3). A man goes down into his field and sees the first ripe fig and his soul desires to eat it, his desire burns inside him – he ties a thread upon it. He remembers and realizes that he is only a mortal human being and that tomorrow grass might be growing through his jaws.

Indeed, it was not decreed that the body should decay in the dust except on account of the sin of the first man who gave in to his desire and ate [the first fruit] from the tree. And because of this, the defilement of the first snake cleaves to him and his progeny after him – impossible to remove, except by means of death. And thus [God] provides a contrary urge in order to purify his substance while a person is still alive.

And this also is the reason for crowning of the first fruit by being the very best of its kind, in order that a person might [be compelled to] restrain his desire even more on account of it. For he controls his urge and rules over his spirit from the beginning of the gathering until [the first fruits] are brought to the temple. ☐

The Teaching (continued)

with its beginning. For this reason the first fruits [in our verse] are called ראשית, reishit.

Our sages, their memory is a blessing, explained [furthermore that the opening words of the Torah], "In the beginning God created . . ." בראשית ברא [which can be read literally as "With reishit God created . . ."], can also therefore be understood as alluding to the mitzvah of first fruits, the very foundation of existence, for it is just this reishit that continually reawakens the spiritual power that comes from God.

And this is the reason the mitzvah [of the first fruits] came after they arrived in the Land of Israel. Parashat Ki Tavo begins, "When you come into the Land . . ." (Deuteronomy 26:10), in order to remember the reishit, spiritual power that brought us out from Egypt and performed miracles for us, and brought us into the Land of Israel, for this is the purpose of the regulation.

"And now behold, I have brought the first fruits ראשית, reishit . . ." (Deuteronomy 26:1). Our sages also said (in Midrash Genesis Rabbah 21:6) "And now lest he [Adam] put forth his hand . . ." connotes teshuvah, for after grasping the truth one needs to turn in teshuvah. For the root of teshuvah [returning] is cleaving to first fruits, reishit, beginning.

And the root of reishit was vouchsafed unto the Israelites that they might be called ראשית, reishit of God's bringing forth, which is to say that they possess the spiritual power for cleaving continually with reishit.

And this also is the meaning of "And Adonai your God will set you on high [above all the nations of the earth]" (Deuteronomy 28:1), as is brought out in Midrash (Deuteronomy Rabbah 7:3): they [the Jewish people] resemble fine oil that when poured from above [always rises to the surface].

And now alas that we no longer physically have first fruits to offer, it is still possible to set everything right with the intentions of the heart. □

Perush: Explaining the Teaching (continued)

energy to begin the new year–as it was harnessed by God in preparation for the creation of the world. Each year, these first fruits reawaken this spiritual energy. We have the opportunity to tap into this spiritual reservoir because the post-Shavuot time, especially the month prior to Rosh Ha-Shanah, epitomizes teshuvah in our preparation for Rosh Ha-Shanah.

The mitzvah is placed on the way out of Egypt–upon arriving in Canaan–because it contributed to the spiritual energy that enlivened our people, moved us out of Egypt, through forty long years in the desert, and finally to a place where we could be home, in the Land of Israel. Now, that the journey is over, meaning that our ancestors have already taken possession of the Land, we now bring the first fruits in the form of teshuvah . □

(149) Ki Tavo: Doing and Remembering

The Teaching from the Sefas Emes, Yehudah Aryeh Leib of Ger

If you fulfill the commandment, obviously you didn't forget it! This couldn't be what the verse means.

It is possible to forget a commandment even though apparently you seem to fulfill it. For instance, you could do it without intending to, in an unthinking, distracted way, or from force of habit, mechanically by rote, all the while your brain and your heart are preoccupied with other matters.

This is what "forgetting" means. So when the text says, "I have not transgressed Your commandments. . . ," it means that I have performed them. And when it says, "and I have not forgotten," it means action was intended, for the sake of unifying the Holy One. □

Scriptural Context

This portion contains various legal and ritual proscriptions designed to lead the people Israel to become fitting partners in a covenant with God. The particular text under discussion is part of a warning to the people of Israel that they keep the *mitzvot* as established by God at Sinai. □

Targum: English Translation Deuteronomy 26:12–14

12) **When you have separated out a tenth of your production in the third year, the year of the tithe, and have given it to the Levite, the stranger, the orphan, and the widow, that they may eat and be satisfied under the protection of your settlements 13)** *then you shall declare before* **Adonai** *your God, "I have cleared out the consecrated portion from the house; and I have given it to the Levite, the stranger, the orphan, and the widow, just as* **You** *commanded me; I have not transgressed your commandments and I have not forgotten.* 14)* **I have not eaten from it while in mourning nor have I cleared it out while in a state of uncleanliness. Neither have I left any of it with the dead. I have responded to the directive of** *Adonai,* **my God and done everything you have commanded me [to do].** □

From the Tradition

This portion contains the well-known text from Deuteronomy 26:5, "You shall then recite as follows before Adonai your God: 'My father was a fugitive/wandering Aramean. He went down to Egypt with meager numbers and sojourned there. There he became a greatly populated nation.'" It is one of the few instances in the Torah where a liturgy of thanksgiving is required. Unlike the festival of Sukkot, on which the American/Canadian Thanksgiving is based and which is communal in nature, this prayer is intended to be strictly personal – although it has found its way into *Haggadot* and the like. □

Perush: Explaining the Teaching

Realizing that the Torah would not teach us something so obvious, the Gerer *rebbe* searches the text for its deeper meaning. Often, we do things habitually without being conscious of our actions. Only when our full consciousness is allied with the performance of a particular *mitzvah* have we "not forgotten" the *mitzvot* of *Adonai*. And only in such a frame of mind can we be united with God. □

Background Menachem Mendl of Kotzk taught that one must not perform *mitzvot* from rote and habit but with vitality, fire, and life. □

(150) Ki Tavo: Garment of Lights

The Teaching
from the Sefas Emes, Yehudah Aryeh Leib or Ger

The Rabbi of Przysucha [probably Simchah Bunem] taught concerning this that all the miracles and wonders that the Holy One did with Israel, since they were supernatural, were only for that particular time. But now, after the entire Torah has been completed for them, indeed the Torah has been made from their lives – made from this into a fixed institution for the generations. They didn't understand it because they were living it! Receiving the torah is allowing your deeds to become it.]

And it is possible to say that the matter of "this day" is actually an allusion to the clothing of all the lights [of the Torah] with deeds, for the Torah was made from all their deeds.

And just this is why receiving the Torah is considered such a great merit for the →

Targum: English Translation
Deuteronomy 29:1-5

1) **Moses called together all of Israel and said to them, "You have seen all that** *Adonai* **did right in front of your eyes in the land of Egypt – to Pharaoh, to his aides, and to his entire country – 2) the amazing actions that you saw with your own eyes, those feats and incredible doings. 3)** *And not until this day has* **Adonai** *given you a heart to understand, eyes to see, or ears to hear. 4) I led you through the wilderness forty years, the clothes on your backs did not wear out* **nor the sandals on your feet. 5) You had no bread nor wine nor intoxicant to drink, so that you would know that I am** *Adonai* **your God."** □

Scriptural Context

It is clear that Moses will not be joining the people whom he has led for forty years through the desert as they enter Israel. But before he dies, he addresses the people once more. He struggles to gather his thoughts as he gathers the people unto him and offers his last oration. □

From the Tradition

When the Bible speaks of a chastisement of Israel, out of fear, people were reluctant to be called up for an *aliyah*, so it became customary in congregations to call for a volunteer (*mi she-yirtzeh*), or it became the duty of the *shammash* (beadle) (cf. Deuteronomy 28:15-68). □

Perush: Explaining the Teaching

Just as many commentators have struggled to understand this introduction by Moses to his final speech to the Israelites, our teacher too explores its meaning. Unlike many of the classical commentators who suggest that the Torah chides the Israelites for not serving as witnesses for *Adonai*, the rabbi of Przysucha asserts that their lives in the desert actually testified to the miracles that God wrought for them. Their journey entered a timeless place in Torah. The Israelites themselves were actually part of Torah since their journey is recorded in it and therefore inseparably linked to God's actions. They did not understand what God was doing, as Deuteronomy 29 asserts, because they were living it. It was their deeds, says our teacher, that illuminated the text so that all could understand. □

Background Although Moses had been commissioned to bring the people out of slavery and into the Promised Land, he died before entering it. The Book of Numbers suggests that it is a result of the incident at Kadesh where the people grumble at the lack of water. Psalm 106:32-33 interprets it a little differently: Moses is blamed for speaking harshly. Yet, in Deuteronomy Moses is denied entry on account of the people: their faithlessness during the incident with the spies as they prepare to conquer the land forces God to turn on Moses as well, for it was then that God declared the Divine intention not to allow him to enter Canaan. □

The Teaching *(continued)*

children of Israel, for the Torah has no fixed measure or boundary. It permeates all creation. Nevertheless the children of Israel merited a garment for the lights of Torah from all their deeds.

And so also the verse in Deuteronomy 26:17, "You have affirmed *Adonai* this day . . ." [which Rashi understands to mean "as witnesses, you have singled out God this day." The explanation is that because of ten utterances the Torah was made complete]. □

(151) Nitzavim: Levels of Turning

The Teaching
from Joshua Sheinfeld

I have heard in the name of Ha-Rav Ha-Tzaddik, Rabbi Shelomoh of Radomsk, author of *Tiferet Shelomoh*: To be precise, it has already been said earlier, "And you turn to *Adonai*, your God . . ." (Deuteronomy 30:2), implying that you made *teshuvah*. But if this be so, why then is "And you will turn" said here a second time?

He [then] said [answering his own question], that before a person makes *teshuvah*, he doesn't even comprehend his sin. Which is to say that he doesn't know that he doesn't know.

And only after the first steps of *teshuvah* does he begin to fathom the enormity of the damage [caused by] his sin: how he sinned, against →

Scriptural Context

The oft-cited passage "including those not yet born," which begins the portion, extends the covenantal relationship throughout the generations. This is Moses' last speech. He lists God's meritorious acts, while highlighting how Israel must act in response. The entire portion expresses the idea of *teshuvah*, which is a fundamental concern to the Book of Deuteronomy. In chapter 30 alone, variants of the word *Teshuvah* (return) appear seven times. □

Targum: English Translation
Deuteronomy 30:5-8

5) **And *Adonai* your God will bring you to the land that your ancestors inherited as a legacy. God will do good by you even more than for your mothers and fathers. 6) *Adonai* your God will open [literally, circumcise] your heart and the heart of your offspring so that you will feel love for *Adonai* your God with your whole self – so that you might live. 7) And *Adonai* your God will curse your enemies and those who hate you, all those who have persecuted you. 8) *And you will return and respond to Adonai's voice, doing all the things I command you this day.* □**

From the Tradition

The Masoretes, the scribal copyists who standardized the Torah text, placed diacritical dots over the eleven letters in the phrase [Deuteronomy 29:28] that emphasized the fact that the fulfillment of the covenant is incumbent on us and our children ad infinitum. The *parashah*, *Nitzavim*, always falls on the last Sabbath before *Elul* – just prior to Rosh Ha-Shanah. Generally, special blessings (*Birkot Ha-Chodesh*) are recited before the annual festival of the New Moon. The *Shabbat* represents the only exception. We are taught that God invokes the blessing for this new month so that the new year might be blessed as well. □

Perush: Explaining the Teaching

The commentator is concerned about the use of the word *tashuv* (you will turn), obviously related to *teshuvah* (literally, "turning"), since in Deuteronomy 30:2, only six preceding verses away, the text had used the word *tashuv* (you will turn). As has happened in previous cases, the question is asked by the commentator, why the apparent redundancy? Here the commentator argues that there are levels to *teshuvah*, to an eventual return to the source. At first, you only have a vague notion of what you had done wrong. Eventually, as you work at it, the implications of your transgression become clearer to you. Thus *teshuvah*, repentance, evolves, moving from level to level. □

Background Radomsk (also known as Radomsko) is located in south central Poland, a town in the province of Lodz. Its Jewish community (which was led by Shelomoh Ha-Kohen Rabinowich – formerly of Wloszczowa – beginning in 1834) was destroyed by the Nazis through a series of deportations. Following World War II, the community was not renewed. □

The Teaching (*continued*)

whom, and so forth and so on. And in this way one ascends from level to level. And on each level one increases in *teshuvah*.

For this reason, it is said earlier, "And you turn to the Lord, your God . . ." (Deuteronomy 30:2), but later on, once one has made a beginning, and drawn oneself near to God, does the person come to the second rung, "And you will turn . . ." (Deuteronomy 30:8). Each time more. Without interruption. Ascending from one level to another level. Through the heights of return, *teshuvah*. □

(152) Nitzavim: Covenant without Romance

The Teaching
from *Shem Mi-Shmuel*

What need is there to make a covenant before they entered the land; wasn't the covenant made with them at Horeb enough?

Said the rabbi of Liadi, the author of the *Tanya*: the making of a covenant between two lovers is not for the present, at a time when their affection and love is strong.

But there will be need for a covenant in the future, when over the passage →

Perush: Explaining the Teaching

The commentator is puzzled by the need to "re-sign" the covenantal contract, when it had already been agreed upon at Sinai (Horeb). He suggests that if we reaffirm our agreement, we may be able to get even closer to God. Like lovers whose bond transcends the original romance and miracles that brought them together in the early years of their love, when you feel far from God, simply open up the Torah as a reminder of the bargain struck at Sinai. □

Scriptural Context

Moses gathers all of the people together in order to offer them his last instructions before his death. The phrase *"Atem nitzavim ha-yom"* (literally, "you are standing today") provides the introduction for the portion. "Today" is repeated six times in Moses' final oration in order to emphasize its importance. □

Targum: English Translation
Deuteronomy 29:9-12

9) **Today, all of you are standing before *Adonai*, your God, even the greatest among you, [namely] your leaders, your tribes, your elders and your officers. 10) [And those of lesser significance] your infants, your wives [sorry], and the itinerant [laborers] who may be camping with you, including the woodcutter and the water-drawer. 11)** *[All are assembled] so that you may now enter into a covenantal agreement with* **Adonai***, your God.* **12) [This is all in order] for you to be now firmly established as God's people so that *Adonai* might be your God, just as God indicated to you and swore to your ancestors Abraham, Isaac, and Jacob.** □

From the Tradition

Mount Sinai is referred to in the Bible by various names, including "the mountain at Horeb" (Exodus 17:6; Deuteronomy 1:6; 4:10, 15; 5:2; 9:8; 18:16; 1 Kings 8:9; 2 Chronicles 5:10; Malachi 3:22; Psalms 106:19) or "the Mountain of God in Horeb" (Exodus 3:1; 1 Kings 19:8); but only once as "Mount Horeb" per se (Exodus 33:6). Horeb comes from the Hebrew root *hrb* (dryness). While there are various scholarly opinions on the relationship of the two names, later Jewish tradition shows the interchangeable use of the names. □

Background Samuel Bornstein (1856–1926), the author of *Shem Mi-Shmuel* (1928–1934) sets forth many of his father's ideas on the *chasidim*. The elder Bornstein, Rabbi Abraham ben Ze'ev Nachum Bornstein, was head of the Bet Din of Sochaczew (Poland). Upon his death, Samuel led the Aleksandrow *chasidim*.

Shneur Zalman of Liadi (1745–1813), whom Bornstein mentions, was born in Liozna, Belorussia. He was the founder of *Chabad* Chasidism. Shneur Zalman reasoned that he knew "a little about learning, but nothing about prayer." Following his marriage, he devoted himself to study, becoming a disciple of Dov Baer of Mezerich. A mystic and charismatic leader who was a great talmudic scholar, he also had a wide knowledge of science and mathematics. In 1797, he anonymously published his *Likkutei Amarim* (collected sayings), which came to be known as the *Tanya*, the principal source of *Chabad*. □

The Teaching (*continued*)

of time, their love will be weakened. Therefore, they make a covenant that the affection might continue even once the causes that originally made them fall in love have ceased.

See, during the lifetime of Moses, miracles were routine and whatever happened was supernatural. But there was anxiety, lest, when they entered the land and matters [like] plowing, planting, and harvesting had to happen according to natural laws, that their love for God might weaken. For this reason, a covenant was made, so that the love might never falter, enduring forever like a tent peg stuck deep [in the earth].

[It would endure] even when they were burdened with earning a living and supporting themselves and [had to depend on] the unpredictability of nature, or when darkness would cover the face of the earth, and there would be sadness and depression.

Even then an Israelite would be able to awaken the love within, and there would be no separation, God forbid! □

(153) Nitzavim: Movin' Along; Standing Still

The Teaching
from Baruch ben Jehiel of Medzibezh

The *tzaddikim*, the holy ones, they are always moving along. All their days they are moving with their spiritual powers from level to level. For them, standing still is incomprehensible except at the hour of communion with God, *devekut*, joining themselves with their Creator.

Moses, our teacher, when he gazed out over Israel and saw that they were "standing," realized that this standing still and not moving [was an indication of their spiritual condition]. He declared that it is no wonder that "you are standing today," for now you are on the highest possible level, "before *Adonai*, your God"–bound in the highest form of ecstasy with the Holy One, face to face, without any dividing screen.

And from such a level it would be incomprehensible to move, rather only to simply stand still and be there. ☐

Perush: Explaining the Teaching

Since we are always on spiritual journeys, our teacher wants to know how we could be "standing [still]." He suggests that one can only stand still during communion with God. Baruch thereby reasons that this is what is taking place at the foot of the mountain–the people are standing so still that not only is movement not discernible but neither are they. ☐

Scriptural Context

For the last time, Moses gathers the people in his last major speech to them. Here the historical imperative is offered to the people. The things we witnessed, our journey, are not only ours. The entire Jewish people owns the journey through the wilderness. In a mystical sort of way, we were all there. ☐

Targum: English Translation
Deuteronomy 29: 9–12

9) **You are standing today all of you before Adonai, your God–your tribal heads, your elders, all the people of Israel, 10) your children, your spouses, even the stranger who is in your camp, from the one who chops wood to the one who draws water–11) to enter the covenant with Adonai your God, which Adonai your God is concluding with you today, and with all its sanctions 12) so that God may establish you today as God's people and He can be your God. ☐**

From the Tradition

The Chatam Sofer, Moses Sofer of Hungary, taught that at the time of the giving of Torah it was said, "I stood between *Adonai* and between you" (Deuteronomy 5:5). It is possible to interpret this according to what I have received from my teacher, a *chasid* in the service of the Gaon, our teacher Rabbi Natan Adler (the memory of the righteous is a blessing): [Throughout] all the days of the life of a rabbi, no student merited [to attain such] exalted height.

In the same way, Joshua did not merit to reveal his light until after the death of Moses. Divine inspiration is not mentioned [likewise] concerning Isaac until, "and it came to pass after the death of Abraham that God blessed Isaac" (Genesis 25:11).

And all the time that Jacob was in his father's house the word of God was not made known [until] "And Jacob went out from Beersheva," only then, "And he dreamed and behold *Adonai* was →

Background Baruch of Medzibezh (1757–1810) was the grandson of the Besht, Israel Baal Shem Tov. He was known to be quarrelsome, boastful, and even vain. ☐

From the Tradition (*continued*)

standing over him" (Genesis 28:12–13).

And this is also [the case] here. Moses said to Israel, [back] then, at Mount Sinai, I was the one who prevented you from meriting to draw near to God. "I stood between God and between you" like a dividing partition, [so that] "you [could] not ascend the mountain."

You were not on a level that you could ascend the mountain, before God. But today, my years and my days are fulfilled; the day of my departure draws near, and there is no power over the day of my death. Now "you are standing today, all of you, [without any intermediary] before *Adonai* your God." □

(154) Va-Yelech: The Last Attainment

The Teaching
from Mei Ha-Shilo'ach, Mordechai Yosef Leiner of Izbica

Moses said this, for on this day he attained ultimate fulfillment: The Holy One sealed the Name upon him.

All the time that a person is incomplete, such a one is able to reach and attain the heights. But such a person is also capable of losing, God forbid, what was attained earlier.

But once one has attained fulfillment, such a one is unable to lose what was attained earlier. Moreover, nothing more can be attained. And that is why Moses said, "I am no longer able to go out and come in."

"To go out," for the Holy One sealed the Name upon him, for now he was unable able to lose anything that he had attained. "And come in," for now there was nothing left to achieve. □

Perush: Explaining the Teaching

Our teacher wants to understand the relationship between Moses' age and the statement "I am no longer able to go out and come in." Mordechai Yosef sees it as describing Moses' ultimate attainment. Here at the end of Moses' life, as he prepares to die, he recognizes all that he achieved. And now finally Moses is describes as needing to attain nothing more.

The teacher reasons that since he was no longer able to go out, it meant that he had achieved the divine imprimatur on his life. □

Scriptural Context

Nearing the end of the journey, Moses prepares for death. We feel his ambivalence in the words he chooses. Disappointed that he cannot join the people whom he has led these past years, he prepares them for the completion of their journey into the Promised Land. □

Targum: English Translation
Deuteronomy 31:1–3

1) **Moses went and said these things to all Israel 2)** *[Moses] said to them, "I am now one hundred and twenty years old, I am no longer able to go out and come in.* **Moreover,** *Adonai* **has said to me, 'You cannot go over there, across the Jordan.'** 3) *Adonai,* **God Godself, will cross at your head. God will wipe out the nations in your path and you will dispossess them [of the Land]. Joshua is the one who will cross as your leader, just as** *Adonai* **has spoke."** □

From the Tradition

In the *Midrash (Petirat Mosheh)*, Moses is seen arguing with God about his death. With each passing hour, a voice is heard from heaven: "Moses, you have only four hours to live ... three hours...." Moses then chooses to petition God: "Master of the world. If I must die for my pupil's sake [Joshua – so that he can become leader], I am willing to conduct myself as his student." God demurs. Then we hear Moses once again: "Let me at least be a fish in the sea, a bird in the air." God again says no. Finally, after arguing for hours to no avail, God strengthens Moses' eyes so that he might see the entire Land of Israel. What lay in the deep appeared to him above, the hidden was plainly in view, the distant close at hand. He saw everything. Seeing that the land would be good to the people he had brought so far, he died at peace with himself. □

Background Izbica Lubelska is a town in Lublin province, Poland. It became known in the Jewish world because of its *tzaddik*, Mordechai Yosef Leiner (d. 1854), a disciple of Menachem Mendl of Kotzk and Simchah Bunem. Mordecai Yosef's writings were collected by his students between the years 1860 and 1922 in *Mei Ha-Shilo'ach*. With his own unique perspective on the notion of free will and determinism, Mordechai Yosef taught "that actions stem from God but thoughts originate in man, and every act committed by man ... is in the hands of heaven and the observance of the precepts or the contrary lies in the hands of God." □

(155) Va-Yelech: The Worst Secret

The Teaching
from Chiddushei Ha-Rim, Isaac Meir Rothenberg Alter of Ger

If there are those who know or even sense that something is hidden, then it is not such a great hiddenness, the disaster is not so great, for then there follows yearning and longing for a Divine revelation. And this shatters every wall, obstacle, and barrier. Indeed, there is no *teshuvah*, no greater turning, than this.

The tragedy is when something is concealed within what is hidden, for then people do not sense that God's countenance is hidden.

The wisdom of the prophets is concealed; there is no searching for God, no desire for Divine mercy or heavenly light. And just →

Perush: Explaining the Teaching

In this comment, the Rim is trying to understand what is

Scriptural Context

As Moses prepares for his death, he appoints a successor, Joshua, who will lead the people across the Jordan into Canaan. Moses' final act is to leave him with final instructions. Our text is taken from this final charge. ☐

Targum: English Translation
Deuteronomy 31:16–19

16) *Adonai* said to Moses, "You are about to lie with your ancestors. As a result the people will go astray after the alien gods in their midst in the land in which they are about to enter. They will forsake Me and break the covenant that I made with them. 17) Then my anger will flare up against them and I will abandon them and hide my countenance from them. They will soon be ready prey. Many evils will befall them. And they will say, 'Surely it is because God is not in our midst that this evil has befallen us.' 18) *Yet I will keep my countenance hidden on that day, because of all the evil they have done in turning to other gods.* 19) Therefore write down this poem and teach it to the people of Israel. Put it in their mouths so that this poem may be My witness against the people of Israel." ☐

From the Tradition

In the biblical idiom, Israel, when it seeks other gods or follows pagan practices, is likened to a harlot. Thus, the relationship between God and Israel is perceived as a holy union, the abuse of that relationship, considered adulterous. Many of the prohibitions in the Torah are designed to prevent the Israelites from coming into contact with foreign cultures and therefore foreign gods, thus preventing the possibility of an "extramarital affair." ☐

meant by the text "hidden countenance." He reasons that if there is a sense that the countenance is indeed hidden, it is so hidden that there is nothing for which to yearn. In other words, if it were really well hidden, one would not realize that it was hidden. Since it was not well hidden, the people yearned for it. This kind of yearning is the greatest kind of *teshuvah*, repentance, of all. He suggests that the kind of hiding is tragic when it is so well hidden that it implies that there can be no searching (for God) for it. That's the tragedy of prophecy – but we are not prophets and can turn to God, and through our longing get going on our journey. ☐

Background In the world of the mystic, there is constant tension between that which is hidden and that which is revealed. Our obligation, we who seek knowledge of the Divine, search out the hidden in the world, hoping that the revelation of God will illumine our way and dispel the darkness. Abraham Joshua Heschel said that the root of the word for world, *olam*, means "hidden." Thus, the world itself conceals from us the mysteries of the Divine. ☐

The Teaching *(continued)*

this is the meaning of "I will keep my countenance hidden," I will conceal that which is hidden from them, I will stupefy their hearts and dull their feelings so that they are not even aware that the splendor of the Holy One is lacking from them. □

(156) Va-Yelech: Defense Witness

The Teaching
from the Sefas Emes, Yehudah Aryeh Leib of Ger

The people of Israel are witnesses to all of God's creation and God's unity, for God is the Creator and the guide.

And through the [religiosity] of the people of Israel, the glory of heaven is made clear. They clarify what heaven sets forth and therefore there is a great need for them to turn in *teshuvah*, repentance, in order to be fit witnesses in the very same way that witnesses for a divorce proceeding are examined for their answers.

And this is the meaning of the "returning of Israel [*ad*] unto *Adonai*, your God." But do not read it "[*ad*] unto," but "[*eid*] witness" [vocalized with the vowel *tzeire* instead of a *patach*]. Just this is the testimony that establishes what is written in the Torah. □

Scriptural Context

While Moses has chosen to leave the entire people with words of instruction, he summons select individuals like Joshua to offer them individual words of guidance. Our text is taken from the main address to the people – near the end of the portion. □

Targum: English Translation
Deuteronomy 31:28–29

28) *Gather to me all the elders of your tribes and your officials, that I may speak all these words to them and that I may call heaven and earth to witness against them.* 29) Because I know that when I am dead, you will act wickedly and turn away from the path that I enjoined upon you. [As a result] in time to come, misfortune will fall upon you for having done this evil in the sight of *Adonai* – vexing God with your [mis] deeds. □

From the Tradition

The great gift of this literature is a recognition, often forgotten in the hurried modern world, that *teshuvah*, repentance, is a road always available to us. No matter how far away we have traveled from our Source, the road home is always made clear for us. The gates of repentance are always open. □

Perush: Explaining the Teaching

The Sefas Emes is intrigued by the notion that Moses calls heaven and earth as witness "against" the people. What is the function of this call, for it is the people of Israel who are witnesses of God's glory? The Sefas Emes likens this witnessing to those who sit in a divorce proceeding. They are there to clarify the claims of the various parties. Likewise, heaven and earth are there to clarify what God had set forth for the Jewish people. Thus, the people need to turn in *teshuvah* in order for them to be regarded as viable witnesses to God's works. □

Background The Sefas Emes once wrote, "Israel says to *Adonai*: 'If the day of redemption is to be long awaited; if the time that Your sheep should be assembled to be taken home has not yet arrived, I implore You *Adonai*, do not let them perish in the long interim. Water the sheep. Go and feed them so that they may have the strength to wait.' " □

(157) Haazinu: The Future of "I"

The Teaching from the Chatam Sofer

We recall that behold, at the first sprouting of Israel's redemption for the Egyptian exile, in Exodus 3:14, the Holy One said to Moses, "I will be who I will be."

Rashi explains this by citing *Berachot* 9b, in the name of our sages, as meaning that "I will be with them in this distress, and that I will be with them through the servitude of yet other kingdoms."

And behold, now in the singing of Moses' farewell song, *Haazinu,* a [present and] future redemption is mentioned, for the Holy One says [again repeating the first person singular pronoun], "Now that time when 'I, I am the One,' has arrived. Then [at the Burning Bush] I spoke in the language of the future, 'I will be,' and now that the time has arrived, I speak in the language of the present, 'I, I am the One.' " □

Perush: Explaining the Teaching

When is the "then" that is included in this text? The Chatam Sofer recalls an event when a reference in time was used as further explained by Rashi—at the beginning of God's redemption when God spoke to Moses. Rashi explains this early statement by referring to the language of the present and the future. "I am the One" is the language of the present—for the time of redemption has arrived. □

Scriptural Context

A beautiful text, this is the final (of three) songs of Moses articulated at the end of his journey. While the earlier songs were integral to the wilderness experience, this last song resonates with Israel eventually living out the drama of God's will for the people: Israel will succeed in body and spirit. □

Targum: English Translation
Deuteronomy 32:39

39) *See, then, that I, I am the One; there is no God besides Me.* **I deal death and give life. I wound and I heal. None can deliver from my hand.** □

From the Tradition

Martin Buber taught in his essay "The Man of Today and the Jewish Bible," in *Israel and the World: Essays in Times of Crisis* (Schocken, 1948): "The lived moment leads directly to the knowledge of revelation, and thinking about birth leads indirectly to the knowledge of creation. But in his personal life probably not one of us will taste the essence of redemption before his last hour. And yet here too, there is an approach. It is dark and silent and cannot be indicated by any means, save by my asking you to recall your own dark and silent hours. I mean those hours in the lowest depths when our soul hovers over the frail trap door which, at the next instant, may send us down into destruction.... But suddenly we feel a touch of a hand. It reaches down to us, it wishes to be grasped—and yet what incredible courage is needed to take this hand, to let it draw us up out of the darkness. This is redemption." □

Background Regarding the many disagreements he had with others, the Chatam Sofer wrote, "There are no quarrels without wounds." □

(158) Haazinu: Heaven and Earth

The Teaching
from Yalkut Yehudah

[How shall we reconcile the subtle difference between Moses' statement in Deuteronomy 32:1 and Isaiah's words as recorded in Isaiah 1:1, "Hear, O heavens, and give ear, O earth"?] What did these two prophets call to the heavens and the earth, that they should listen to their voice? According to *Midrash Mechilta* (Exodus 12), the prophet needs to demand the honor of the parent *and* the honor of the child, which is to say, the honor of God and the honor of Israel.

Elijah demanded the honor of the parent but not the honor of the child. And Jonah demanded the honor of the child but not the honor of the parent. And, on account of this, their prophetic teachings were cut short. Jeremiah demanded the honor of both parent and child and his prophecy was doubled.

This has already been clarified by Elijah, the Gaon of Vilna, who noted that we read in Isaiah 6:8, "Then I heard the voice of *Adonai* saying, 'Whom should I send? Who will go for us?' " "For us," the implication is that Isaiah would go for God's sake and for the sake of Israel, that he would demand the honor of the parent and the honor of the child. →

Scriptural Context

Only one chapter in length, unusual for a Torah portion, this section comprises Moses' last song. Spoken close to the eve of Moses' death, the poem embodies the spirit of the prophet as he leaves an "ethical will" for the people he has led through the desert. □

Targum: English Translation
Deuteronomy 32:1–3

1) *Give ear, O heavens, and I will speak, let the earth listen to the words of my mouth.* 2) **May my discourse come down as the rain, My speech distill as the dew, like showers on young growth, Like droplets on the grass.** 3) **For on the name of** *Adonai* **I call; give glory to our God.** □

From the
Tradition

Rabbi Nachman of Bratzlav wrote: "How do you pray to God? Is it possible to pray to God with words alone? Come, I will show you a new way to sing to God – not with words or sayings – but with song. We will sing and God will understand us." □

Perush: Explaining the Teaching

Our teacher is concerned about two things in the text and he resolves both questions together. First, there is a similar text in Isaiah, which he recalls, that simply reverses the language in regard to the heaven and the earth. Obviously, there must be a reason for the reversal of language. In both cases, what is it that Moses or Isaiah called out that would demand the attention of the heaven and earth?

Citing a text from the *Mechilta* and assigning it to all prophets – beyond Isaiah – Yalkut Yehudah suggests that the prophet demands the honor of the parent (read, God) and the child (read, Israel). The prophecies were cut short of those prophets like Elijah and Jonah who did not demand the honor of both. He corroborates this understanding by recalling a comment of the Vilna Gaon. →

Background Elijah ben Solomon (1720–1797), known as Der Vilner Gaon or the Gaon of Vilna, was the greatest rabbinic authority of east European Jewry. He became a bitter antagonist of Chasidism, demanding the meticulous observance of the minutiae of rabbinic regulations. He did not believe that *devekut* and *kav-vanah* could make up for belated services. In this regard, the Vilna Gaon remarked, "Can a child be told when to approach his father?" Yet, he thought worship was too lengthy and deleted many *piyyutim* and encouraged participatory singing. □

The Teaching (*continued*)

When prophets demand the honor of the parent, they would appeal to the earth, which is to say, to those who dwell on the earth. and when they demand they honor of the child, they would appeal to the heavens, which is to say to "our parent, who is in heaven."

This may be the explanation why Moses, [who] after all was the closest any prophet ever got to heaven, demanded the honor of the child and Isaiah, who was very close to the earth, demanded that Israel honor God. □

Perush: Explaining the Teaching (*continued*)

Once he has resolved this part of his question, the commentator goes on to resolve the subtle differences in the text he originally perceived. Moses, who according to tradition was the greatest of all prophets and therefore got the closest to Heaven (God), demanded the honor of the child. Isaiah, on the other hand, demanded that Israel honor God. □

(159) Haazinu: Rain and Dew

The Teaching
from Rabbi S. Z. Ulman

Everyone knows that there can be speaking words, which is hard, and talking, which is soft. Similarly we have occasional rain, which is a blessing for all vegetation. There are plants that thrive on rain and plants that would be injured by too much. And thus showers are good for the grass; these grasses require light rain.

And corresponding to them are people who only need compassion while others need stern justice. This is the scriptural lesson. "Give ear, O heavens, let me speak...." Speaking here connotes "hard." "Let the earth hear the words I utter..." connotes "soft."

This is not surprising. It can be explained by likening it to rain and dew. Just as there are plants that can easily survive on dew alone, there are plants that require rain. Some grasses thrive on heavy rainfall while other vegetation [thrives on] occasional showers.

It is the same with human beings: Some need gentle speaking; others require hard talk. Each one receives what is best according to his or her needs. Therefore, just as people need to offer a blessing for the good things that befall them, so too do they need to offer a blessing for the bad, because everything is for the best.

And this is the reason the text says, "For on the name of *Adonai* I call . . . ," [for] Divine compassion. "Give glory to our God," evokes stern justice. □

Scriptural Context

Our text is taken from the last words Moses leaves for the people. In this text he recalls the desert journey, a final effort to suggest his hopes and aspirations for their future. □

Targum: English Translation
Deuteronomy 32:1–3

1) *Give ear, O heavens, let me speak; Let the earth hear the words I utter.* 2) *May my discourse come down as the rain, My speech as the dew, like showers in young growth, Like droplets on the grass.* 3) *For on the name of* **Adonai** *I call; give glory to our God.* □

From the Tradition

Among the many attempts to define the 613 commandments, *Shirah Le-Chayyim* (Warsaw, 1917) attempted to insert the 613 precepts into the 613 letters of *Haazinu*. □

Perush: Explaining the Teaching

Our teacher, Rabbi Solomon Ulman, is intrigued by the kind of words that Moses describes in referring to his own speech. What is actually meant by such a description?

The poetry works. Words like rain can be soft like morning dew that gently offers itself the earth's vegetation, tending to its growth. Or words can be like torrential rains that destroy and uproot.

Just as plants need different rains to nurture their growth, people need different words, as well. There are times when gentle speech is required and there are times when harsh words of rebuke are needed. Know well the kind of words needed and speak them well, warns our teacher. All words, when properly delivered are of the living God. □

Background Rabbi Solomon Zalman Ulman was head of the *bet din* of Yastritz. The *bet din* is a rabbinical court of three, formed primarily for purposes of decisions in religious (and formerly civil) matters, as well as for limited liturgical/ritual purposes. □

(160) Ve-Zot Ha-Berachah: A Secret Burial

The Teaching
from Rabbi Yerucham Varhafig

Why is the burial site of Moses concealed from human eyes? Because it is revealed and known by the Holy One that in the future the Temple will be destroyed and Israel exiled from their land. Perhaps they would come to the grave of Moses at that time and stand in tears and supplication. And, Moses would arise and nullify the decree!

It is possible to give still another explanation.

If they knew the location of Moses' burial, all Israel would rush to fulfill the commandment to bring Moses' bones to the Land of Israel, just as Moses had done with the bones of Joseph. Indeed, it is suggested in *Deuteronomy Rabbah* 2:9 that "the Holy One said to Moses, 'Should you be buried near those who died in the wilderness, then they will enter the land by your merit, and you will go at their head.' "

If so, it is proper that they not know the location of the bones of Moses in order that the wilderness generation go up [to the Land of Israel] and he be at their head. For if others brought up the bones of Moses, who then would bring up the wilderness generation! □

Scriptural Context

This Torah portion, read only during Simchat Torah serves as an epilogue to the Torah. It reports the death of Moses and the assignment to Joshua, Moses' designated successor. Near the end of the portion is the well-known phrase, now part of Israel's collective memory: "Never again did there arise in Israel a prophet like Moses." □

Targum: English Translation
Deuteronomy 34:5–8

5) So the servant of *Adonai*, Moses, died there, in the land of Moab, at the behest of *Adonai*. 6) *God buried him [Moses] in the valley in the land of Moab, near Bet-Peor; and no one knows his burial place to this day.* 7) Moses was a hundred and twenty years old when he died; his eyes were undimmed and his vigor unabated. 8) The Israelites cried [over his death] on the steppes of Moab for thirty days. □

From the Tradition

While Jewish tradition acknowledges the greatness of Moses – even calls him a prophet – we are reminded that he was merely a man. Little is really known about him, and the place in which he was buried has been hidden from the Jewish people throughout its history – to keep him human. □

Perush: Explaining the Teaching

Rabbi Yeruham Varhafig asks a question that many teachers have pondered: Why indeed did God choose to hide the specific location of Moses' burial place from the people of Israel? He offers two possible reasons; both suggest the potential inherent in human actions to change God's decree. God knew that (on the eve of their entering the Promised Land) the Jewish people would one day be exiled from it. God thus feared that the people would pray at Moses' gravesite and encourage Moses to rise and nullify the decree!

The real reason, he suggests, is that the Israelites would try to carry Moses' bones into Israel – as Moses had done with the bones of Joseph. Our teacher even recalls a text from the *Midrash* that would really confound God's plans. If the bones were near those who died in the wilderness, they might be allowed to enter the Holy Land as well. As a result, the merit of the wilderness generation would be confused with Moses' merit. God wanted only those who had rid themselves of slavery to enter the Promised Land truly free. □

Background The mystics believe that if one prays on the gravesite of a holy person, one's prayers will be answered more readily. In a metaphysical sort of way, the prayers of the individual get intertwined with the merit of the righteous person. □

Index of Names

Index of Biblical Verses

Index of Biblical Verses

Index of Talmudic Verses

About the Authors

Rabbi Lawrence S. Kushner is rabbi of Congregation Beth El in Sudbury, Massachusetts, and is widely recognized as a leading theologian and authority in Jewish mysticism and Chasidism. He was the first rabbinic chairman of Reform Judaism's Commission on Religious Living, and he is also on the faculty of Hebrew Union College–Jewish Institute of Religion, New York. Rabbi Kushner is the author of numerous books and articles, including the acclaimed *God Was in This Place and I, i Did Not Know* and *The Book of Letters: A Mystical Alef-Bait.*

Rabbi Kerry M. Olitzky, D.H.L., is director of the School of Education at Hebrew Union College–Jewish Institute of Religion, which is at the forefront of innovative Jewish education. He is the author of numerous books, monographs, and articles, including *The Official Handbook for Jewish Kids, Twelve Jewish Steps to Recovery: A Personal Guide to Turning from Alcoholism and Other Addictions,* and *A Glossary of Jewish Life,* with Rabbi Ronald H. Isaacs. Dr. Olitzky is executive editor for *Shofar* magazine.